Democracy and Public Space

D0293250

Democracy and Public Space

The Physical Sites of Democratic Performance

John R. Parkinson

OXFORD
UNIVERSITY PRESS

OXFORD
UNIVERSITY PRESS

Great Clarendon Street, Oxford, OX2 6DP,
United Kingdom

Oxford University Press is a department of the University of Oxford.
It furthers the University's objective of excellence in research, scholarship,
and education by publishing worldwide. Oxford is a registered trade mark of
Oxford University Press in the UK and in certain other countries

© John Parkinson 2012

The moral rights of the authors have been asserted

First Edition published in 2012
First published in paperback 2014

Impression: 1

Published in the United States of America by Oxford University Press
198 Madison Avenue, New York, NY 10016, United States of America

British Library Cataloguing in Publication Data

Data available

ISBN 978–0–19–921456–3 (Hbk.)
ISBN 978–0–19–967694–1 (Pbk.)

Printed in Great Britain by
CPI Group (UK) Ltd, Croydon, CR0 4YY

To my father, L. J. Parkinson,
who started this;

Sarah Penelope Randall Parkinson,
who was born half way through;

and Thomas Henry Randall Parkinson,
whose imminent arrival pushed me to finish.

Contents

Preface

This book started with a discussion with my father on a long drive across the centre of the Australian state of Victoria. Dad is a retired architect and architectural historian, and we were arguing about whether democracy and great architecture went together. Initially, I contemplated writing something exploring that argument, but it is an argument that has been had many times in various contexts, and I had nothing particular to add to it. What I found instead was that issues of physical space and the built environment were largely off the agenda of democracy scholars – indeed, I found claims that physical space was unimportant in modern democracy, but felt that this could not be right. As someone who has lived in cities as diverse as Singapore, London, Hong Kong, Wellington, and Canberra, I was aware of the difference that spatial arrangements can make to people's lives; and given the present spread of physical defences around state buildings and other public spaces, I became increasingly concerned that space for the expression of democratic rights and claims was being eroded in Western democracies. Although the initial discussion was far removed from these subsequent concerns, it was the spark that ignited the rest. So, thanks for an inspirational argument, Dad.

Time to start thinking about these issues was provided by the University of York's Anniversary Lectureship scheme. Part of what convinced me to pursue it was the critical but engaged and stimulating reception it received from friends and colleagues in the Research School of Social Sciences, Australian National University – particular thanks to Geoff Brennan, John Dryzek, Bob Goodin, and Jeremy Shearmur. As usual, these contributors should be absolved of all blame for what follows.

Further assistance came from a Small Research Grant from the British Academy (SG 44244) which allowed me to visit more than a dozen cities around the world. In those cities I was met with great generosity by a group of organizations and individuals who include:

- in Ottawa: Marc Bosc and Robert Gaudette of the House of Commons; Heather Lank and Marysa Oueriemmi of the Senate; Pierre Dubé and Mark Kristmanson of the National Capital Commission; George Pollard of

Carleton University; plus Matt Behrens of Toronto Action for Social Change.

- in Washington, DC: Brett Anderson of the American University, who gave me a personal tour of the nooks and crannies of the city; Gael Murphy, Code Pink; Toni Griffin, District of Columbia; Julia Koster, National Capital Planning Commission; Joe Goldman and Carolyn Lukensmeyer of AmericaSpeaks; plus Setha Low, Columbia University; Michelle and Bill Hormuzdiar in New Haven; and the Sikorsky family in Minneapolis/St Paul.

- in Mexico City: Alejandra Moreno, City Centre Authority; René Cervera García, the Mayor's Chief of Staff and Vidal Larenas of the city government; and the Department of Urban Development and Housing.

- in Santiago: the Morales family; Alfonso Donoso; and Alfonso's rugby-mad friends during the 2007 World Cup quarter-finals.

- in Tokyo: Hiroshi Ota and Kaori Ito of Tokyo University and the Tokyo Picnic Club; and Yukio Maeda, Tokyo University.

- in Hong Kong: Peter Cheung at the University of Hong Kong; Richard Tsoi, Sha Tin District Councillor and convenor of the Power for Democracy group; Martin Lee QC and Patrick Lau, Legislative Councillors; and community activist Verdy Leung.

- in Wellington: the Rt Hon Margaret Wilson, Speaker of the New Zealand House of Representatives; Liz Mellish of the Wellington Tenths Trust; Gerald Blunt, Wellington City Council; Helena Catt, Chief Executive of the Electoral Commission; and Sandra Grey, Victoria University of Wellington.

- in Canberra: Neil Savery of the ACT Planning and Land Authority; Annabelle Pegrum and Andrew Smith of the Australian National Capital Authority; Hilary Penfold QC, head of Parliamentary Services; Sarah Miskin of the Parliamentary Library; Ann Jackson-Nakano; Simon Niemeyer and Kersty Hobson; plus Kim Dovey, University of Melbourne.

- in Cape Town: the people of the township of Langa, especially the Tsoga Environmental Resource Centre; the staff of the District Six Museum; Melanie Atwell, for another marvellous walking tour; Pat Hill, Cape Town City Councillor; Gideon Brand, City of Cape Town Council; and Ruben Govender, the Public Relations Unit of the South African Parliament.

- in London: Iain Borden of the Bartlett School of Architecture, University College London; Muir Morton, Deputy Serjeant-at-Arms, House of Commons; the chair, members, and staff of the House of Lords Constitution Committee; and Sarah Gaventa of the Commission for Architecture and the Built Environment.

- in Athens: Manolis Polychronides, University of Athens, and his partner Jen, who took me from conservative to radical Athens and back again; Seraphim Seferiades, Panteion University; and Terrel Carver of the Political Studies Association who organized for me to be there.

- in Douglas: Sian Hoggett, who first alerted me to Tynwald Day, and her father Paul Hoggett, former Chief Constable and guide par excellence; Roger Carey, Isle of Man International Business School; and Roger Sims of the Manx Museum.

- in Appenzell: Charlotte Reinisch and Denise Traber of the University of Zürich, and the *Ratschreiber* of Canton Appenzell Inner-rhodes.

There are others not named here because they preferred to remain anonymous. My sincere thanks to them too, and to the dozens of unnamed people on park benches and street corners, on buses and trains, in queues and waiting rooms in every city who took the time to chat with me about the places they lived in or were passing through.

I am grateful for permission to reprint material from the following:

John Parkinson, 2009, 'Symbolic representation in public space: capital cities, presence and memory', *Representation* 45(1): 1–14, by permission of Taylor & Francis. In addition, numerous individuals and organizations have generously supplied photographs, which are credited in the text.

My thanks to my former colleagues at York, especially members of the ever-incisive Theory Workshop, who helped dissect Part I in particular; to David Atwell for his assistance with the South African visit; and Simon Parker for guiding me into urban theory. Thanks also to my new colleagues at the University of Warwick who generously provided me with time to finish the production process. For their comments and criticisms I would also like to thank the organizers of, and participants in, the Representation and Democracy Symposium, University of Birmingham, and the Comparative Politics Workshop at Nuffield College Oxford, May 2007; the Democracy: Theory and Practice Conference, Manchester, November 2007; the Political Studies Association Conference, Swansea, April 2008; plus numerous other workshops in the United Kingdom, Australia, New Zealand, and Canada.

Finally, thanks to Dominic Byatt and Lizzy Suffling at Oxford University Press for their enthusiasm and patience; and to Carolyn, who kept up the encouragement while doing the usual hundred hard things at once, not the least of which was bringing our two gorgeous children into the world. My love and admiration are boundless.

JRP
Alderminster, April 2011

List of Figures

List of Tables

1

Introduction

We live in an online, interconnected world. The public sphere, that realm of political talk and action between the state and society, burst out of the market and the coffee house long ago, but in recent years even the pages of newspapers and the broadcast media have been superseded. Now, the public sphere is virtual, digital, and dispersed across billions of desktops, laptops, mobile phones, and PDAs.[1] As a result, the public sphere is not just a bourgeois indulgence but a global phenomenon. Revolutions in the Arab world are coordinated and cheered on via Facebook and Twitter; not only is the news of a tsunami in Japan told through video and commentary shot by ordinary people from their balconies and rooftops, but important parts of the global response are coordinated online as well. Individuals find that their words and actions suddenly have a global reach, for good or ill: the pronouncements of a US official about British elections on Australian radio would once have passed unnoticed, but now strain relations (Elliot, 2010); gunsight video exposing the casual brutality of a military helicopter crew spreads worldwide (Wikileaks, 2010). And amongst all the blogging, tweeting, and social networking, the stone of the Palace of Westminster and the expanse of the National Mall are increasingly marginal, increasingly irrelevant.

Or so we are told. This book argues that matters are not that simple. It starts from the premise that while a growing proportion of political communication uses digital means, the things that are communicated involve real people who take up, occupy, share, and contest physical space. Often, those who deny the importance of physical space confuse the medium and the message: by focusing on the means of communication, they overlook what is communicated. While revolutions most certainly *are* televized,[2] what television, YouTube,

---

[1] Personal digital assistants: an increasingly outdated term itself, following the rise of mobile devices that blur once-solid lines between phones, music devices, computers, cameras, diaries, maps, and more.

[2] With apologies to the late Gil Scott-Heron (1971).

Figure 1.1. Demonstrators in Tahrir Square, 2011
Photo by Ramy Raoof, Creative Commons Attribution 2.0 Generic license.

Twitter, and others disseminate are pictures and narratives of physical events, not just streams of digits. The digits encode narratives and pictures of contests over physical space, performed by flesh-and-blood people. What was coordinated and communicated in Cairo in 2011, just as in Kiev in 2004, was not virtual, but the prolonged and mass occupation of public space by citizens (Figure 1.1).

From that starting point, this book argues that democracy depends to a surprising extent on the availability of physical, public space, even in our allegedly digital world. It also argues that in many respects the availability of space for democratic performance is under threat, and that by overlooking the need for such space – or arguing against that need – we run the risk of undermining some important conditions of democracy in the modern world.

Take the example of modern representative assemblies. It is common to deride them, especially when all one ever sees is the monkey-cage antics of Prime Minister's Question Time or the partisan posturing of televized committee hearings. But one of the great virtues of these institutions is that they force politicians onto a single stage where they must make their arguments and decisions in public. As I argue in detail in Chapter two, this has two important democratic benefits: it makes scrutiny of the powerful easier, and it provides symbolic cues that signal the importance of those decisions for the rest of us. A democracy that lacks a single site for binding collective decision-making is a more-easily attenuated democracy, because it is one that is taken less seriously by its citizens, and one in which decisions can too easily pass undetected and undefended. The fact that some legislatures honour this requirement more in the breach is not an argument against the principle; it is an argument for fixing the practice, and in Chapters five and six I look at assemblies in detail to see how they function as public spaces.

Similarly, think about the everyday freedom to walk down the street in a democratic society. This is such a commonplace freedom that the vast majority of us, political scientists included, do not stop to think about it. But the fact is that in a great many cities that freedom is rather more limited than appearances suggest and, I will argue, democratic values require. With the very funny exception of the one protest it was designed to control, there is at the time of writing a law in Britain that means one cannot walk or sit within a mile of Parliament wearing or carrying anything that might constitute a political protest (Figure 1.2) – a 'Stop the War' badge, a cake iced with the word 'Peace', a comedy red nose[3] – without prior permission from the Metropolitan

Figure 1.2. G20 protest policing, London, 2009
Photo by 'bayerberg', licensed by Creative Commons.

[3] All real examples. For discussion, see Chapter seven, pages 158–9.

3

Figure 1.3. CCTV surveillance, Singapore
Photo by 'Isderion', licensed by Creative Commons Attribution-Share Alike 3.0 Germany.

Police Commissioner. This strikes most people who hear of it as ridiculous, and battles are being fought to overturn it, but other, more subtle restrictions apply in city streets every day: restrictions on where one can canvas for elections, where certain *kinds* of people can walk, certain neighbourhoods that one cannot enter without a pass key, and so on. The restrictions are enforced not merely by police officers but by unaccountable operatives in CCTV control centres, by private businesses, and by the very design features of city streets (Figure 1.3). What blinds us to these restrictions is that they apply only when we perform certain kinds of roles: in particular, they apply when we act as politically engaged citizens, not when we act as shoppers or employees on a lunch break, say. One of the aims of the book is to understand when those restrictions are justified, and when they are not.

Not only is it the case that democracy requires physical space for its performance, it can be the case that only certain kinds of spatial arrangements will do, or that certain arrangements amplify or mute particular behaviours that democrats find valuable. For example, academics have argued that the layout of Beijing universities facilitated the Tiananmen student protests by easing communication among activists and encouraging the building of a collective identity separate from the party-state identity (Zhao, 1998). Equally, it has been argued that spatial arrangements can undermine a sense of 'we', as in

Figure 1.4. Two-tiered Minneapolis
Photo by Michael Hicks, licenced by Creative Commons.

Minneapolis where the elevated, covered walkways between buildings reinforce divisions between office-dwelling haves and street-level have-nots (Byers, 1998) (Figure 1.4). There are those who agree with Winston Churchill who, after the British House of Commons was bombed in 1941, argued that it should be rebuilt exactly as it had been – rather small and rather inconvenient as a working space – in order to preserve what he saw as Britain's valuable adversarial political culture. 'We shape our buildings, and afterwards our buildings shape us' (Commons debates 28 October 1943: col. 403–9). Thus, parliamentarians in New Zealand and South Africa have debated changing their seating arrangements to encourage more consensual behaviour; organizations like the Commission for Architecture and the Built Environment attribute various powers of health and well-being to well-designed buildings (CABE, 2002); while an art historian recently went so far as to claim that Russian President Putin has become more dictatorial not because of his

5

personal characteristics but because the buildings of the Kremlin have made him so (Thurley, 2007). Regardless of what one thinks about some of these claims, there is something appealing about extending an idea common in political science – that institutions structure political behaviour – and asking whether this is true in a physical, bricks-and-mortar sense as well. Perhaps, as Frank Lloyd Wright thought, it is possible that there is an 'architecture of democracy', a building and planning style that embodies and embeds democratic values (Wright, 1939).

The idea that democracy depends on physical space in various ways runs counter to the current orthodoxy in democratic theory and wider political science. Issues of physical space are almost entirely off the radar of scholars of politics. Those very few political theorists who use the term 'public space' use it interchangeably with 'public sphere' or 'public realm'. They generally take it to be a metaphor that refers to the myriad ways in which citizens separated in time and space can participate in collective deliberation, decision-making, and action (e.g. Benhabib, 1992; Nagel, 1995). Hénaff and Strong (2001: 35) go so far as to claim that 'the literal meaning has almost been wiped out'. Of course, the study of the virtual realms of democracy has been extremely fruitful. From the standpoint of normative democratic theory, the issues are scale and complexity: the members of large-scale, complex societies cannot all gather together in a physical forum to argue, deliberate, and decide; yet they need to participate in public debate in some way if that society is to be called democratic, even if only to debate their choice of representatives. Online worlds, therefore, offer attractive alternative venues for democratic deliberation, making the idea of active, engaged democratic citizenship thinkable and achievable at scales beyond the city state, even beyond the nation state. But while the pursuit of metaphorical conceptions of public space is clearly a worthwhile endeavour, and one that is doing much to broaden conceptions of democracy, important risks arise if that becomes an exclusive focus. I will spend a large part of the book setting out these risks, but in brief, they concern a loss of connection between political elites and masses, and an increasing isolation of elites from mass concerns; a loss of a sense of 'we' that underlies any effective democracy; and a loss of connection between people's narratives about themselves and their community and the physical environment that 'emplaces' those narratives. Each of these things, while not fatal to democracy, weakens it in important ways and may, collectively, prove damaging in the long run. And yet, by and large, political scholars have not noticed, and are failing to call attention to, the erosion of some fundamental conditions for democratic performance.

That is not to say that no one has noticed: they have. Urban sociologists, architectural theorists, and human geographers especially have been attentive to issues of public space and democracy for some time now. Sociology, for one, has been said to have undergone a 'spatial turn' following the work of Edward Soja (1989), although Soja and others have followed a much older thread of work from Georg Simmel in 1903 (1950) and Walter Benjamin in the 1920s and 1930s (1999) that focused on the ways in which social structures and power relationships are embedded in and reinforced by the built environment of cities. Since then, writers like Mike Davis (1990) and Richard Sennett (2002) have provided rich and widely cited narratives of how those same relationships have played out over time and space. Sennett, in particular, has been widely influential in noting what he calls the 'fall of public man', which he traces through the loss of spaces in which people can act as citizens, and a preference for spaces through which people transit, or act as consumers and displayers of their consumption. This theme has been picked up and explored in many different contexts, but a common one is city development projects that effectively take large swathes of former public space out of the public realm and control it, commercialize it, and commodify it, such that perfectly ordinary, everyday uses of space become no longer possible – parking a bike, having a picnic, and sitting and talking. That is to say nothing of the control of expressly political purposes, something that will be taken up at length in Part II. One of the major aims of this book is to draw these shifts to the attention of political scholars of democracy – it is a significant move that is being overlooked, and is rendering some of the usual nostrums about liberal democracy looking more and more tired.

The literature that I lump together under the banner of 'urban theory', following Parker (2004), has its own blind spots. To a scholar of policy and democracy in a mainstream political science department, two things are particularly striking. The first is that all sorts of public activity are often treated as categorical and normative equivalents: that encountering members of the public in playful settings is normatively the same as engaging in binding collective decision-making, for example. The second is that the idea of democracy is either taken as a background assumption not worth exploring or is taken to be something roughly equivalent to freedom. In some work, this generates unintended irony. There are writers who decry the privatization of public space on the grounds that people can no longer 'do what they want' in it, which merely pits one liberal individualist claim against another without providing any reasons to choose between them. I shall spend some time in this book providing reasons – liberal reasons – to choose between some competing claims on the use of space but also argue that, for the most part, democracy is the means we use to make such choices, not something to which we can appeal to make the choice for us.

There is some work in urban theory that is much more conceptually aware and rigorous. Notable among more recent contributions is that of Clive Barnett (2003) who rejects the formal, institutional, and somewhat bloodless accounts of democracy that dominate political theory and political science, and instead provides a dynamic account based on public claim-making and the invocation of different publics in different sites (see also Iveson, 2007). Barnett draws most on post-structuralist resources, although he is at pains to point out that he is interested not in 'caricatured oppositions' (2003: 197) but in the overlapping concerns between liberal, post-structural, and other approaches. He is also explicitly interested in the 'cultural conditions of democracy'. This project is somewhat different. I share Barnett's focus on claim-making, but focus on the *physical* conditions of democracy rather than its cultural conditions, although one of the key points to emerge in Part I is that one cannot get away from the social construction of what sociologists call 'place'. I also look most particularly at physical sites rather than media sites, although one of the key reasons why I think physicality matters to democracy is its importance in generating images for media consumption and transmission. I also stick with a liberal conception of democracy – one with a deliberative and performative twist, admittedly, but still liberal in its foundations – because I think that the physical still matters on a liberal understanding of democracy. Liberal theorists should not, I think, dismiss the importance of physical space simply because they reject the account of democracy that underlies most spatial analyses.

This book thus has two audiences. Its primary audience is scholars of democracy, communication, and planning in mainstream political science and policy departments; its secondary audience is urban theorists. While the primary aim is to alert political scholars to the importance of the physical, drawing on resources from the urban theory literature, the secondary aim is to highlight some important differences in the way key political concepts are handled in urban theory, especially the concept of democracy and the public/private distinction. Therefore, in Chapter two, I spend what will doubtless seem to a political theorist an unconscionably long time setting out a political definition of democracy and the implications of that definition for the study of public space; but it is important that I do so because the political definition has significant departures from that implicit – it is rarely explicit – in urban theory. Chapter three is targeted at both audiences. It concerns the public/private split, which is, in my view, problematic in both political and urban theory. In that chapter, I set out reasons to think that the public/private distinction masks at least four finer-grained distinctions, and that therefore objects and practices that might be public in one respect are private in others. Both these chapters help us make better sense of the tensions and contradictions that arise in battles over public space. I argue that one of the big faults of the urban theory literature is a tendency to appeal to concepts of democracy and public to resolve such conflicts, when more often than not the concepts of democracy and public *give rise to* those conflicts. The big fault of the political literature is that it has barely noticed physical space, or dismisses its importance too abruptly.

I will set out the plan of the argument in more detail shortly. Before doing that, I want to sketch out the approach taken, including a brief discussion of the case studies.

Questions, Approach, and Cases

This is a work that blends political theory with the principles of comparative political and policy studies, using observation and interviews to ground the discussion in lived experience. While it is thus a long way from analytic political theory as usually practised, it attends to the call that many democracy scholars have made in recent years to be more inductive and less deductive, and to attend to the way that democracy is actually performed rather than be driven entirely by ideal models. One of the stand-out exponents of this way of working in recent years has been Michael Saward (2003, 2006, 2010), but it is a call that has been made in various ways by Dryzek (2000), Fung (2003), Mansbridge (2003), and Smith (2009). Having said that, ideal models are useful because they help us ask better questions of political activity. They help us attend to what is present in the real world, and what is not, especially when we use multiple models to highlight different aspects of political action. Thus, my approach has something in common with that of those like Andrew Rehfeld (2006, 2009) who operate not just in normative political theory, nor in empirical political science, but in space that overlaps both, using conceptual tools and focused observation to analyse policy and politics. This is space shared with a number of policy and planning scholars like Frank Fischer (1990, 2009), John Dryzek (1990, 1997, 2006), and Maarten Hajer (2003, 2009), among others.

Therefore, the broad approach taken here is to start with some conceptual work about democracy and its requirements for public space, teasing out what we mean by 'public', 'space', and 'public space' along the way; and then to go looking in the real world to see what public space is available in democratic cities, how it is used, how it is constructed, and how it is controlled. In short, what space is needed in a democracy, and do real democracies provide that space?

Because these questions are broad, the conceptual apparatus I deploy is likewise broad. I have found it useful to start with a deliberative conception of democracy – something I set out in detail in Chapter two – because it is a conception that is founded on ideas of the interchange of claims and arguments in the public sphere. However, deliberative democracy has some important blind spots, and so I supplement it with a 'performative' account of democracy. It treats performance and drama not as metaphors to help explain democracy but as the way that democracy really works. Drawing on the dramatic theory of Kenneth Burke (1969), the political communication theory of Edelman (1976, 1988), and a long-standing tradition of narrative analysis in policy studies,[4] the performative account alerts us to the *staging* of democracy: the need for and utility of particular platforms for the performance of particular roles (cf. Barnett, 2003; Hajer, 2005). By distinguishing between the actors in a democracy and the different roles they play, it gets beyond the frankly arid 'structure versus agency' debate that has persisted for far too long now in British political science (for a critical discussion, see Hay, 2002) and helps us see democracy as a creative, iterative, dynamic thing rather than a fixed set of abstract relations among institutions, or between elites and masses (cf. Saward, 2003).

With respect to the idea of the public and private, I have found the work of Raymond Geuss especially helpful. Geuss, too, stresses the importance of focusing not on abstractions in isolation but on how concepts are deployed in 'some relatively concrete context of human action' (2001: 107). In doing so, he identifies numerous separate and sometime contradictory ideas that get bundled together under the 'public' and 'private' labels. I use his insights to criticize both political and urban accounts of the public and public space, and develop instead a novel set of four criteria for judging the 'publicness' of any given space or structure: accessibility, use of common resources, common impact, and public role performance. Ownership, the criterion frequently suggested by political theorists, is missing, for reasons I explain in detail in Chapter three. Real public spaces can meet one, two, three, or all four of those criteria. Which ones *democracy* requires is another matter, and something I specify in some detail, but I argue that focusing only on the accessibility criterion, as urbanists tend to do, or on ownership, as political theorists sometimes do, leads to a tendency to foreclose debates about public space. Indeed, it leads to attempts to argue that the concepts of democracy and publicness could resolve arguments over the provision, use, and control of space in cities, when my view is that tensions in these concepts are what open the debates in the first place. As I argue in detail in Part II, more limited conceptions fail to make sense of those conflicts; I think my broader approach offers a way forward.

The final bit of conceptual architecture is to deal with questions of what effects, in principle, spatial arrangements can be said to have on political behaviour; that is, to what extent, and how, might space limit democratic action, if at all? In Chapter four, I set out a continuum of effects from the

---

[4] Including Dunsire (1973), Stone (1988), Hood and Jackson (1991), Fischer and Forester (1993), Hood (1998), and Hajer (2009).

10

mandatory – a wall or barrier being a paradigm case – to the purely conventional processes through which symbols cue certain kinds of behaviour. To do that, I draw on two theoretical sources: semiotics, and the sociological distinction between 'space' and 'place' (Gieryn, 2000), the former denoting physical entities and settings and the latter denoting those settings filled with meanings, symbols, social practices, narratives, power relations, and so on.

Having done the conceptual groundwork, I then attempt to answer the second question – what space do democracies provide? – by a mix of observation, interview, and secondary research on eleven capital cities around the world. The cities are: in Europe, London and Berlin; in North America, Ottawa and Washington, DC; in Latin America, Mexico City and Santiago; in Australasia, Wellington and Canberra; in East Asia, Tokyo and Hong Kong; and in Africa, Cape Town. In addition to those primary locations, I also occasionally draw on material from, and personal visits to, Athens, the town of Appenzell in Switzerland, and various political sites on the Isle of Man; Valparaíso, the seat of the legislature in Chile; and New York, New Haven, and Minneapolis in the United States.

The first point is that the primary eleven are all capital cities with the exception of Hong Kong, although Hong Kongers like to think of themselves as citizens of a city state as much as citizens of a grander entity, and so I do not think it too big a stretch to include Hong Kong in a list of capitals. I focus on capitals because they are the symbolic and formal centres of their nations' respective public spheres. Of course, I realize that a great amount of public engagement with politics takes place in entirely different cities, even outside urban centres, but time and resources were limited and I could not visit everywhere I wanted.

The selection was done with comparative requirements in mind (King et al., 1994), although practicalities were important too. Given that one of the views I explore is the idea that different spatial arrangements affect democratic behaviour, I chose a mix of cities that were purpose-built, organically developed, or a mix of the two; and I followed Goodsell (1988a) by balancing cities whose legislative assemblies were of neoclassical or modern design, and those with different shaped debating chambers. Given that I think that political culture might play at least as important a role in determining democratic dynamics as the spatial arrangements, I used three indicators of culture to further balance the sample: I tried to get to at least two cities in each continent; a balance of majoritarian and consensual polities (following Lijphart, 1999); and a balance of democracies that ranked high, medium, and low on Inglehart and Welzel's measure (2003) of democratic effectiveness. As Table 1.1 shows, in these aims I was partially successful. There are five purpose-built and rebuilt cities to six organic ones (although classifying London as organic is debatable). Assembly styles include six

11

Table 1.1. Cases and selection criteria

	Capital type	Legislative building style	Chamber shape	Institutional arrangements	Democratic effectiveness
London	O	T	II	M	H
Berlin	M	T/M	C	C	H
Washington, DC	P	T	F	M/C	H
Ottawa	P	T	U	M/C	H
Mexico City	O	M	C	n/a	L
Santiago/ Valparaíso	O	M	F	n/a	M
Canberra	P	M	U	M/C	H
Wellington	O	T/M	U	C/M	H
Tokyo	M	T	F	C	M
Hong Kong	O	T	U	C	L
Cape Town	O	T	U	n/a	M

Notes:
Capital type: O = organic; P = purpose-built; M = mixed;
Legislative building style (Goodsell, 1988a): T = traditional, usually neoclassical; M = modern; T/M = mixed, traditional dominant;
Chamber shape: C = semi-circular; II = oppositional benches; U = U-shaped, with oppositional front benches only; F = broad fan;
Institutional arrangements: C = consensual; M = majoritarian; M/C = mixed, with majoritarian features dominant; C/M = mixed, with consensus features dominant; n/a = not rated in Lijphart (1999);
Democratic effectiveness (Inglehart and Welzel, 2003): H = high; M = medium; L = low.

traditional, three modern, and two mixed with a reasonable cross-section of chamber shapes. The sample is dominated by states with a mixed institutional style rather than pure consensual or majoritarian democracies. Where the set is most skewed is towards developed democracies with highly effective legislatures. It is rather dominated by colonial cities, G8 cities, and not the more marginal. There is only one city in Africa, and one that is hardly representative of the continent. This was forced on me by resource limits and the political economy of international air links. While the G8 capitals are all nicely connected, flying between South Africa and Brazil, for instance, is a great deal harder than one might think. Including Delhi and different African cities into round-the-world tickets proved impossible and side trips would have been ruinously expensive. Given that, there is certainly a bias to my sample, but I call attention to that fact wherever it seems important in the narrative that follows.

In each city, I tried to do five things:

1. interview legislature managers, city planners, police authorities, local urban academics, and protest organizers, especially those who organized anti-war protests from 2002 onwards;

12

2. visit the assembly buildings and other important buildings of the formal public sphere, on a casual, walk-up basis;

3. visit major parks, plazas, and sites of important historical events;

4. use local public transport to get a sense of how easy it is to get around each city; and

5. walk around a lot, talk to people in cafes and on park benches, observe, take notes, and photographs, to get a feel for the place in a less purposive way.

Time constraints meant that I interviewed those who were available more than deriving a rigorous comparative sample. Where there were gaps, I filled them in with information from online sources and the secondary literature. The biggest omission is that in only one place – the Isle of Man – was I able to arrange interviews with local police. I am not going to speculate on the reasons for that, but simply note it. In all, I conducted interviews with sixty-three people, categorized as in Table 1.2.

I also need to explain a couple of points of terminology and scope. To readers in parliamentary democracies, focusing an account of the formal public sphere on legislative assemblies may seem a fairly uncontroversial thing to do, but to those in presidential or semi-presidential systems, to use Linz's categories (1994), it is anything but that. Thinking about the formal public sphere in the United States, for example, might lead one to protest that such a study should, at the very least, include not just the Capitol Building but the Supreme Court, the Library of Congress, and the White House, let alone the DC assembly and all the other centres of public debate at state, county, and municipal level. I agree in principle, and in some cases I mention the offices and palaces of presidents. Nonetheless, I do spend more time on assembly buildings themselves, for three reasons: available space; the fact that the tiny literature on the buildings of democracy also focuses on legislative assemblies; and because, with a few exceptions, I found access to assembly

Table 1.2. Interviewees by occupation

Assembly members and staff	16
Protest and community organizers	14
Academics	13
Planning authority staff and advisers	9
City councillors and staff	8
Local residents not otherwise counted	8
Police	1

Note that, with the exception of the 'not otherwise noted' group, the categories above overlap: academics serve on city councils or agitate about public space; planning authority staff sometimes spoke with their 'residents' hat on, sometimes as publishing academics. Family and group discussions have been counted as just one instance. I have not noted the countless and fruitful conversations with taxi drivers, tour guides, people on park benches, and so forth.

buildings very much easier. The issue of accessibility is something taken up in detail in Chapter six.

By 'assembly buildings' I mean primarily the buildings that house the assembly chamber(s), elected representatives and their staff, services staff, libraries, committee rooms, and so on. Rarely does this mean one building. Sometimes it means distinct and commonly identified precincts, as in Cape Town; sometimes it means buildings that have less obvious linkages, as in Wellington; and sometimes it means a mixture, as in Ottawa. In some cases, not all the assembly buildings are even in the same city, as in Chile, with the Congress building in Valparaíso, but a lot of assembly business conducted in Santiago. Some elements may not be enclosed structures at all, like the *Landsgemeindeplatz* in Appenzell or Tynwald Hill on the Isle of Man. But my scope generally stops there. I do not generally consider buildings housing government departments, even if their ministers are accommodated in them; I do not look at constituency offices, although they get a mention, and consider only national assemblies rather than state, provincial, district, and city assemblies. There was enough to visit in each city as it was without going into every federal and sub-state government office as well.

This is a minor point, but perhaps it is also worth explaining why I tend to use the word 'assembly' in preference to some common alternatives. 'Legislature' is the more usual term in the United States, but it focuses too much on law-making as the business of democracy when, following the 'governance' turn, we know that publicly binding decisions are often made well outside formal representative institutions, often without a specific law being enacted to make things happen (Pierre, 2000). That is to say nothing of the non-decisional drivers of and constraints on policy. 'Parliament' might be an attractive alternative because of its etymological links with talk, focusing our attention on the deliberative features of democracy, but that word is perhaps too closely associated with Westminster and Westminster-style democracies. 'Assembly', like legislature, might be objected to on the grounds that it focuses too much attention on the debating chamber, when the work of democracy goes on in committee rooms, lobbies, corridors, offices, cafes, and bars in and around the legislative precinct. However, I will argue that democracy requires single stages on which representatives assemble for its scrutiny role to be performed effectively. Therefore, despite my personal preference for 'parliament' and the image of talk that it entails, I use 'assembly' throughout to focus attention on that normative requirement.

Finally, let me set out what this book is *not* about. For a start, it is not a book primarily about spatial justice. Questions concerning access to and distribution of land and resources, and the group and individual narratives that are anchored to particular sites arise, especially in Part II when I consider the production and availability of public space, but that is just one aspect among many. Second, it is not a complete evaluation of public space in the cities under study nor is it an attempt to explain urban theory to political scientists and theorists. It has narrower concerns than that, specifically to tease out what a liberal deliberative account of democracy requires in terms of public space, and how well modern cities provide it. Thus, while I discuss issues like the way that power relations are embedded in the built environment, the counter-movements and counterpractices that attempt to reclaim space from private or oligarchic control, the idea that there is a 'right to the city', and so on, these are not the central concerns.

Outline of the Argument

The book is in three parts. Part I, *The Theory of Democratic Public Space*, does the conceptual groundwork, setting out a theory of democracy's requirements for public space, defining democracy, public, and space along the way. Part II, *Public Space and Democratic Performance*, offers a more grounded analysis of my cases, showing how the theoretical requirements are met, or not, in real life, focusing first on the formal public sphere and then on the informal. Part III, *Evaluating Democratic Space*, summarizes the main points but does so in the context of a set of proposals for improving some measures of democracy to take spatial requirements into account, and is illustrated by a tentative comparative evaluation of my selected cities based on the observational and interview work.

The theoretical work starts in Chapter two by setting out a fairly standard, political definition of democracy following the deliberative turn, one that focuses on making binding collective decisions about all manner of public claims. The point of the definition is to emphasize that democracy is a set of principles and decision procedures for resolving conflicts; it is not in itself a set of principles that can resolve conflicts *ex ante*. But I then link that standard account to the more novel ideas about the necessity of narration and performance, arguing that drama should not just be used as a metaphor to help us think about democracy, but that democracy really does proceed in a dramaturgical fashion. From that starting point, I build a performative account of democracy that specifies a number of roles that need to be played, including roles for every member of the *demos* and roles for elected, selected, or self-selected representatives. Chapter two then closes by setting out, in broad terms, the theoretical linkages between each role and the kind of stage – the kind of physical public space – that the performance of those roles requires. In doing so, I draw on Kenneth Burke's concept (1969) of the 'scene-act ratio', by way of Hajer (2009), arguing that while for some roles and some narrative content pretty much any stage will do, for others there are very specific

15

requirements. In particular, I argue that public claim-making requires highly visible stages, which limits the range of possibilities in interesting ways, and that binding collective decision-making and scrutiny of the decision-makers require not just visible but single stages, putting decision-makers under the spotlight and keeping them there. The implications are these: it is a functional requirement of democracy that binding collective decision-making takes place in a single, visible, and accessible venue; and it is a requirement of democracy that public claims be made in places that are conducive to being noticed and taken seriously by the rest of the *demos*. From those two claims, a great deal follows.

Having produced a working definition of democracy, Chapter three offers a working definition of public space. It starts with the public/private distinction, arguing that it is misleading because it overlies a set of quite different, often-competing distinctions concerning the nature of 'the public', the places where they gather, and the things that the public is or should be concerned about. This leads me to abandon the idea of a single public/private distinction, and offer instead a four-fold definition of public space that

1. is openly accessible; and/or
2. uses common resources; and/or
3. has common effects; and/or
4. is used for the performance of public roles.

Along the way, I specifically abandon the idea that it is ownership that defines whether space is public or private, because ownership turns out not to track the other categories, and fails to deal with a set of public goods that cannot be packaged up and parcelled out. I then argue that democracy *requires* public space in sense 4 and may sometimes require it in sense 1, but set out reasons to be cautious, and that democracy *is concerned with* public space in senses 2 and 3. In response to the argument that the requirement for physical public space is overstated, and that democracy can happily move online, I highlight the losses for communication when that occurs and the reliance on physical events by the media, and point out a crucial confusion between medium and message that underlies the objection.

Chapter four wraps up the conceptual work by considering claims that spatial arrangements affect political behaviour. This matters for the overall project because it helps us understand exactly what is at stake politically when it comes to battles over public space. It deepens our answer to the question posed in the last chapter: public space is all very nice, but does it *matter* in the modern world? My answer is that it does, but in complicated ways. I start by drawing on some concepts from sociology and semiotics to distinguish between 'space' as physical settings and 'place', which is those settings functioning as symbols, anchor points for memories, narratives, norms, and power relations. I argue that it is often the symbolic associations that do the political work, not the symbol itself, and while that makes the effects no less real, it also means that the effects are changed by things other than mere bulldozing or interior design. I also consider how likely it is that democratically important public space will be provided in an environment characterized by the deliberate removal of powers from elected governments to unelected decision-makers like property developers and business associations. While these political-economic battles are not the primary focus of this study, they are very important for understanding the degree to which my normative injunctions can be realized in present-day democracies. They help alert us to the sources of many conflicts over public space.

The case analysis then begins with two chapters examining how legislative assemblies function as public space. Chapter five focuses on assemblies as stages for the performance of democratic roles: first as symbolic statements of national identity (narration); second as stages for the performance of grand national rituals; and third as sites for deliberation and decision-making. Along the way, I engage further with arguments about the alleged behavioural effects of assembly buildings, and while some of these claims are clearly nonsense, buildings and their interiors nonetheless send behavioural cues because of the symbolic associations that have built up around certain formats and layouts *in particular contexts*. This implies two things: first, that democrats should value assembly buildings for their role in cueing onlookers to take the proceedings inside – binding collective decision-making – seriously; and second, that the symbolic associations of buildings and rooms can be changed, often simply by changing, visibly, what goes on in them. That said, I do also argue that certain kinds of spatial effects genuinely are physical and not symbolic – the size of a chamber has an impact on acoustics and the ability to visually engage one's interlocutors that is not merely conventional, for example, while speaking from a central lectern in an assembly strips out some – but not all – of the status cues that come with other arrangements.

Chapter six continues the focus on assembly buildings, but this time from the requirements of public space. In particular, I argue that while assemblies were once extremely open to very limited *demos*, they are increasingly inaccessible, in obvious and subtle ways. The obvious methods include security measures that quarantine visitors as a dangerous contagion. More subtle means include turning assembly buildings into museums and tourist attractions so that the work that goes on in them, or should go on in them, disappears from public view. I use these observations to make the first of several points on a recurrent theme in the book: that the buildings of the formal public sphere are increasingly and systematically excluding people as citizens, purposive publics, and privileging incidental or leisure publics. The major exception in all this is the Canadian Parliament, whose members have fought battles with security advisers about maintaining citizen access to Parliament Hill and Parliament Buildings themselves. I conclude by making my first modest proposal: to continue the focus on assemblies as working buildings in which binding collective decisions are made, yet encourage purposive engagement with those decisions by active citizens, by creating an institution called Public Question Time, something that is already a feature of local government meetings in parts of the United Kingdom and Australia.

The theme of the legitimacy of purposive publics continues in Chapter seven, which considers the importance of space for public protest, especially space directly adjacent to the buildings of the formal public sphere. As with Chapter five, this chapter is structured around the types of space available for the performance of different democratic roles and the effects that different spatial arrangements can have. By contrast with the assemblies discussion, it is the case that layout matters a great deal more, especially proximity to the sites of the formal public sphere and the ability of a site to hold a large number of people that *look like* a large number of people. I argue that proximity to decision-makers matters for two main reasons: (*a*) so that decision-makers cannot insulate themselves from public displeasure; and (*b*) so that protestors themselves can cloak their claims in symbols of national importance, associating their claims with the self-same dignity that elected representatives draw on when making their claims and decisions. Nonetheless, there is an interesting tension between using such spaces and running the risk of ritualization, in which one's claims disappear into the background and the performance becomes an empty shell, and I note the ways that some activists advocate for dealing with that inevitable tension. This means that I take a highly unfashionable view, arguing not only that public spaces in front of assemblies should be maintained but also that they should be maintained relatively empty and featureless so that large purposive crowds can gather when they need to, and not be crowded out of the space by landscaping, plantings, fountains, seating galleries, and all the other 'programming' that some urban designers celebrate. But I also spend some time in Chapter seven on two factors that mean that such space is getting harder and harder to use: the privatization of public space, and its policing. It is with respect to these last two issues that the problem of the delegitimization of political engagement re-emerges.

The case study work wraps up in Chapter eight with a look at the wider fields of democratic engagement in the cities under study. I focus particularly on the representative functions of space in cities, looking at the ways in which people build up their impressions of the membership of the *demos* both through direct encounters and through the symbolism of the city. The degree to which certain narratives and experiences are anchored in physical form has a significant impact, I argue, on the degree to which different people feel included in the city, and thus the degree to which they feel they have a stake in the democratic performances and decision-making that take place within it. Along the way, I look at the variety of ways in which cities stratify citizens and how public transport systems can either reach across or reinforce those divides. But I also look at some of the conflicts that arise in the context of public parks, with particular layouts favouring some purposes over others, with politically valuable purposes losing out in many instances while noting the value of escaping purposive publics too. We need to get away from it all sometimes, something that both political scientists and urbanists can too easily forget.

Part III sums up the major claims in the book before deriving from those a set of qualitative, evaluative criteria and applying them to the cities under study. Because of the broad-brush nature of the work, the evaluation is necessarily tentative – each city deserves a detailed qualitative research project of its own – and so the conclusions are offered as hypotheses for further testing. But still I offer some broad qualitative judgements about the relative democratic merits of the cities under study, showing how some provide many more of the requisite spaces than others. What a particular group of people should *do* with a city that does not provide the requisite space is complicated, and I end up following the implications of the analysis by arguing that in most cases grand redesign is simply unnecessary, because people can change the meanings of buildings, and the behavioural cues that they send, by changing the ways they use them. Sometimes there is a need to rebuild, but less often than might be imagined.

The book ends with a hope about the study of democracy: that even if the reader is not persuaded that physical stages are needed for the performance of democracy, he or she will recognize that democracy is nonetheless a performance, and a rich and fascinating one at that. This has important implications for political scholarship, focused as it currently is on rationality in all its guises.

But now, I move on with the argument, starting in Part I with the theory of democratic public space.

Part I

The Theory of Democratic Public Space

2

Democratic Theory, Democratic Performance

I suggested in Chapter one that implicit in much of the sociological, geographical, and architectural literature on public space is a thin, under-theorized account of democracy. This thinness matters because while writers in these traditions are more aware than most of the conflicts that arise in the use and control of public space, they tend to assume that the democratic answer to such conflicts is always relatively simple and straightforward. Throughout this book I will argue, on the contrary, that the requirements of democracy pull in multiple directions when it comes to space, and that appeals to the concepts of 'public' and 'democracy' are what open many conflicts, not what resolve them. The tensions are not simply the result of rampant privatization or securitization, important though those things are, but internal to democratic and public norms themselves. This means that implementing the injunctions that emerge from some branches of urban studies will not necessarily make the problems it uncovers go away. Quite the reverse, it may exacerbate them. So, we need a thicker understanding of democracy and the public, and this chapter tackles the first of those concepts. I begin by setting out my take on democratic theory. As those who know democracy theory well will immediately spot, my take has fairly orthodox foundations, focusing as it does on decision-making rather than democratic culture, for instance. But it is also one that follows the so-called 'deliberative turn' in democratic theory, and so, rather than focusing on elections and formal institutions, my account takes seriously the processes of opinion formation and narration in the public sphere, and the ways in which public claims are transmitted to formal institutions for action. If I can demonstrate that even currently orthodox democratic theory requires physical public space, then I will have achieved something important.

The second step is to connect that account of democracy with an understanding of politics that is one of the present orthodoxy's blind spots: that democracy is not merely the interplay of arguments and reasons in some abstract public sphere but is performed by people, with aims, on stages. This

23

performative, dramaturgical understanding of democracy has roots in classical understandings of politics, and it is odd that this understanding has fallen into disrepute at a time when otherwise democratic theory is highly attentive to talk, communication, and interaction. Sometimes one gets the feeling that modern democratic theory has become disconnected from real people, and has drifted off into an abstract realm of ideas and reasons, a criticism related to that made some years ago by Young (2000: 37–40). Yet Young reminds us that even if democratic activities are things that can make us irritable or anxious, or make us wish we were doing something else, democracy involves *activities* none the less: demonstrating, petition-gathering, arguing, voting, persuading, discussing, and eyeballing (2000: 16). As I hope to show, this is true even of apparently 'disembodied' notions of democratic engagement that emphasize not people and their decision-making processes but discursive threads (Dryzek, 2000: 74–5) or storylines (Hajer, 2003: 104–5) that persist over time and space. While discursive threads may appear to have an existence independent of the people who pick them up and use them, they depend on being 'grounded' in activity, performance, and physicality to a degree that is sometimes not appreciated by theorists of the public sphere.

So, the aims of this chapter are to fill out our understanding of democracy such that we are alerted to the variety of performance that a reasonably standard account of democracy can demand, and then its requirements for physical stages on which those performances can take place. Readers familiar with democratic theory in mainstream political studies may wish to skip the first section, and pick up the thread again when I come on to the performative aspects. Chapters three and four will then set out a descriptive and normative theory of the stages themselves.

A Political Definition of Democracy

It is common to start discussions of democracy by picking apart the word's etymology, 'rule by the people', and then problematizing each bit: who are 'the people', what does 'rule' mean, and how is that rule exercised (e.g. Held, 2006: 1–2)? I will touch on each of those issues, but I want to begin with a different question: why democracy? What is it that theorists think democracy is *for*?

The common answer is that democracy is primarily a way of making collective decisions and that those decisions are primarily about three things: how to distribute scarce resources or, in Laswell's famous phrase (1958), 'who gets what, when and how'; the interests and power relations that structure that distribution; and the normative issues of who should get what, and how to structure society so that they get it.[1] 'Resources' on this account might include familiar things like time, money, and various physical goods, but it can also include information and information technology; welfare-related goods like health and happiness; or other abstract goods like ability, opportunity, autonomy, and liberty (Raz, 1986).

What distinguishes democratic means of making these collective decisions from non-democratic ways is

- the idea that those making the decisions are 'the people' or their duly authorized and accountable representatives;

- that those people are treated as *political* equals, despite their evident inequalities in other respects (Dahl, 1989: 89);

- that, following what is called the 'deliberative turn' in democratic theory (Dryzek, 2000: v), proposals for collective action or inaction need to be defended, or at least defensible, in public if they are to have any binding force for others;

- that decisions should reflect the 'wishes' (May, 1978: 1), 'felt interests' (Saward, 1998: 51), or 'settled preferences' (Goodin, 2003: 1) of citizens (Saward) or persons affected (May and Goodin) (i.e. one of the reasons why democracy is valued is because it is a set of decision-making procedures to make sure that what we want – 'we all' or 'we most of us' – goes); and

- that subject to these and various subordinate procedural requirements being met, the decisions are binding on winners and losers alike, although people are free to attempt to review decisions, sometimes on a regular basis.

Each of these points raises many questions, and involves continuing arguments. I will survey the relevant controversies in a moment, but for now want to emphasize that for scholars of politics, democracy is a collective decision-making mechanism designed to help 'us' decide what to do, and to resolve disagreements over who gets what. In liberal democratic theory, these conflicts arise when private demands on resources conflict; when one group's exercise of freedom conflicts with others' desire to exercise the same thing; say, when the accumulation of private property means that others cannot afford to house themselves decently; or when the insistence of a few on playing thrash metal at high volume means others' pursuit of other pleasures

---

[1] Alternative approaches include the democratic culture approach following the seminal work of Almond and Verba (1963), which focuses not on decisions but on the habits of mind, values, and daily practice that underpin democratic institutions. Nonetheless, my view is that those are *underpinnings*, not democracy itself, which is why I stick with the mainstream 'collective decisions' view. Recent, accessible discussions of the subject matter of politics are Leftwich (2004) and Stoker (2006).

25

is shattered. Other theorists have a broader account of how such conflicts arise, but all implicitly or explicitly agree that democracy is about sorting out common issues without dictatorship, domination, or shooting at each other (Przeworski, 1999).

The key point to note is that this political definition of democracy has an important point of contact with urban theory, and an important point of divergence. The point of contact is that for democracy to work there must be some sense of 'we', some appreciation of the fact that my exercise of personal freedom can impact on others' abilities to do the same thing, or impact on the collective resources that we all need to draw on. Urban theorists like Watson (2006), therefore, are right to worry about the degree to which space is structured to ensure that groups are separated from one another, atomized into subgroups who see only their internal interests, not their common interests with others. They are right to worry about gated communities, about commuters who lead lives separated from city dwellers, and about the loss of space for genuine cross-community encounter, if these things feed a politics in which sectional interests fight to maintain their privileges rather than taking the claims of the disadvantaged seriously (Connolly, 1991).

Where the political definition diverges from the urban is on the idea that some negotiation over the use of space is essential, because space is itself a resource that needs to be shared. It is, for example, presently fashionable to celebrate downtown skateboarding as the reclamation of streets and plazas from private corporations and the private police they hire (e.g. Borden, 2001; Stevens and Dovey, 2004) (Figure 2.1). While rebellious acts may be necessary to force open space that should not be closed or overly regulated (cf. Young, 2001), there is an obvious rejoinder: that space that has been colonized by young people whizzing around on skateboards is no longer 'public' for the elderly, or for parents with very young children, among others. A collision between a boarder and an 80-year-old, no matter how fit and healthy, can result in serious injury to the older person, even death. For public space to be genuinely accessible to all, there must be rules that regulate interactions between individuals, a freedom for each consistent with a like freedom for all (following Rawls, 1971), not individualistic anarchy. In some of the urban theory literature, democracy is treated as if it were solely a matter of individual liberty. That is a mistake. It is about how we resolve conflicts over the exercise of such liberty, and other resource claims.

Returning then to the definitional points identified above, they raise several prior questions: who is this 'we', do proposals need to be defended in public or merely defensible, how many of us have to agree before a decision is democratic, and why think that it is what we want that should be decisive? The last question can be dealt with most quickly. The competing view is to want the 'right thing' to be decisive, regardless of our individual preferences on the

Figure 2.1. Sharing space with skateboarders, San Francisco
Photo © Jack Simon, by permission.

matter, and followers of this requirement tend to be suspicious or simply dismissive of democracy, preferring elite-based choice mechanisms instead (e.g. Riker, 1982, and his followers). It is not necessary to pursue that argument in detail here, other than to say that the democratic response is that right answers to questions about what we should do collectively are not generally lying around waiting for the wise to uncover but are rather the result themselves of more democratic, deliberative processes. Even when right answers do exist prior to democratic creative processes, that does not instantly lead to the conclusion that it is right in politics to implement those answers without recourse to democratic deliberation (Walzer, 1981), partly because implementation requires justification to those affected, and partly because of the 'who judges the judges?' problem (Estlund, 1993). A more serious challenge is the claim that while 'getting what we want' is the right thing to aim at, democratic decision-making mechanisms are the wrong way of getting it. Instead, Hayek (1960) and his followers recommend market mechanisms that, when operating under the conditions of perfect competition and full information, are able to coordinate the individual actions of millions of people in such a way that they are given 'what they want' without any one decision-maker having to figure out all the permutations and implications. The problems with this view are well-known, particularly when it comes to the failure of markets to provide public goods, including public space, and I will take these issues up again in Chapters four and eight.

More recently, elements of the 'right decision' view of the point of decision-making have reappeared through the influence of deliberative democracy, the most significant development in democratic thought in the last two decades. Deliberative theory is a way of thinking about democracy that emphasizes not the decision-making moment but all the processes of opinion formation and public debating that go on before matters come to a vote. There are several major variants of deliberative theory (Hendriks, 2006; Parkinson, 2007b). One camp draws inspiration from Habermas's 'ideal speech situation' (1984) and focuses on the procedural conditions likely to produce free, rational communication between equals: reasonably full inclusion, equal treatment of participants, systematic information, and a preference for deliberating together until consensus or something like it is reached (see Cohen, 1989). The other camp has more in common with Habermas's sociology (1996) of democratic societies, and thus focuses on large scale debate in the public sphere, from the 'informal', messy, creative public sphere in which experiences, interests, and opinions are woven into storylines (Hajer, 1993) that are shared, discussed, challenged, and transmitted around society, to the 'formal' public sphere of legislatures, courts, and ad hoc institutions that develop law and policy out of those narrated demands. But both camps emphasize rational decision-making, both in the guise of better inputs into decision-making processes by including more diverse experiences and better quality information, and in the guise of better outputs that are supposed to emerge from freely deliberative encounters. The latter is enhanced by an important feature of deliberative democratic theory: the publicity principle. This is the Kantian idea that having to defend one's views in public has a disciplining effect on what one proposes, because one has to put forward proposals in terms that others can accept. 'Me, me, me' does not persuade others to give you the resources you want; 'It's good for you too', or, 'It's the right thing to do', is more likely not only to produce a positive reaction but also to change the nature of the proposals to ensure that people really can see collective benefits, or the justice of the claims being made. This is another way of making a point already made: that the 'right thing' to do in politics is often the result of inclusive, democratic encounters, not something that pre-exists them, hiding under rocks waiting to be found by clever truth hunters.

Herein lies the answer to a commonly expressed question about deliberative democratic practice: do proposals for action need to be publicly defended or merely publicly defensible?[2] The former implies that nothing should be done

---

[2] There is another possibility: 'not defended in public at all', or *in camera* deliberation (Parkinson, 2006a: 136–7). On the value of secrecy, see Dean (2001).

in a democratic society without it first being tested by the harsh light of publicity and associated public debate. The latter implies that just going ahead and doing something is fine so long as one can imagine defending one's actions in public. Goodin (2003) notes how paralyzing it would be if we expected every single public decision to be made through actual participation, and calls attention to the virtues of internal deliberation – imagining, pondering, thinking – as a necessary starting point and foundation for all sorts of decisions. The other route is to consider how different democratic requirements might apply at different points of the decision-making process, a 'sequencing' approach (Parkinson, 2006a). The idea is that the strict democratic criteria should be applied most rigorously at those points of the system where (a) disagreement is most sharp and (b) where a binding collective decision is about to be made. This gets us away from insisting, unreasonably, on all the panoply of elections and accountability at points in the deliberative system where it does not matter so much. What are those points? Previously, I have discussed this in terms of standard, linear models of the policy process (Parkinson, 2006a: 166–9): problem definition and agenda-setting, deliberation over alternatives, the decision-making moment itself, and post-decision implementation – what Catt (1999) calls 'define, discuss, decide, implement'. To foreshadow something later in this chapter, however, I now think the first step conflates some important democratic roles. Drawing on the macro theorists of deliberative democracy and governance,[3] it is important to signal more clearly that what precedes all the formal steps of decision-making is the generation of narratives in the informal public sphere, narratives about experiences of conflict over collective resources, the impacts of public decisions, normative claims about what should be done to whom, and so on – 'discourse', in other words. Given that, I think it is right to insist on fairly strict democratic criteria at the decision-making moment; but in the early stages, what is needed is to encourage much wilder, looser, informal discourse generation. The key is then to ensure that there are formal agenda-setting processes that capture the variety of narratives circulating on particular topics and feed them into the formal decision-making processes. The precise detail of how this works is not important right now: I have made specific utopian proposals elsewhere (Parkinson, 2006a), and anyway the precise form should vary from context to context and be the result of experimentation and tradition as well as principle (Saward, 2003). For the moment, what matters is the point that we do not need to insist on publicly defending every single element that circulates around a deliberative system – there is a time and a place for everything.

---

[3] Mansbridge (1992, 1999), Habermas (1996), Dryzek (2000), Young (2000), and Hajer (2003).

Moving on to the 'Who are "we"?' question, there are two main answers: all affected interests and those resident in a particular place (Goodin, 2007). The latter approach tends to be advanced by those who take boundaries, especially national boundaries, as more or less natural, appealing to ideas of 'communities of memory' (Bell, 1993), people who share founding or defining experiences, culture, traditions, symbols, and so on. This is not a terribly satisfactory approach in my view. From a sociological point of view, it seems more plausible to think that communities of memory are fictions devised in order to legitimate regimes, identities, and boundaries, to exclude as much as include, and to naturalize the relationships thus formed – in other words, that they are effects as much as causes; social and political constructs, not natural phenomena (Anderson, 1991). What those stories are often legitimizing is certain people's claims to control not territory for its own sake but the resources that come with a given territory: food, commodities, climate, and even the myths and narratives that are told about those territories, along with the access routes to those things. This means that they can be used to rule out claims to common resources by some disadvantaged people against wealthier others by ruling that the other is not part of 'us', and so has no claim on 'our' collective resources; or, on the contrary, by swamping and assimilating invaded or colonized groups, to deny public claims on the grounds that the larger 'we' does not agree. The former case was daily practice in apartheid South Africa, in which non-whites did not count as members of the *demos*; the latter is now seen in Australia, where Aboriginals' claims are regularly swamped by claims of what is good for 'Australians' generally.

Incidentally, I am thinking here of territorial control not just in the sense of individual ownership and exploitation. The discussion is meant to include the idea of guardianship as well, the husbanding of land for its own sake or the sake of future generations. This is the idea of guardianship that goes with being *tangata whenua*, 'people of the land', commonly wielded by New Zealand Māori in defence of claims to physical territory, and the stories, genealogies, resources, power, and respect that come with guardianship of such land. I have heard many an English farmer express similar sentiments: the land is not 'theirs'; they hold it in trust, and must manage it well while it is in their care.

The alternative way of thinking about the *demos* is to define it in terms of 'all persons whose interests are affected'; or, as recent work by Dryzek and Niemeyer (2008) would suggest, 'all relevant discourses'. For the moment, it is not necessary to spend too much time on the distinctions between these two formulations, other than to say that the 'discourses' formulation recognizes the point that, on any given question, the variety of impacts and opinion is rarely endless but rather is grouped into a much smaller and more manageable number of distinct experiences and positions, and that what democracies need to ensure most of the time is that the variety is captured rather than every single voice. This might seem to go against the political equality criterion of democracy, which asks that everyone gets a say. How most modern-day, large-scale democracies handle this is through the 'great invention' of representation (Mill, 1992 [1819]), in which everyone gets a say on choosing representatives, but then the representatives are supposed to get on with re-presenting the varied experiences, interests, and opinions of their constituents, subject to numerous accountability mechanisms and the authorization of regular elections. Other representatives too have a role: there are those who claim to speak for others without anyone having appointed them or authorized them, yet still make valuable contributions to enriching collective understanding of the situations faced by others (Saward, 2006); and there are those who speak for those who cannot, such as the natural environment, or the interests of animals, or those who are considered not to have the developed capacities needed to be effective advocates on their own behalf.

Of course, sometimes territories are a rough way of dealing with the 'all affected' injunction. As Goodin (2007: 48) points out, this is because those who live together in particular localities have certain kinds of interest that they share with their neighbours, and much of the time and for many issues these proximate bonds are what matter: sorting out roads and road rules, access to public services provided by local agencies, and so on. Still,

> the correlation between territoriality or nationality or history and shared interests is far from perfect. Not every person who lives in a given territory is affected by the actions and choices of every other person in that territory; not every person in the territory is affected by every collective decision of the demos constituted on the basis of residence in that territory. (Goodin, 2007: 48)

To that we might add that not every person affected by the actions or inactions of those in charge of a particular territory live in that territory. Therefore, while community of identity is clearly an important motivator in politics, and while it is often the default concept that people appeal to when thinking about who constitutes the *demos*, democratic theory points in a different direction: that it is those who are affected who should be the relevant *demos*, and that territoriality is only a rough, convenient shorthand that sometimes includes the relevant people, but sometimes does not.

From a spatial perspective, the conflict between these two answers, all affected interests and territorial groupings, has interesting implications. As will be seen in Chapter eight, for example, this turns out to be a central battleground when it comes to the democratic management of capital cities, because capitals are both places where the nation-state represents itself –

through monuments, large public buildings, the naming of parks and streets, the siting of ceremonies, and so on – and places where people live and work. Residents' need for a living, livable city can easily conflict with commuters' need for speedy access, which in turn can conflict with outsiders' demand for a national, symbolic city, as will be seen in the cases of Washington, DC and Canberra in particular. The key point to stress now is that this conflict is one that arises not because of democratic failure, but because it is inevitable in large-scale, multilayered and interconnected societies in which whatever one group does with a spatial resource affects what others can do with it. One cannot wish these conflicts away by appeal to democratic principles; they are the things that democratic principles are meant to help us cope with. Being democratic, in terms of responsiveness to the people's wishes, always involves dealing with conflict.

Moving on to the 'how many of us' question, there is an ongoing debate between those who prefer the majority decision rule (the option with 50 per cent plus one supporters wins), and those who prefer consensus (nothing is done until everyone supports one option). Defenders of the plurality decision rule (the option with the most supporters wins) are thin on the ground (see Goodin and List, 2006, for a defence in limited circumstances). It is not necessary to resolve this and other controversies here. The point to stress is that, whichever way you look at it, democracy requires very large numbers of people to agree on a course of action. Even a plurality winner in a society of a few million people is still based on the preferences of an awful lot of people, and in practical democratic politics we tend to judge the strength of positions not just by the deliberative criterion of 'the better argument' but also by the number of people lined up behind it. We take headcounts as an indicator of strength of feeling and issue importance, and, after deliberation, as the means of deciding what people think is the right course of action. While numbers are not sufficient to legitimate courses of action, they nonetheless matter a great deal, and that turns out to have important implications for performing democracy, a point I will return to later in this chapter.

The final definitional point concerns the scope of democracy, and here we touch again on issues that closely concern writers on public space. In what Held (2006) calls 'protective' liberal thought, or 'minimal' models of democracy (Przeworski, 1999), the scope of democracy must be strictly limited to establishing and maintaining a framework of rights that allows individuals to pursue their private projects free from the interference of others. That returns us to the earlier liberal definition of democracy as means of sorting through the conflicts that arise when we all try to claim the same resources at the same time, but it also relates to debates in the literature on public space because of the way that the more libertarian versions of this conception insist on bracketing off individual property rights from the purview of democracy (e.g. Nozick, 1974). Political geographers are concerned about what happens when private property rights are combined with the concentration of property in a relatively small number of hands, leading to the diminishing availability of common, public space, and I will deal with this topic extensively in the next two chapters. The competing vision is of a more expansive scope for democracy, one that is concerned with developing the full potential of citizens, considering the relevant 'resources' not in a narrow sense of a framework that guarantees free private action but in its most expansive sense of all the 'goods' of life. This is connected with competing accounts of liberty, the negative 'freedom from' and positive 'freedom to' accounts so eloquently expounded by Berlin (1958). The risk of the expansive, positive approach is that political life comes to overwhelm everything else; if the personal really is political, as the old feminist mantra has it, then there is no area of one's life that the collective cannot peer into. In response, Held (2006: 283) argues that while an expansive scope for democracy seems better justified in terms of a full account of the resources needed for citizens' autonomy, nonetheless we might want to halt at the borders of 'the sphere of the intimate'. Held offers no clear definition of what the sphere of the intimate might involve – he lays it down as a theoretical challenge for others – but this very topic has been debated extensively in feminist theory for some time now, especially over conflicts within feminist thought over the imperative on the one hand to expose the political nature of apparently 'private' domestic relationships, and that on the other to set clear boundaries on the state's ability to interfere with the workings of women's reproductive capacities. Again, I will deal with this extensively in the next chapter where I tackle the definition of public and private space.

* * * * *

What we have thus far is a definition of democracy that emphasizes collective decision-making over matters of common concern, among all those affected by the decision or their duly appointed representatives, using at least a majority decision rule. This has skipped over many issues, blithely ignored some controversies, and covered enormous territory very quickly, but it has focused on issues in mainstream democratic thought that will turn out to have direct bearing on questions of public space. However, there is relatively little here of our everyday experience of democratic debate and decision-making. There is plenty of 'discussion' but little sense so far of people doing it, little sense of how it is performed. Political debate is grounded in real activity, and in the next section I provide an account of that activity, an account that provides the basis for the discussion of stages for the performance of democracy, which comprises Part II.

33

Performing Democracy

Drama is a problematic label at a time when otherwise democratic theory is concerned with rationality and communicative competence. This is because drama carries with it an implication of insincerity – if one is 'playacting', one is putting on a show in order to manipulate (Harrington and Mitchell, 1999: 1) – although actual motivations may well include the sincere desire for mutual understanding, or the reinforcement of social bonds and identities, or problem solving (Bandura, 1982). Thus, drama is viewed with the same suspicion that some deliberative theorists like Spragens (1990) and Chambers (1996) view rhetoric. However, not all view rhetoric with suspicion. O'Neill (1998), for one, views it as an essential part of interpersonal communication, and overcomes the normative worry by pointing out how people in real deliberations are perfectly capable of making rational judgements about rhetorical claims. To think otherwise is to worry, along with religious literalists, about the 'lies' told in the theatre, as if audiences were not sophisticated enough to distinguish between fictional stories and the 'truths' they convey. I think we can apply the same reasoning to political drama. Some amount of dramatic spectacle, I argue, is empirically necessary for reaching and persuading audiences in politics, and what we need is dramatically educated audiences, not some grand censor or Master of the Revels approving every political script before it can be performed.

Thinking of politics in performative terms has a long history. In ancient Greece, it was quite commonplace to equate politics and drama (Hindson and Gray, 1988: 31), both requiring the same rhetorical skills to move an audience. When the *ecclesia*, the assembly of all Athenian citizens, moved from the Pnyx to the Theatre of Dionysus in the fourth-century BC, the distinction was blurred even further. This view persisted well into the early-modern period. Public men were often 'dramatists, courtiers, scholars and politicians' all rolled into one (Walker, 1998: 1). Indeed, one of the primary means used by the powerful to legitimate their rule was the public spectacle (Backscheider, 1993; see also Barker, 2001). Later, the connection becomes more of an analogy, something one finds in Edmund Burke, who draws repeated attention to the idea that parliament is a great, dignified 'theatrical exhibition hall for dramatic talents' (Hindson and Gray, 1988: 28), full of actors acting out a grand play. More recently, Whitehead (1999, 2002) uses some of the features of drama – conflict, leadership, persuasion, narrative tension and resolution, dramatic time, motives, character development, and public/private personas – as a heuristic device with which to analyse democratic transitions. Otherwise, most branches of political scholarship have long abandoned serious comparison between drama and politics.

It persists nonetheless, in political communication; in the study of social movements; and, as a minority sport, in policy studies. There is a rich thread of scholarship that has analysed the policy process as a battle between competing grand narratives, with good guys and bad guys, tragedy and comedy, and the selection of salient facts to bolster or undermine particular storylines.[4] Among these, Hajer (2005, 2009) argues that policy stories are not merely narrated but performed, staged, and dramatized, because this is what political communication in a 'mediatized' age demands. The modern media does not merely transmit words; it transmits still and moving pictures, taken by journalists, and also by passers-by on mobile phones, or captured on security cameras and shared on newspaper websites and YouTube alike. In that environment, intentional communication becomes highly performative, and Hajer spends much time showing the degree to which political images are the intended or unintended results of a scripted performance, in which issues of staging, lighting, audience access, symbolism, and interaction between actors are all important. Thus, Hajer extends the scope of political communication analysis by scholars like Edelman (1976, 1988), who have long insisted on the 'spectacular' nature of familiar political action and engagement.

It is important to stress that on this account, narrative structures and dramaturgy are not just heuristic devices to explain political processes; it is how politics really proceeds. Political actors make sense of the world in dramatic terms because it is the tool that allows those actors to attempt 'to create order and structure in potentially unstable situations' (Hajer, 2009). Fitting people and events into a narrative structure is the necessary first step in preparing to do something about a situation; dramatization is the tool we use to communicate those narratives to the audiences we need to persuade to act, or to remain inactive. Without narrative, complexity would overwhelm us – we would literally not know where to start. Without dramaturgy – that is, without the ability to present the narrative in a physical way through a staged event – we significantly undermine our ability to attract the cameras and thereby fail to transmit our narrative to the wider *demos* in the modern era.

This is more than an empirical point about how people in the real world communicate; it is a theoretical point about the conditions of democratic communication. However, while performance is not optional, the choice of performative style is, and here Sanders (1997), Young (1999), and others are surely right to highlight the degree to which certain sites and styles of performance tend to be privileged over others in political contests: the committee room over the school gate, for example. Therefore, to enter into political

---

[4] Notable examples include Fischer and Forester (1993), Schon and Rein (1994), and Stone (2002). Related work includes Dunsire (1973), Majone (1989), and Hood and Jackson (1991).

debate is to participate in a clash of which issues to narrate, a clash of performative styles, a clash of attempts to cast people as villains and heroes, a clash of what facts and values count as salient to the story, and to challenge attempts to close political contests with some variant of 'and they lived happily ever after' or perhaps, following Stone's analysis of policy stories, 'and they would have lived happily ever after had it not been for the interference of X' – insert your favourite bogey-man.

While descriptive political theory or 'comprehensive doctrines' (Rawls, 1996) offer alternative ways of structuring our understandings of the world, and while they are sometimes wielded in public debates, they are almost always used as tools in a performance rather than replacements for it. Bad guys are sometimes bad guys because they do not possess the valued theory, or are said not to understand the theory they espouse; just as good guys are sometimes good guys because they do possess the valued theory and wear it like a merit badge. British Prime Minister Margaret Thatcher did not discourse learnedly on neoliberal theory; she used mantras from it as a means to beat those who attempted to wield alternative weapons, to paint those alternative weapons as outdated, and to cast those who used them as the enemies of 'sensible' people. Therefore – and apologies for treading on toes now – it makes little sense to me to analyse the political theory of political leaders because it strikes me as odd to expect them to have a political theory in the first place. Rather, it makes more sense to look at the particular theoretical nostrums used alongside other narrative weapons, examining the use they are put to in a wider performative context.

I will defend the idea that democracy *depends* on performance in more detail in the next chapter. For now, I want to push the dramatic idea a little further to draw attention to the roles that democracy requires citizens to perform, which gives us some purchase on the kinds of stages required for performing them. On the basis of the preceding definitions and my own model of the deliberative system (Parkinson, 2006a), the main roles are:

- articulating interests, opinions, and experiences;
- making public claims
  - defining collective problems or defending existing arrangements,
  - requesting action or inaction on collective problems,
  - expressing, setting, and defending norms, and
  - making claims on public resources;
- deciding what to do, or what not to do, to address public claims, including weighing up options; and
- scrutinizing and giving account for public action and inaction.

I distinguish between general articulation of interests, opinions, and experiences on the one hand, and making specific public claims on the other,

36

because (*a*) the former does not automatically imply the latter, yet (*b*) is an important resource for the latter. As Kingdon (1984) points out, there are many issues and conditions that attract our attention, but not every one of them comes with a demand for collective action in response. In his terms, this is what separates a 'condition' (that there are rich and poor, for example) from a 'problem' (despite its persistence, the gap between rich and poor is only sporadically on the public agenda in neoliberal societies). I think it is worth including articulation of conditions in an account of democratic roles, because without it, the claiming role has no foundation in lived experience; because it suggests that one of the key democratic roles is to encourage people to talk about conditions that one might want to raise to the status of problem; and because it is how real people deliberate, swapping narratives about experience before attempting to draw more general lessons from those experiences (Parkinson, 2006*a*: 139).

Given the political equality criterion of democracy, these are roles that all members of the *demos* should be able to play to some degree. However, in a large-scale society, there is necessarily some role separation between the vast majority and specialist representatives who perform some of these roles on their behalf. This may not be a matter of rationality and efficiency, as Kateb (1981) argues, but necessary for achieving what in Britain is now called 'joined up' decision-making, ensuring that issues are considered in the round, relative to other public claims, rather than piecemeal. Given that some specialization is necessary, we can add the following roles, some of which will be more often than not performed by representatives, whether elected, selected, or self-appointed, and some of which will be undertaken by everyone. Those representative roles are:

- re-presenting experiences, opinions, and interests to other representatives;
- making, checking, accepting, and challenging claims to represent (Saward, 2006);
- leading, by proposing ends and means, norms, and standards;
- communicating decisions and reasons to other members of society; and
- making claims to public office and deciding between competing claimants.

The first supplementary role includes making actors in the formal public sphere aware of the narratives and claims circulating in the informal public sphere, and vice versa. This is particularly a role for the so-called attentive publics, especially journalists, bloggers, and advocacy groups, and also for artists (dramatists, even) and competing political parties (one of whose roles is to look for chinks in their opponents' argumentative armoury), or even the formal scrutiny role of bodies like the Audit Office or the Committee on

Standards in Public Life in the United Kingdom. This in turn leads to a distinction between the full-time role of the directors of such organizations, and the part-time role of other individuals who may devote a great deal of time and resources to supporting a cause on a regular basis, or who may take only an occasional interest, responding with time and money, voice, or vote when an issue that concerns them closely is brought to their attention.

There are, of course, many other things that governments and states do: provide security, enforce law, provide public goods, and so on. But these are things that governments of all stripes do; they do not emerge from the requirements of democracy per se. I do not also mean to imply that representation roles automatically map onto a centralized, hierarchical form of state organization. Formal public spheres exist at fairly local levels too, in the shape of parish, town, and county councils, for example. Equally, a deliberative system can form around a particular issue in a particular place, with ad hoc institutions set up to deal with it (Parkinson, 2006a: 177). It is a mistake to equate the formal public sphere with central legislatures alone.

It is important to separate democratic roles from the actors who perform them. For one, single actors can play multiple roles: this is commonly the case with elected representatives who not only have private and public roles to keep separate but also can have multiple public roles as party members, constituency representatives, government members, and so on. For another, consider the important democratic role of scrutinizing the legislative programme of governments. In many countries, this scrutiny role is played primarily by an upper house; in others, it is played by sub-committees of the legislature; and in yet others, it is played by courts, or legislative analysts offices (as in some US states), or academics, or quangos, or any number of other appointed and self-appointed watchdogs. Now, effective scrutiny requires independence from those people whose actions are being scrutinized, which tends to mean independent resources and tenure – one's ability to scrutinize the powerful is seriously compromised if one owes one's job to those same powerful individuals. In the United States, this is one reason why the members of the Supreme Court are appointed for life – no President can kick out justices whose decisions they do not like. In the United Kingdom, the present House of Lords performs a similar role: life tenure frees up members to scrutinize the government's programme, regardless of who actually secured them their ermine robes. This provides some logic to what would otherwise be a puzzling feature of British democracy: the unelected nature of the upper house (Parkinson, 2007a). Putting aside historical explanations of how the situation came about, it is normatively most puzzling when seen in isolation; when considered from the perspective of roles in a democratic system, it makes a great deal more sense, although that is certainly not to say that the British arrangements need no improving. The point is that while

38

roles and actors have many linkages – it would not do to have too young an actor playing the 'four score and upward' King Lear, and it would not do to have a government crony playing the role of Chief Justice – that still leaves a great deal of room for creativity and local tradition in assigning democratic roles to individuals and institutions, and some room for doubling up the roles assigned. Therefore, I do not propose to provide a detailed cast list to match the dramatis personae above: the precise actors assigned those roles will vary from context to context. Still, I can make some general comments about what should go on in the formal and informal public spheres, respectively.

It is on this point that I go further than Hajer (2005), who suggests that it is meaningless to seek a general account of links between political acts and their appropriate scenes, drawing on Kenneth Burke's idea (1969) of the 'scene–act ratio', and that instead it is only worthwhile looking at how particular ratios are constructed in particular cases. Of course, the scene–act ratio involves more than just scene and act – there is also actor, audience, script, time, author, and so on – and I agree with Hajer that what links these elements is highly variable and interdependent; but high variability does not mean that there are *no* limits within which the variation takes place.[5] I think we can theorize what those limits might be, and here I offer some thoughts on appropriate setting.

The first democratic role is narrating political issues with each other, not only helping form their own views but also distributing opinion and story-lines through the system as a whole. When it comes to spatial performance of this role, the limits are very wide indeed. Narration takes place in all sorts of settings: at the informal end of the deliberative system, it happens in homes, pubs, clubs, at work, in the street, or wherever people interact (Mansbridge, 1999); at the formal end, it happens when witnesses are called to give evidence to parliamentary committees, or when representatives narrate stories about the impact of policy on their constituents. It happens virtually, of course, in magazine and newspaper stories, in documentaries, and in blogs and other online forums; but it happens in physical settings too. Indeed, one of the ways that we might be able to tell whether we have a healthy democracy, I suggest, is by the degree to which the narratives that are told at street level are conveyed, represented, in formal decision-making moments, so that decision-makers know how it feels to be on the receiving end of the decisions they make.

---

[5] In a completely different context, Heffernan (2002) makes a similar point, showing that the somewhat tedious argument over whether there was or was not a consensus on policy in Britain after the Second World War misses the point that ferocious policy arguments can take place within relatively narrow bands of possibility, narrow paradigmatic ranges, yet appear no less oppositional and conflictual to participants.

An important point arises here. Private political narrative is more than casual interaction, something that is indicated by the frequently encountered taboos in many cultures about discussing certain topics with strangers. In Britain, for example, there is a strong taboo against talking about money, sex, and politics even with fairly close friends. In Chile, I found that people approach political topics extremely warily, partly because of their recent history of deadly political conflict but also because of a more general reticence to talk about potentially conflict-generating topics too quickly, before one has had a chance to establish some grounds of trust and friendship with that person. Therefore, most private talk is about establishing social bonds, not sorting out the problems of the world. While there is a great deal of cultural variation on this point, the tendency in many northern European and Anglophone countries is to talk about political subjects only among friends whom one can trust to share opinions, or at least trust to adhere to norms of civility to one's host. This is related to the points that Sunstein (2002: 176) makes about group polarization, an effect in part of 'people's desire to maintain their reputation and their self-perception', which reinforces the tendency of people to socialize and deliberate with the like-minded rather than those with differing experiences, in isolated 'deliberative enclaves' rather than as fellow members of a single *demos*. This has both positive and negative consequences – positive for sub-altern groups whose experiences might easily be swamped in the wider public sphere by the stories of the majority, negative in terms of encouraging extreme views to develop without the moderating influence of engagement with alternative points of view.

When we expect narration to happen across the boundaries of experience and enclave, or when we expect conflict to arise, we tend to move narration to particular, designated settings where conflict can be encouraged yet contained, to place it in a more formal setting, with formal rules of engagement to civilize conflict, perhaps controlled by a mediator or chairperson. This can be fairly hierarchical and formal, as with committees that operate in conjunction with norms of having a dignified, sometimes raised, place for the chairperson; or fairly egalitarian, with participants sitting in a circle but still using a moderator to encourage norms of respect (Dryzek, 1987).

All this is to show that the limits of the scene–act ratio when it comes to the narration of experience depend on whether the experience being narrated involves conflict with others present at the same time, which in turn depends on local norms about what constitutes acceptable and unacceptable topics of normal, unmediated interaction. When it is 'safe' topics with friends or strangers – the weather, say – the range of possible stages is extremely broad; when it is 'unsafe' topics with friends, the range is narrower, more private, less 'in the street' because of the risk of causing conflict with others nearby; when it is unsafe topics with strangers present, it is narrower still, moved to committee rooms or other neutral territory like library rooms – one case I have written about extensively used rooms at the local football club (Parkinson, 2006a: 1). These points present a challenge to the too-quick equation of democracy with open, unrestricted engagement across boundaries of difference that is found in much of the urban theory literature. I have argued that as an empirical matter narration, for one, does not work that way; Sunstein provides a further argument that enclaves can be normatively valuable from the perspective of sub-altern groups, helping them create spaces in which they can narrate their experiences and interests without being swamped by the experiences of dominant groups.

Interestingly, note how different this is from narrating experience in virtual settings. On the radio or online, people do not worry so much about offending each other because they are not physically present: they cannot pick up on body language, cannot be physically attacked, often cannot even be personally identified because of the use of online identities, and thus can get away with casting the other as a one-dimensional opinion carrier rather than a flesh-and-blood person with feelings, goals, and interests. I will return to this point in the next chapter when I ask whether physical public space is necessary for the health of democracy.

The second democratic role, making public claims, has much in common with narration, and thus shares elements of its scene–act ratio. Indeed, it is important not to think that the roles require *separate* stages: clearly, a particular setting can and often does involve all the roles, with people narrating experience, on the basis of claims that that experience is representative of some wider group, in order to back up claims for action on one's own behalf as well as on behalf of others. Still, the specific act of making public claims requires that the rest of the public is paying attention somehow, and that in turn implies another set of restrictions on the range of possible settings. Thus, scene–act ratios are neither identical for different democratic roles, nor entirely separate, but have areas of overlap.

We can think about the settings for making public claims in direct and indirect ways. In small-scale groups where all the members of the relevant *demos* can physically gather together in one place, public claims can be made directly in front of the assembled masses, as in the Athenian *ecclesia* or the Swiss *Landsgemeinden* (Reinisch and Parkinson, 2007) (Figure 2.2). In large-scale societies, the *demos* simply will not fit into the forum anymore, so claim-makers either require mediated ways of making the whole public aware of their claims, in cases where the whole public still is the final decision-making authority (as in referendums), or require ways of making representatives aware, in cases where decision-making power is with a representative body of some sort. These overlap: in a democracy, part of what makes decision-

Figure 2.2. Landsgemeinde Canton Glarus, 2009
Photo by Marc Schlumpf, www.icarus-design.ch licensed by Creative Commons.

makers take notice of a claim is to convince them that the wider public has noticed and takes it seriously too.

The stages for such activity are not unlimited. In any of these cases, simply 'talking among yourselves' in out-of-the-way places will not do – getting noticed and taken seriously is what matters, which means that claims need to be made in publicly visible and accessible places. Most obviously, groups can organize demonstrations at sites of power or sites of symbolic importance, perhaps adding a march from one site to another. The more the people who turn out, the bigger is the impact, recalling the importance of numbers as a short-cut to calculating the significance of a point of view. It is relatively easy for decision-makers to dismiss letters to the editor as the rantings of a few cranks, but much harder to dismiss millions demonstrating in the streets. It could involve spaces that the media regularly monitor anyway, because they are spaces where the powerful and decision-makers gather: legislatures, courts, and meeting venues for the G-8 or the World Economic Forum. It could involve stunts designed to attract the television cameras – remembering that news is about the unusual, the extraordinary, not the commonplace – such as Greenpeace scaling smokestacks, or disability activists chaining themselves to inaccessible buses, although the 'taken seriously' requirement sometimes means that movements face difficult choices about when to behave soberly and engage with the powerful, and when to throw the toys

Figure 2.3. Claim-making in public space – climate change protest on Big Ben, London, 2009

Photo © Nick Cobbing/Greenpeace, by permission.

out of the cot (Barnes and Oliver, 1995: 115) (Figure 2.3). For some, a reasonably successful strategy is to split themselves into collaborative and insurgent wings, one wearing suits and sober miens, the other causing the stir that gets the suits invited round the table (Dryzek et al., 2003). But for all these approaches, visibility is paramount, and as will be shown in later chapters, this can present particular challenges in some cities. In Minneapolis, with its raised network of 'skyways' connecting downtown buildings, it is hard for public demonstrators to attract the notice of fellow citizens walking one or two levels above the street; in Bangkok the situation is often reversed, with marchers either having to use elevated roads, passing fairly harmlessly over the heads of their fellow citizens below (Dovey, 2001), or occupying ground-level space that tends to provoke violent state responses. In other cases, there is no obvious centre where the powerful gather, no focal point, such as in South Africa with its four-fold capital and a fifth dominant city, Johannesburg. Or, access to symbolic sites is strictly limited or controlled, as in London where the already-limited space for protest is being even more constricted by security barriers, permit systems, and heavy policing. I will discuss many of these examples in more detail in Chapter six.

Another important aspect of this performative account of democracy is the role of audiences. It is a commonplace observation in dramatic studies that no theatrical 'event' can exist without the audience (Sauter, 2000); it is always aimed at communicating with or involving someone. Likewise, claim-making

43

is always directed at an audience, persuading others to think something or do something. Standard deliberative accounts do not distinguish well between performers and audience: in classic models oriented around the ideal speech situation, participants are alternatively speakers and listeners, all engaged together in the attempt to achieve mutual understanding. Get beyond even fairly small numbers of participants, however, and some role specialization emerges, with the majority taking more of a supporting role, or a seat in the stalls, while the few occupy centre stage. When that happens, communication can become less about achieving mutual understanding with one's interlocutors, and more about persuading the audience, depending on where the decision-making power lies. For example, no one, I imagine, would expect a debate between a group of presidential candidates to result in one of the leaders being persuaded by something another said, stroking his chin thoughtfully and responding, 'There is something in what you say, I shall have to reconsider my position.' Rather, the aim of such events is to convince the audience that one's ideas are right (logos), to engage their emotions on your side (pathos), and to convince them of your good character (ethos – to use Aristotle's categories of rhetorical proof), at the expense, rather than to the mutual benefit, of one's opponents. Furthermore, the primary audience may not even be in the same room. This was clearly the case with a deliberative poll (Fishkin, 1997) in Australia: some of the expert witnesses and some of the small-group spokespeople in the televized plenary question-and-answer sessions realized that their primary audience was not their fellow panellists or randomly selected participants in the chamber, but the television audience. Some, therefore, and completely rationally, chose to play to that gallery rather than engage in micro-deliberative reasoning together (Gibson and Miskin, 2002). The point to emphasize here is that in large-scale democracy, even though the audience might not be physically present at all, and even though the performance might be conveyed to them by virtual means, their virtual presence nonetheless affects what kind of performance is undertaken, and the imperative of reaching them determines the choice of stage: it must be highly visible, or made so by attracting media attention.

When it comes to the decision-making role in democracy, I tend to the view that binding collective decisions are best made by elected representatives in legislatures or councils, or directly by referendum. In the case of referendums, it is because of the clear act of consent to a specific proposal that such mechanisms entail. In the case of elected representatives, it is because their hold on office is dependent on the pleasure of their constituents; other kinds of representative, like the self-appointed or randomly selected representatives, cannot be held accountable for their actions so easily, and so should not hold the power to make decisions that are binding on the rest of us (Parkinson, 2006a: 152–4, 171–2). Here too the setting range is narrower again. We need not get quite so carried away as Edmund Burke who thought that parliament should be

> ...imposing and majestic. It should overwhelm the imagination of the populace, and awe them into acquiescence. The arena should be the architectural summit of human achievement, vast, impressive and sublime. (Hindson and Gray, 1988: 31)

It is possible, for example, to stage binding collective decision-making in much less grandiose style, as the Swiss cantons of Appenzell Inner-rhodes and Glarus do at their annual outdoor *Landsgemeinden*, held in the main town square each Spring (Reinisch and Parkinson, 2007). Nonetheless, even though the *Landsgemeinden* take place outdoors, they are still physical assemblies that take place in a single location, and are surrounded by dignifying rituals that have remained largely unchanged for several hundred years. This is important for two reasons. The first is that the staging signals that the event really matters and that the decisions reached there have an impact on thousands or even millions of people. The rituals of seriousness cue us into taking the proceedings seriously, although that, to my mind, is a good reason for ditching *some* of the wigs and regalia worn in the UK parliament, simply because they no longer signify anything serious and dignified, but something outdated, out of touch, and doddery. The same applies to voting: I think it is useful that one has to go physically to another public building – often a school, or a church, or a council office – and go through the physical performance of an act of voting, because it helps reinforce the importance of the action (Figures 2.4a and 2.4b). Voting for one's leaders or a ballot proposition has much more impact on the lives of one's fellow citizens than voting on the latest C-list celebrity game show or shopping online, and it is important to mark that difference by an appropriate performance, such as having to turn out to a polling booth, or come to the town square on *Landsgemeinde* day. The action and the setting impresses people with a toned-down, ideally more egalitarian, but still somewhat Burkean sense of significance, and should not, in my view, be replaced by the option of clicking a mouse or pushing the red button on the television remote control. Making voting easier in these ways might, I suspect, have the unintended consequence of making it seem less significant, and so a narrow range of staging options is a valuable thing.

The other reason is hinted at by something else Burke says: that being a member of a legislature means that one is 'on a conspicuous stage, and the world marks our demeanour' (quoted by Hindson and Gray, 1988: 21). Many political leaders and writers have remarked on how exposed that stage can be. Orgel (1975: 42) quotes James I as saying, 'A King is as one set on a stage whose smallest actions and gestures all the people gazingly doe behold'. When considering the fourth, scrutiny role of democracy, it is a significant advantage to have a single, readily identifiable and prominent stage on which the

Figure 2.4a. The rituals of democracy 1: voting in a school hall, New Zealand, 2008
Photo by Simon Lyall, public domain via Wikimedia Commons.

Figure 2.4b. The rituals of democracy 2: the state opening of Parliament, London, 2009
Photo © UK Parliament. Parliamentary material is reproduced with the permission of the Controller of HMSO on behalf of Parliament.

powerful must perform. It puts the powerful under the 'spotlight' – more theatrical language – and keeps them there. This, I suspect, is one reason why people find the existence of 'off-stage' political actors so troubling. It is not just that these people are unelected yet still influential, not just that they are hard to hold accountable for their actions, but that they cannot be clearly seen on the stage. They cannot be located in a physical sense and thus have the light of publicity shone on their words and actions.

Conclusions

In this chapter, I have covered an enormous amount of territory, so it is worth spending a moment summing up the key points to provide a reference point for the remaining discussion.

I have started with a definition of democracy as decisive public reasoning on common issues among all affected interests. The common issues concern resources, but that word is broadly understood to include both physical and abstract: money and liberty, as well as food and welfare more generally. Democracy requires some sense of being mutually affected, a sense of 'we', but does not, contra some urban theorists, boil down to mere negative liberty – it is a means of resolving conflicts over liberty, among other things. Contra those who advance territorial conceptions of the *demos*, I have argued that 'we' should also be defined expansively, using a variety of representatives to handle the inevitable scale problem that arises from wanting to have all relevant perspectives taken into account in public decision-making. Democratic theory at present emphasizes deliberation as the right means of debating issues – inclusive, more-or-less informed deliberation among equals oriented to consensus, with the right thing to do often being created in the democratic encounter rather than found lurking under a rock somewhere. However, there is ongoing debate about what the right decision rule is, with partisans of majority rule and consensus dividing on what they think will be more transformative, and what protective of the status quo. I have not taken a position on that debate, but simply argued that the number of people lining up behind a claim is an important indicator of how important people find the issue and, after deliberation, what people think is the right course of action. To all this, I have added a fairly expansive scope criterion (cf. Dryzek, 1996: 4–6), subject to further discussion of the public/private boundary.

I have then attempted to add more flesh and blood by providing what I think is a novel account of what performing democracy requires. I have briefly made a case – and will expand on this in the next chapter – for thinking that narration is an essential first step in any democracy that aims at solving real problems, and that performance is necessary to bring narratives to the attention of fellow citizens. Democratic performance involves four primary roles: narrating interests, opinion, and experience; making public claims; deciding about those claims; and scrutinizing and accounting for decisions and actions. In addition, representative structures introduce a set of roles to do with representing, leading, deciding, communicating, and competing for office, along with a role to do with judging and choosing between competing claimants for office. The other key role distinction arises between performers and audiences, which means that the classic theoretical conflation of participants in deliberative democracy into a single category cannot apply in real world deliberative democracy at the large scale. Roles and actors are separate: different contexts divide the roles up in different ways, some actors perform more than one role and some roles are performed by more than one actor. This does not mean that any actor can play any role – attentive publics perform important aspects of the scrutiny and representation roles that others cannot, for example – nor does it mean that there is *no* relationship between roles and stages. Instead, it is possible to theorize what the limits are to the possible stages associated with different roles: a wide range of stages for narration, but not boundless thanks to local norms about what safe and unsafe topics might be; highly visible stages for making public claims; and a dignified and preferably single stage for making collective decisions and for scrutinizing the acts of the powerful.

This chapter has started to look at public space from the point of view of the demands of democratic roles. This is important because it helps us understand why public space matters to democracy, and why I think political theorists are wrong when they dismiss the value of the physical, giving all their attention to the virtual realms of public engagement. I will deal with objections to that view in the next chapter, but before that need to engage more with this idea of public space. Space can be public in more ways than those that democracy requires, and have more impacts on democratic engagement than those discussed here. Therefore, the next chapter starts by analysing the concepts of 'public' and 'public space'. This discussion results in another set of analytic categories, which will be used to analyse real democratic spatial issues in cities around the world.

3

Theorizing Public Space

Having deepened our definition of democracy, the next task is to do the same with the concept of public space. The two are closely related because some ideas of 'public' are built into the concept of democracy, the 'we' and our collective concerns that are the agents and subjects of democratic action.

The standard starting point for this sort of discussion is the more general distinction between public and private, but it is a problematic starting point because there is no single distinction to make. Instead, I argue that what is really at stake is four sets of other distinctions between accessible and inaccessible places; things that are related to collective concerns and resources versus things that are not; things that affect us all without discrimination, as opposed to things that just affect us individually; and things that are owned by the collective or the state, as opposed to individually owned things. From this discussion, I derive a four-fold definition of public space, but one which drops the ownership criterion, and problematizes many of the markers of public space that dominate the urban theory literature. We end up with four ways in which space can be public, ways that may or may not overlap. I then argue that two of those ways are functionally necessary for democracy, and attempt to overcome objections based on the claim that physical public space no longer matters in a networked, online world.

The Public/Private Distinction

There is no such thing as *the* public/private distinction, or, at any rate, it is a deep mistake to think that there is a single substantive distinction here that can be made to do any real philosophical or political work. When one begins to look at it carefully, the purported distinction between public and private begins to dissolve into a number of issues that have relatively little to do with one another.... To repeat this as a methodological point: it is not the case that we must or should adopt a two-step procedure, *first* getting clear about the public/private distinction,

49

assuming all the while that there is a single distinction to be made, and *then*, having discovered where the line falls between public and private, going on to ask what we can do with that distinction, what attitude we should adopt toward it, what implications making the distinction correctly might have for politics. Rather, *first* we must ask what this purported distinction is *for*, that is, *why* we want to make it at all. To answer this question will bring us back to some relatively concrete context of human action, probably human political action, and it is only the context of connecting the issue of the public and private to that anteced-ent potential context of political action that the distinction will make any sense. (Geuss, 2001: 106–7, original emphasis)

The public/private distinction has been a cornerstone of liberal politics and liberal democratic theory. The traditional distinction is between a private sphere of activity that is the 'locus of initiative' in which free individuals make autonomous decisions, and a public sphere 'where the rules of associa-tion are defined and the problems to which it gives rise are resolved' (Baechler, 1980: 269). Thus, the public/private split is taken to be constitutive of democ-racy itself: it creates normative room for citizens to exercise individual auton-omy free from interference by others, and a public sphere in which conflicts between the results of those autonomous decisions can be resolved, or at least discussed. Precisely where the boundary between public and private should lie, though, is a matter of intense debate. For example, a major strand of feminist political thought has shown how the liberal insistence on privacy can be used to hide the political dimensions of domestic arrangements, which led some to want to push the boundary of legitimate public concern well towards the private end of the scale. In the context of debates about fertility, however, the trend has been somewhat reversed, with many writers arguing instead for strict limits on the degree to which the public can encroach on women's decisions about their bodies (Cohen, 1996).

What Raymond Geuss does, summarized in the quote above, is to point out that in part such conflicts arise because the concepts 'public' and 'private' are not things one can draw a sharp line between, but instead depend very much on the particular purposes and values that we have in mind when wanting to make the distinction, and that those purposes and values are the things we should be focusing on, not attempting to foreclose debate by appeal to the categories public and private. Geuss makes particular use of Dewey's definition of the public as being 'all those who are affected by the indirect consequences of transactions to such an extent that it is deemed necessary to have these consequences systematically cared for' (Dewey, 1924: 12). Geuss (2001: 84) argues that this is relative in four senses:

> ... first, it depends on the level of social knowledge of the possible consequences of acts. Second, it depends on what we allow or disallow to count as 'conse-quences' of action. Third, it also depends on the value judgments of the members

50

of the society and thus on their views and decisions about what consequences 'need' to be controlled. Finally, it depends on an initial decision about who is considered to be 'directly concerned.'

Thus, for Geuss, any appeal not to interfere with something because it is private is tautological: it 'says that we should not interfere because that is the kind of thing we think we ought not to interfere with' (2001: 84). The same formulation clearly applies to claims that something is public: we should interfere with this other thing because it is the kind of thing we think we ought to interfere with. To repeat, appeals to the publicity or privacy of something are actually appeals to other values that are bundled up in the labels 'public' and 'private'.

We can discern four broad categories of things that people commonly appeal to under the guise of public and private. Drawing on the rather diverse resources of Dewey (1924), Arendt (1958), Waldron (1988), and Geuss (2001), we can include in the 'public' bundle the following ideas:

1. Freely accessible places where 'everything that happens can be observed by anyone', where strangers are encountered whether one wants to or not, because everyone has free right of entry (Geuss, 2001: 52). This is a concept very similar to Arendt's first sense of 'public' (1958: 50). These are places where the spotlight of 'publicity' shines, and so might not just be public squares and market places, but political debating chambers where the right of physical access is limited but informational access is not.

2. The things that concern, affect, or are for the benefit of everyone, Arendt's second sense of 'public' (1958: 52). This realm includes 'common goods' (Hardin, 1968), goods like clean air and water, public transport, and so on; as well as more particular concerns like crime or the raising of children that vary in their content over time and space, depending on the current state of a particular society's value judgements and discursive battles.

3. The people or groups that have responsibility for that realm covered in (2), which might include rulers, or 'public figures', or might be defined more broadly to mean all of us: 'the public' as a noun, not an adjective.

4. Things which are owned by the state or the people in (3) and paid for out of collective resources like taxes: government buildings, national parks in most countries, military bases and equipment, and so on.

In the private bundle, we can include the following:

1. Places that are not freely accessible, and have controllers who limit access to or use of that space.

2. Things that primarily concern individuals and not collectives, following Dewey's formulation.

51

3. The people who primarily deal with such items; or rather, following the distinction made in the previous chapter, the roles that people play when they are so dealing, referring to the common distinction between politicians' 'private' commercial and family interests and their 'public' roles managing collective resources and concerns.

4. Things and places that are individually owned, including things that are cognitively 'our own', like our thoughts, goals, emotions, spirituality, preferences, and so on.

There are several points to note here. First, it is important to separate out items 1 and 4 on both lists. At first glance, the ownership criterion may not appear to be separate at all. For some theorists, the right to limit access flows from ownership of a particular space or thing, so that ownership *defines* whether something is public or not (Pennock, 1980). This may seem to be obviously the case when it comes to some kinds of property – my home, my briefcase (Christman, 1994: 6) – but not so obvious when it comes to others. In Britain, for example, National Parks are made up of privately owned parcels of land, but people have the right to wander across that land uninvited and with remarkably few restrictions. A few years ago, I heard a representative of English Heritage bewailing the loss of open access to 'public space' that occurs every time a church, privately owned by the Church of England, is sold and converted into a home or flats (BBC, 2005): village churches especially are usually unlocked and accessible by anyone, whether they are confirmed members of the church or not. Equally, there are buildings and spaces that are public in the sense that they are owned by the state and consume common resources, but to which there are more limited rights of entry: national parks in most other countries, military facilities, the offices of government departments, and even legislatures.

This only seems confusing when we fetishize 'public' and 'private' and treat them as single concepts. In the briefcase and home example, what is really at stake is not privacy per se, but protecting individual autonomy, individuals' projects, thoughts, desires, and predilections from interference by other people, again because we think that these are things that other people should not interfere with. In the military case, what is really at stake is the value of secrecy when it comes to the instruments of national security, and while we might want the military to be subordinate to elected leaders and accountable for their actions and inactions, that does not mean that we need to insist on full public accessibility – to do so, it is often argued, would be to undermine their effectiveness. So again, the public/private distinction is not really doing any work here: other values are at stake.

The ownership dimension can also be misleading because it divides goods into separate packages that can be assigned to some particular individual

52

(Waldron, 1988: 38–41). However, some kinds of good are not separable: they cannot be subdivided without destroying them, and involve and affect many people without distinction. One obvious example is clean air: parcelling up ownership of the airspace above separate territories on the ground is common practice in terms of things like air traffic control, but is problematic when it comes to industrial air pollution when emissions from privately owned chimneys come to affect not only the lives of people near the plants concerned, but people thousands of miles away. This is one of the issues that have caused so many problems for the United Nations' various climate change protocols, with the competing demands of some industries and countries to be able to pollute 'their' air coming up against the demands of others to reduce global emissions as part of a fight against distant environmental impacts and global warming. As will be seen shortly, some kinds of space are best characterized in this 'public good' fashion, under heading two above, and not as publicly owned goods under heading four.

The second major point to note is that item 2 on the public list might seem to put things unjustifiably in terms of human use. Here, I am thinking of green theories of value in which the natural world has intrinsic value, not instrumental value solely in terms of its utility for humans (Goodin, 1992). To the extent that humans have a role on some versions of these theories, it should be restricted to a duty of guardianship, not a right of exploitation. That might well be true, but it strikes me that this is one of those contexts in which Geuss would exclaim, 'Exactly!' The right debate to have is not whether the natural world is 'public', but whether it has innate value that should be respected by humans or whether it is merely a resource for our use or some combination of the two, and thus how humans should treat it. The public/private label forecloses that debate.

Third, there are many things that do not seem to fit neatly into either bundle. For example, think of cultural practices of ethnic minorities that primarily concern their collective but not the whole society, assuming for a moment that those living inside the boundaries of a given state are the relevant people to include in the 'whole' society. Think of debates over the wearing of headscarves in France, or the denial of speaking rights to women at many Māori formal occasions in New Zealand, or First Nations whaling along the north-west coast of the United States and Canada. This suggests that the way I have characterized the bundles above is too dichotomous, too 'all or nothing' in character, and that there are intermediate collectivities between everyone and the individual that might include family, clan, caste, ethnicity, and so on. Solving this problem is partly the point of Arendt's triple distinction between private, social, and public. Again, however, appealing to the public–private distinction, or a private–social–public distinction, is to foreclose more useful debate on the values that are actually central to such cases,

53

such as how majorities should treat cultural minorities, indigenous and otherwise, living in the boundaries of given states.

Fourth and finally, as Geuss is at pains to point out, the bundles are not internally consistent: things that appear public on one criterion can be private on another. However, I am going to postpone discussion of this point for a moment because I want to illustrate it with examples from public space. The important conclusion for now is this: a general discussion of public and private gets us only a short way, and to go further we need to contextualize more. Therefore, it is now time to 'spatialize' the discussion, to see if we can distinguish what 'public space' might be, and I start by taking the four categories of public above and applying them to space.

Defining Physical Public Space

The first kind of public is itself spatial, and is that which most often appears in the urban theory literature, whether architectural, geographical, or sociological origin. It is freely accessible space, particularly space in which we encounter strangers.

The broadly accepted definition is based on a distinction between (*a*) a realm of individuals, their minds, and bodies, and extensions in terms of family and property, especially the home and the car seen as a metallic, mobile extension of the body and personality; and (*b*) a common realm of streets, plazas, parks, malls, and buildings where access is unrestricted and strangers interact with each other (Madanipour, 2003; see also Hénaff and Strong, 2001). Indeed, interaction with strangers is taken to be emblematic of public space, implicitly and explicitly contrasted with the world of the home, family, friends, and those one chooses to invite and interact with (Lofland, 1998: 7–8). Although this is not always acknowledged, in between are a series of gradations, 'liminal' spaces where the private and the public collide, such as in Benjamin's famous example (1999) of the city arcade in which privately owned buildings arch over publicly accessible footpaths, shielding pedestrians from the elements but also inviting them into the privately controlled commercial world whose doors open invitingly off the paths themselves. For urban theorists, it is at these boundary points between public and private space where much of the conflict they study arises: conflicts such as that between businesses' interests in attracting the 'right kind of customer' and the 'wrong' kind's intentions – right, even – to walk wherever they choose (Dovey, 1999); conflicts between individuals' desire to do what they want with their homes, and neighbours' desire to present a 'nice' built environment; conflicts between haphazard, creative, and unscripted encounters between people and the highly scripted, controlled encounters preferred by some spatial designers.

While the idea of open accessibility is fundamental to many definitions of public space, the associated emphasis on strangers and unscripted encounters is more complex than some authors acknowledge. For one, the strangers emblem is often discussed in terms of the absence of choice about whom one encounters, yet in family groups there is no aspect of choice either. It is a well-worn truism that one can choose one's friends but not one's family, yet family is always included on the private side of the ledger, not the public, so choice cannot be the defining element of private space, nor its lack definitive of public. For another, there is, in Western societies at least, what Goffman (1963) calls 'the principle of civil inattention' or 'disattendability', which is the norm that in publicly accessible places people should behave in unobtrusive ways, or least 'avoid being systematically obtrusive' (Geuss, 2001: 13). Now, Geuss and Goffman present this norm as being universal, and as being about respecting others' freedom to pursue their ends with minimal interference, something that lines up neatly with a negative liberal understanding of freedom (Berlin, 1958). It is not clear to me that this is so. In many cultures, the principle at work is often *attendability*, the norm that strangers must be acknowledged, welcomed, perhaps tested, integrated, or shunned, but certainly not ignored – that would be the height of rudeness. Still, one could present Goffman's principle in more general terms as a requirement that people act in public within locally accepted limits, because following the rules, whatever they are, signals to others that one can be trusted, can be communicated with, and can be treated as a fellow member of the relevant 'public' rather than an outsider, an 'other'. Thus, the status of strangers is ambiguous in public space. A stranger can be someone you do not know personally but who nonetheless acts in expected ways: they might be strangers but they do not act strangely. Likewise, someone who is well-known can act in unexpected ways, and it is that expected/unexpected distinction that is the target of normative controls, not simply the known/unknown distinction (Figure 3.1). In public space, one certainly encounters people one does not know, who are strangers in the sense of 'not an acquaintance or family member', but one nonetheless expects those strangers to behave in familiar ways. This does not mean bland conformity: we might *expect* teenagers and young adults to behave in boundary-testing ways; we might *expect* designated individuals performing particular roles to do the same: Socratic philosophers, say, or *fa'afafine* men performing women's roles in Samoa. We also might tolerate more boundary-pushing from group members than outsiders. This means that while the known/unknown distinction is not irrelevant, it is a mistake to think that it is the only consideration when it comes to thinking about the definitional markers of public and private space.

Furthermore, there are many kinds of public events in public space that are even more scripted and impose quite rigid standards of behaviour, well

Figure 3.1. A controlled, expected breach of disattendability – 'Ricoloop' at the Bern Street Music Festival 2007

Note the permit around Ricoloop's neck, and the arcade in the background. Photo Philipp Zinniker, licensed by Creative Commons.

beyond everyday norms and boundaries. Think, for a moment, of major ceremonial events in which the rituals of membership of a given polity are acted out, rituals like the installation of Presidents, fireworks displays in central parks on national holidays, parades given for sports people or military heroes, and so on. This is what Goodsell (1988*b*) calls ceremonial space, in which identities are presented to 'the public' in sense 3. Spaces that are used for national events often come with reserved norms of behaviour even when not being used for formal events. In Santiago, for example, people do not attempt to have picnics in the open spaces at either end of the presidential palace, La Moneda, even though the space behind it is quite conducive to spreading a blanket out on the lawn. Now, there is a heavy military police presence around La Moneda deterring picnickers and hacky-sack players; but in Canberra a similar taboo applies to the upper reaches of Federation Mall even though the officers of the Australian Protective Service or Australian Federal Police are nowhere near so obvious. Once again, this does not mean there should be no room for challenges to the rules on the one hand, or good old playfulness on the other – far from it, and I will deal with both of these points in later chapters. The point that follows from these observations is that there *are* scripts for many encounters in public space, rules that do not seem to diminish the 'publicness' of the space, most obviously in sense 4 where we are talking about space that is publicly owned; perhaps also in sense 2 referring to things like common rituals, collective expressions of membership, values, history, and memory; and in sense 1, referring to the idea that for some public events or some public spaces while everyone is welcome in a physical sense, they need to modify their behaviour to ensure that they do not clash with others too much, following liberal egalitarian injunctions already mentioned about freedom for all consistent with a like freedom for each. In other words, precisely how we should react to the features of a particular space when it comes to unscripted encounters with strangers depends very much on the uses and purposes of the space in question.

I will set out a rough outline of the *democratic* purposes and requirements of public space later in this chapter, but before I do that I want to consider quickly the spatial analogues to the other three kinds of 'public' noted above. The second meaning of 'public' is those things that concern, affect, or are for the benefit of everyone. In spatial terms, one could generate a very long list indeed, and the following is just meant to be suggestive rather than exhaustive, but on the basis of my city visits the sorts of space that fit into this category include:

- public recreational facilities like parks, baths, promenades, arenas, concert halls, and so on;
- other public facilities like libraries, schools and assembly rooms, public toilets, some places of worship, and even cemeteries that can take on the characteristics of mini-cities in their own right;
- the built environment of the city, which not only shapes such things as the availability of light and air but also is of concern to those who want a beautiful city (however that is defined), or a city that preserves memories and heritage, among other things;
- the natural environment surrounding and sometimes penetrating the built environment, considered as a recreational facility and as the broader ecosystem of which built environments are a part; and
- infrastructure, including power, water, and transport systems allowing people to access all these things, including not just buses and trains but, in a few cities, public bicycle schemes; or, at the very least, public roads and parking systems.

Thinking about the public in senses 3 and 4 allows us to add a few more items to the list:

- the spaces for the performance of specifically democratic roles – narration, claim-making, decision-making, electing, etc. – such as legislatures, town squares, speakers' corners, and broad avenues;

- monuments and streetscapes where the *demos* represents itself to itself, anchoring identities and memories; and
- spaces owned by 'the public' for other collective purposes, such as security (police, military and intelligence facilities), and the housing of other public servants (government office buildings) (Figures 3.2a–d).

I will take up detailed discussions of these things in Part II: developing a more detailed account of these kinds of places is the primary aim of those chapters. For the moment, there are some general points to make about the nature of public space that emerge from this list.

The list helps us drive a further nail into the coffin of the idea that what distinguishes public and private space is ownership alone, and that accessibility flows from ownership. A building might be a privately owned, separate entity, and thus fit into the private list under item 4, but it also has a public face, and goes with other buildings to make up the built environment, which affects everyone living in or passing through its shadow and thus fits into the public list under item 2. In other words, public space cannot just be treated analytically as a class of property, one that happens to be owned by the state or some other collective body. Rather, in many cases it needs to be treated more like other public goods, in sense 2. Therefore, relevant to some kinds of public space will be the usual issues that arise with other public goods, namely

Figure 3.2a. Road to a defence communications facility, Northern Territory, Australia
Photo by 'Schutz', licensed by Creative Commons.

58

Figure 3.2b. Peckham Library, London
Photo www.CGPGrey.com licensed by Creative Commons.

Figure 3.2c. Nijmegen 1 radio studio
Photo by 'Lj-jlong', licensed by Creative Commons.

ensuring their continuing existence given the free-rider problem, preventing the 'tragedy of the commons' (Hardin, 1968). Nonetheless, we might still want to include in the idea of public space those spaces that are owned by the collective: by the central state, by local government, by publicly funded agencies, and so on. This is less because of their ownership per se (sense 4) than their relationship to collective resources (sense 2): going back to the previous chapter, one of the fundamental things that the public in a democracy decides is how to allocate collective resources (maximally) or to hold accountable those who make allocation decisions (more minimally). That means that we can include in the idea of public space those things to which the public does not normally have *access*, and so are not public in sense 1, such as military bases and the private offices of senior officials, but which are nonetheless public in sense 2 because they consume common resources and have purposes related to collective goals. Likewise, we can include some things that are privately owned but that have collective impacts, like the built environment generally or, in many cities, where 'public' facilities are controlled by private companies, like bus systems, leisure facilities, and so on.

The other problem to note here briefly is that a given territory can have multiple geographies, multiple boundaries, which leads to disagreements over what counts as space of common concern. I will come back to this point when I discuss the 'space and place' distinction in the next chapter, but interesting

Figure 3.2d. Tokyo Picnic Club promotional poster, 2005
Photo © Tokyo Picnic Club, by permission.

60

examples arise in disagreements over land access and use when there is a clear split in the *demos*, two or more separate *demoi*, such as between indigenous people and the descendants of settlers in states like Australia, New Zealand, and Canada, or in Northern Ireland where Catholic and Protestant neighbours have entirely different patterns of use of what on an ordinary road map looks like the same territory.[1] This means that even physical space has socially constructed elements, and that public space will necessarily be a topic of political contestation, involving fights over who is the relevant 'we' at any given point. Indeed, putting forward claims to be the relevant 'we' is often a strategy used to foreclose disputes over access to space and thus who controls the resources – material and cultural – that come with it.

So, to sum up, physical space can be 'public' in four major ways. It is space that

1. is openly accessible; and/or
2. uses common resources; and/or
3. has common effects; and/or
4. is used for the performance of public roles.

Some space can be public in all four senses, like large central plazas on which I focus in Chapter six. It can be public in just some of the senses, like recreational and other 'public' facilities (senses 1, 2, and 3) or legislatures (senses 2 and 3, but only limited access), discussed in Chapter five. Or it can be public in just one of the senses, including privately owned and tenanted skyscrapers (sense 3), and most Anglican churches in England (sense 1, the exceptions involving senses 3 and 4 when it comes to royal weddings and public mourning). Examples of space that is public only in sense 4 might include privately owned locations that are used for public purposes, such as the conversations about collective matters that go on every day around the kitchen table, whether among family and friends or among dissidents gathered away from the watchful eye of the state, the activity determining the publicness of the space more than any intrinsic features of the space itself (Benhabib, 1992: 78; also Mansbridge, 1999).

I have removed ownership from the list because it was found not to track the values and goals that were really at stake. There are privately owned things that are public in all of the other senses, and publicly owned things whose importance is best captured by sense 2 only. I have also dismissed the definitional sufficiency of 'unscripted encounters', arguing that encounters in public space are always scripted by culture, law, or physical barriers, and that it is 'strangeness' rather than being a 'stranger' that is more important when it

---

[1] Shirlow (2001). Thanks to Roger Mac Ginty for the example.

comes to controls on deviation from the script. This usage helps bring to the foreground the frequently observed conflict between accounts of what space should be accessible and what not, what should be controlled and what not, and who should exercise control and who should not, related to claims of competing *demoi* in particular locations. This turns out to be a fundamental dimension of conflict over public space in the examples drawn out in Part II.

We are now almost fully armed with a working definition of public space. All that remains is to connect this with the discussion in the previous chapter about how certain democratic roles require certain spaces for their performance. Along the way, however, I need to deal with a serious objection: that this 'requirement' is overstated, and that in an age of rapidly advancing communications technology, public space has moved from the plaza and onto the airwaves and Internet. This is the concept of public space that dominates political theory, and one that increasingly operates in urban theory, and my brief survey of this focuses on Jürgen Habermas and his account of the 'public sphere'.

Democracy, Public Space, and the Public Sphere

In Chapter two I set out an account of democratic roles linked with specific settings for their performance, using Kenneth Burke's idea (1969) of the scene–act ratio. It was a very broad account, but nonetheless suggested some limits to the kinds of setting appropriate for different roles: fairly wide for narration but not boundless thanks to local norms about what safe and unsafe topics might be; highly visible stages for making public claims; and dignified and sometimes singular stages for making collective decisions and for scrutinizing the acts of the powerful.

The question that then arises is whether democracy really does *require* physical space in the strong sense that I have suggested so far. Critics of that thought appeal to the idea that public space is much, much more than physical settings; that it has largely moved onto the airwaves or the Internet and has become 'virtual', and that, on the contrary, democracy can continue in a vibrant form without *any* physical setting at all.[2] Some versions of this argument involve treating 'public space' and the 'public sphere' as being one and the same thing – Nagel (1991) and Benhabib (1992) use the terms interchangeably – but I think it is useful if we distinguish between 'the public

---

[2] This criticism has been levelled at me in various forms at various workshops and conferences, but was presented in its strongest form by John Keane at the Representation and Democracy Symposium, organized by the Political Sociology Group, Department of Sociology, University of Birmingham, on 16 May 2007. My thanks to John for the objection.

sphere' to designate the myriad ways in which people participate in collective deliberation about political action (Calhoun, 1992: 1) and 'public space' in a more limited sense to designate the physical settings in which such engagement takes place.[3] Therefore, the question I want to examine is whether democracy can thrive without public space in this more limited sense, and to understand that we need to take a moment to consider the broader concept of the public sphere.

Habermas (1989: 27–31) and others following him distinguish the public sphere from the economic sphere on the one hand, and the state on the other. The distinction between the public sphere and the economy is fairly straightforward: in the former, people coordinate by gathering and discussing, coming to agreements about courses of action and modifying individual views; in the latter, individual preferences remain unreconstructed, with coordination occurring through the price signals that result from the interaction of supply of and demand for goods and services.[4] The distinction with the state has been somewhat blurred in more recent work, but originally Habermas asserted that the public sphere arose as a bourgeois reaction against the power of the personalized state, offering an alternative legitimating site for political agreements and proposals for action. In later work, Habermas has distinguished between an informal public sphere of civil society institutions and a formal public sphere of legislatures and courts (Habermas, 1996), but one can still broadly see a distinction between the formal public sphere and the state: the state in a democracy is not the same as parliament or the courts, and formal public spheres can emerge on an ad hoc basis around specific issues in specific locations, and are not coterminous with ongoing, central, national institutions.

The development of new communications technology has meant that we now have the means not only of reading each other's views and debates via pamphlets and newspapers but also of engaging directly with people widely separated in space via the Internet, increasingly actively and in real time rather than in a pre-recorded or passive fashion via the traditional media. The attraction of these technologies from the standpoint of democratic theory is

---

[3] This distinction turns out to be useful in another way, when thinking about the effects of public space on political behaviour. I deal with this in the next chapter when considering the 'space/place' distinction.

[4] Here, I merely repeat the standard line in the literature, but I am not convinced that the collective/individual distinction maps on to a society/market distinction. In any market, communicative coordination is absolutely essential for getting large numbers of people to prefer brand x to brand y, on the basis of creating brand identification and spreading stories about who wore what, who dined where, and what's hot and what's not. Indeed, listening to many conversations in cafes and bars might lead one to the opposite conclusion – that successful marketing relies heavily on communication that creates and reinforces a *social* preference, not at all the tailoring of supply to the aggregate of individual demand. This is a side issue for my present purposes, however.

enormous because they help us focus on policy and law formation processes that occur well beyond the confines of formal institutions in legislative complexes, presidential palaces, and the plazas that front onto them. The members of large-scale, complex societies cannot all gather together in a town square to argue, deliberate, and decide, let alone fit into the debating chamber; the idea of a virtual public sphere allows us to see that they can nonetheless take a crucial role in constructing problems and solutions well before those matters get on to the formal political agenda. This has led some writers on democracy to assert that the virtual public sphere is now pretty much all that matters (Hénaff and Strong, 2001: 35).

One way to respond to such claims might be to consider the point that interpersonal communication is easier and more civil face-to-face, the former because of how much online worlds filter out non-verbal cues, making communication more ambiguous and massively less fluent (Jaeger, 2006; Kock, 2007), and the latter because of the way that physical separation and online pseudonyms allow name calling and demonization (Sunstein, 2001). Thus, participatory and deliberative democrats have long emphasized the importance of face-to-face interaction both in terms of enhancing communication and increasing civility, although face-to-face interaction also needs to be relatively small-scale interaction because one just cannot keep track of the reactions and non-visual communications of more than five to seven participants at a time (Parkinson, 2006a). Therefore, this defence of physical space works only for relatively small-scale settings like parliamentary and party committee deliberations, minipublics (Fung, 2003), and so forth. Of course, even in small-scale settings it might be objected that face-to-face interaction still need not be physical interaction: it might involve videoconferencing or some other technology instead – even 3D holography of the kind imagined in Isaac Asimov's *The Naked Sun* might become possible one day. Projection technology is developing rapidly, allowing better resolution and thus more detail and many more people to be projected. But then, the same scale objection arises, because the problem is not technical limits to *projecting* people's images but perceptual limits to *keeping track* of participants' reactions.

Still, the face-to-face defence only works at the small scale. We need other defences of the idea that physical stages are somehow a necessity at the large scale, and when it comes to the other democratic roles physical presence does indeed seem to be a necessary element in many cases. I argued in Chapter two that demonstrations are very valuable in showing decision-makers the sheer scale of public displeasure, and that campaigning organizations still go to enormous lengths to create, stage, and publicize physical events – 'actions', as many call them – aimed at attracting large numbers of participants and media coverage. Now, the media might transmit discourse in 'virtual' ways, but the *things* that they transmit are very often stills or film of physical events, involving political actors in specific physical locations. Broadcast media in particular require pictures, pictures of physical events performed by people, to illustrate symbolically in one or two images something that might otherwise take hundreds, even thousands of words to say. The same is true of the Internet, where video sites like YouTube (http://www.youtube.com) are rapidly encroaching on the territory even recently dominated by blogs. And is it not interesting that while virtual spaces like Second Life (http://secondlife.com) feel the need to mimic the physical world, attempts by 'real life' organizations to use it for real life purposes have proved less than resoundingly successful? One of the more interesting examples of this in recent years was when the French far-right party *Front National* opened a virtual office in Second Life only to have it picketed, attacked, and destroyed by a variety of activists (Au, 2007), leading to a complete retreat and reversion to physical engagement using physical infrastructure, something that cannot be quite so easily destroyed by cyber-activists. According to contributors to the blog cited above, the denizens of Second Life are suspicious of activities that 'blur the line' between the physical world and the online world, preferring their politics offline and their fun online, which leaves me wondering to what degree the public sphere has shifted online.

The fact that physical political events are frequently staged shows how important political actors think it is to get the right image out, because they are keenly aware of the fact that certain images of an event support one storyline and one set of interests rather than another (Edelman, 1988). Examples are legion. One of the more notorious in recent years was US President George W. Bush landing on the deck of the USS Abraham Lincoln on 1 May 2003, clambering out of his aircraft in a flight suit to the delirious cheers of the assembled sailors, and declaring 'Mission accomplished' in Iraq (Figure 3.3). Every element of that event was designed to attract media attention and communicate symbolically – the choice of ship (Lincoln, the great emancipator), the flight suit, and the tail-hook landing in the Persian Gulf (the President as Commander-in-Chief, bravely sharing risk with those under his command). Other examples are less dramatic but are nonetheless staged. At a more homely level, think of the 'fireside chat' radio broadcasts by F. D. Roosevelt between 1933 and 1944, or of the bid by the then-Leader of the Opposition in Britain, David Cameron, to present himself as 'just like us' by posting a video online of himself in his kitchen helping with the washing up, acting like a dad, surrounded by symbols of home, family, and normal life. The pictures were meant to communicate, 'I'm like you, I understand what it's like for you' – to express his ability to re-present the lived experience of other people. The pictures – or, in the case of radio, the visual images conjured up in listeners' imaginations – achieve something that merely saying the same thing cannot, because of the way we assess credibility. We distrust what people say

65

Figure 3.3. Staging George W. Bush on the USS Lincoln, 2004
US Navy photo (public domain) by Photographer's Mate 3rd Class Tyler J. Clements.

about themselves; we trust more when we can see for our own eyes the person in settings and performing actions that back up the words. For political leaders, therefore, physical settings are absolutely essential for building rhetorical *ethos* – the settings provide the *ethos* cues far more effectively than words.

Supporting points have already been made about the need for physical stages to perform other democratic roles. When it comes to binding collective decision-making, I have claimed that a *dignified* setting is necessary for impressing on participants the fact that the decisions affect millions, even billions of others – it helps participants take what they are doing seriously. I have also argued that having a *single* location helps with the scrutiny role, and while I do not think that either of these points means that we need to go along with Burke and overwhelm onlookers by the majesty of legislative architecture – I am much more a fan of Giurgola's Australian Parliament than Lutyen's Indian one – I *do* think that this means that national assemblies help not only to encourage face-to-face engagement between those advancing opposing political claims but also to facilitate scrutiny of those engagements, ensuring representatives remain accountable to the rest of the public.

So far, I have been discussing space that is public in sense 4, space for the performance of democratic roles. Types 2 and 3 are not functional necessities but the subject matter of democracy. They are included among the things that the *demos* is concerned about, because they concern either collective resources like recreational space, the production of cultural and informational goods, and so on; or they are included among the things that affect everyone indiscriminately, like the built environment, air quality, and so on. Things are different when it comes to space of type 1 – we might well think that it is necessary for the functioning of democracy too. This is space in which a sense of 'we' is created, space in which one encounters other members of the *demos* and recognizes them as people one must take into account one's own decision-making. This is a fundamental of democracy: the need for democratic decision-making itself does not arise unless each of us sees our actions impacting on others, and recognizes those others as having claims on us. If one encounters or recognizes only a limited range of others, then one takes only a limited range of impacts into account, and takes seriously the claims of only a limited number of those affected instead of 'all those affected'. Thus, spaces in which one can encounter the *demos* in all its variety have an important democratic function – they help us see and recognize others and make us more willing to take their right to make claims on us seriously when we encounter them in political debate. It is not the claims they make that are important here; it is recognizing them as rightful claim-makers that matters, and I will deal with this extensively in Chapters seven and eight when discussing the symbolic landscape and places of encounter of capital cities.

I diverge once again from many urban theorists, however, on the question of what kinds of space matter here. When observing the fact that in many cities one encounters only a small subsection of the whole *demos* in city streets, parks, shopping districts, and waterfront developments, many urban theorists tend to interpret this as if it were not just a loss of openness and accessibility of public space – that is, a type one loss – but a complete loss of publicness and thus *democratic* space tout court. The lack of awareness of the different meanings of 'public' leads them to declare the 'fall of public man' (Sennett, 2002) when actually they may only be referring to one kind of publicness. It is perfectly conceivable that a city faces a loss of type 1 space but an increase of type 4, which would represent a net *gain* for democracy and not a net loss. Here, I am thinking of places like, once again, the Swiss *Landsgemeinden* cantons where national parks (type 3) and spaces to sit and enjoy random encounters (type 1) are almost non-existent, yet the central town squares are transformed once a year into uniquely thriving type 4 spaces without parallel in the Western world. These are spaces where one gets to experience what my research assistant Charlotte Reinisch called 'direct democratic shivers': it is strangely unsettling, as an outsider, the first time one experiences a crowd of 8,000 people voting by simultaneously raising their hands. Until then, the *demos* is a fairly abstract notion, represented by poll samples and turnout figures, and seen in dribs and drabs at polling booths on

67

election day. Afterwards, the *demos* gains a great deal more solidity, having encountered it in all its variety. Fishkin (1997: 163) relates a similar experience when a colleague of his sees for the first time a stratified random sample in the shape of real, flesh-and-blood people gathered together in one room at the start of a deliberative poll – the same applies any time we gather a minipublic in a citizens' jury or an electronic town hall process (Smith, 2005). One of the aims of Part III will be to set out a framework for judging patterns of gain and loss of different kinds of public space in democratic cities, based on evidence gathered from the cities under study.

Of course I agree that public parks, waterfronts, and so forth should be openly accessible to all comers, and that we should encounter people of all sorts in these places. What I am calling into question is whether *type 1* losses damage democracy; type 4 losses, yes; but type 1 losses? Of course, some spaces are of both types. It is hard to imagine democratic space of type 4 not also being of type 1 in some sense – even parliaments are open to the public via television cameras if not in person. However, one can easily imagine type 1 space that is not also type 4: most city parks, waterfronts, shopping centres, and so forth do not have a particularly political character, even if they are sometimes used for political purposes – and sometimes should be more open to such use. I agree that gathering a variety of people from different back-grounds is good for developing an awareness of the variety of the *demos*, and helps people think of themselves as 'we', which in turn helps people take others' claims more seriously. My doubt is on the basis of whether this means we just require more space of type 4, or whether we need type 1 as well. Resolving this question will be a central aim of Part II.

One final set of objections attacks the *necessity* of physical public space: a critic might well concede that physical settings are all nice to have, all en-hancements, but none is necessary. My response to that is to ask the reader to imagine a society in which one is not free to undertake any of these activities. In a society where one is not free to demonstrate, public claims can be dismissed as the rantings of a few malcontents. In a society where parliament becomes 'virtual', we lose the ability to identify readily those who are sup-posed to be in control and therefore who we can call to account when things go wrong. In a society where all voting and decision-making shifts online, I suspect that debate would become less civil, more polarized, and also taken less seriously, such that politics just becomes another game show, and a rather tedious one at that.

It might then be argued that we already live in such a society. In many countries, it is becoming more and more difficult to gain direct access to representatives because of the hyping up of security worries and the fact that, in differentiated polities (Rhodes, 1997), it is increasingly difficult to identify decision-makers anyway let alone press public claims upon them; so dispersed are governance networks and the mechanisms of control. All the more reason, goes the objection, not to worry about access to physical public space and engage with the powerful virtually. In addition to pointing to the other reasons why physical engagement is nonetheless important, I have one final response: that mass, physical engagement is useful not just when demonstrators eyeball the powerful but also when the demonstration is publicized, televized, and watched by the powerful. That transmission depends on news values – whether the event is 'significant', unusual, narratable, and salient to target audiences (Iyengar and Kinder, 1987) – and one factor that goes into that calculation is the number of people involved. Millions in the streets make news; a few hundred do not, unless they themselves are unusual, like bankers demonstrating in June 2006 in London against the extradition to the United States of three of their fellows (Coleman, 2006). As political activists have understood for years, it is not the issue per se that gets coverage, it is the dramatization of the issue, and that often requires physical action, creating pictures and a story, in physical public space.

To object to the importance of physical public space on the grounds that virtual transmission of messages matters more these days is to focus on the medium to the exclusion of the message that the medium transmits. It is my contention that the message still matters – that demonstrating the sheer scale of popular anger still matters – even in a world in which the public sphere has burst out of the coffee house, beyond the confines of the central plaza, and onto the airwaves.

Conclusions

In this chapter, I have argued that the public/private distinction is a misleading one, because it conceals the fact that underlying it is a set of quite different, often-competing distinctions concerning the nature of 'the public'; the places where they gather; the set of things that the public is or should be concerned about; and those things that affect them all, or some significant subgroup. Having abandoned the idea of a single public/private distinction, I then came up with a four-fold definition of public space that

1. is openly accessible; and/or
2. uses common resources; and/or
3. has common effects; and/or
4. is used for the performance of public roles.

I then argued that democracy *requires* public space in sense 4; may possibly require it in sense 1, but set out reasons to be cautious; and *is concerned with* public space in senses 2 and 3. In response to the argument that the requirement for physical public space is overstated, and that democracy can happily move online, I highlighted the losses for communication when that occurs, the reliance on physical events by the media, and pointed out a crucial confusion between medium and message that underlies the objection.

The conceptual work is now almost complete. We have a working definition of democracy and a working definition of public space. In the next chapter, I wrap up the theoretical work by examining some models of how public space influences political action, and the political economy of public space: that is, how likely is it that the space theoretically required will actually be delivered, given existing modes of spatial production? That will provide the final element of conceptual scene-setting needed for the case studies in Part II.

4

Place and Politics

We shape our buildings, and afterwards our buildings shape us.

Winston Churchill, 28 October 1943

A skyscraper shouldering itself aloft at the expense of its more humble neighbors, stealing their air and their sunlight, is a symbol, written large against the sky, of the will-to-power of a man or a group of men – of that ruthless and tireless aggression on the part of the cunning and the strong so characteristic of the period which produced the skyscraper. One of our streets made up of buildings of diverse styles and shapes and sizes – like a jaw with some teeth whole, some broken, some rotten, and some gone – is a symbol of our unkempt individualism. (Claude Bragdon, 1918: 6–7)

In the introduction, I noted how frequently one comes across assertions that patterns of bricks and mortar, and stone and steel shape political behaviour. One can also find work arguing that physical forms are themselves the result of larger, macro-political forces: the structure of the capitalist system that leads to particular patterns in the built environment, which in turn shape behaviour (Agnew, 1987; Sennett, 2002). These are not new arguments. Modernist architects like Louis Sullivan, Claude Bragdon, and Sullivan's pupil, Frank Lloyd Wright railed bitterly against 'grandomania', wanting to replace it with an architecture that would develop democratic citizens (Duncan, 1989: 150) – although not to the extent of actually letting *people* have an input into the design of their buildings (Wright, 1939: 20–1).

This last chapter of Part I teases out precisely what is being claimed in these kinds of statements, and how robust the claims are at the conceptual level. This matters for the overall project because it helps us understand exactly what is at stake politically when it comes to battles over public space. It deepens our answer to the question posed in the last chapter: public space is all very nice, but does it *matter* in the modern world? I begin by examining the micro-level claim, that physical form affects political action. I argue that it does, but in nuanced ways that have to do with the distinction between 'space', the form itself, and 'place', that form filled with cultural, political, and historical associations, the form as *used* by people in a particular context. This then leads to the idea that form itself is structured by its processes of production, the political economy of space, and I argue that while different political economic structures are likely to deliver different kinds of public space, this matters less than believers might fear, and more than sceptics might think. The chapter concludes with a summary of the interpretive framework that will be applied in Part II to understanding particular cases, and in Part III to construct criteria for evaluating public space in democratic cities.

Form and Political Behaviour

Why might we think that physical form matters to politics? There are some very obvious cases that help illuminate the issues. First, there are walls: unless they are merely relics, pierced by unpoliced openings like the walls around Avignon or York, walls can prevent access to services, fellow citizens, and political fora. Such walls constitute an unfreedom in a basic liberal sense, and the wall building in Israel–Palestine is a prime example, with many Palestinian Israelis deprived of the ability to work, gain access to services, or contact or engage with other fellow-citizens and representatives, limiting their ability to operate in even minimal ways as free members of the society (Figure 4.1). Notice that it is not the mere presence of a wall that is important here: they need to be guarded somehow, whether directly by people or indirectly by electronic means. Still, the point is that such physical forms matter for politics when they present barriers to the expression of rights and freedoms. Relatedly, there might be forms that do not prevent action so much as mandate it. Examples are harder to find, but we might think of roads in this way: while it is physically possible to sit down in the middle of the road, the fact that it is dedicated to traffic means that it is most unwise without stopping the traffic first. Even when roads are used for political purposes – a march, a demonstration – the norm is that people *move* down the road. Generally, we stand still for marshalling or speeches in parks and squares at the ends of roads, rarely in the middle of them.

Second, there are some forms that do not prevent or mandate the expression of certain actions and freedoms in any absolute sense, but which, more softly, *limit* the extent to which certain actions can be expressed, or which *facilitate* a small range of actions. Here, one of the common examples is Clausewitz's injunction to 'command the heights', because the occupier of an elevated position can see what his enemies are up to more effectively; and because the facts of gravity make it easier to lob one's missiles down than to lob them up

72

Figure 4.1. Israel–Palestine wall near Bethlehem, with evocative graffiti
Photo Henry Duval and Marc Venezia, licensed by Creative Commons.

(Gieryn, 2000; Hirst, 2005). It is not impossible to attack a raised position; it is just a lot harder. One can think of parliamentary analogues: ambitious representatives want to ensure that (*a*) they are seated near their leader so they get their face on television more often; and (*b*) their offices are handily placed so that they casually encounter or gain access to those in charge of portfolios, the whips, influential committee chairs, and so on.

The general point is that certain kinds of space encourage encounters while others do not (Gieryn, 2000: 477; Sennett, 2002). For example, it is argued that proximity encourages interaction and the development of community, and here some writers celebrate the way that the front steps of houses can operate as a kind of community space where neighbours meet and children play, especially when the footpaths are broad and the traffic not overwhelming. Neighbourhood cafes, bars, shops, libraries, and other amenities all contribute to a sense of belonging and encounter, it is said. By contrast, other city forms encourage transit, although one needs to be careful about assuming precisely what forms have what effects. It is not the case that open plan offices, for example, encourage more interaction. Instead, the removal of physical walls tends to make people put up psychological and communicative barriers in their place – people become ferociously protective of 'their' cubicle and communicate less often than when there are walls and doors that people can pass in and out of and engage in a more intimate and controllable fashion (Block and Stokes, 1989). As with office space, so it is with blank city squares, according to Sennett (2002): encounters are encouraged not by a blank canvas but by furniture and 'breaks' that encourage people to stop, sit, and take in their surroundings.

A related example of this same general point is to consider the way that space, in Gieryn's terms (2000), 'emplaces difference and hierarchy'. For example, one of the ways in which the patterns of exclusion set up under the old South African Group Areas Act continue is through the strict spatial separation of suburbs and townships, with the latter cut off from other parts of cities not by fences and police but by infrastructure: motorways, railways, large drainage systems, power lines, and golf courses (increasingly), all of which create large buffer zones, seas in which the townships are islands, cut off from the mainland of South African urban life. More subtly, planning regulations and the fragmented, individualized property system create incentives by which only certain kinds (and certain costs) of houses are able to be built in certain areas, which means that only certain kinds (certain income classes) of people can afford to buy homes in those areas. This does not necessarily mean that one *cannot* get into or out of such exclusive zones; even without private security guards patrolling exclusively upper class neighbourhoods, crossing these boundaries require more conscious effort, a deliberate decision as opposed to relying on chance encounters. Because people tend to go with the flow rather than against it, these patterns mean they are much less likely to encounter others, less likely to understand others' needs and desires, and less likely to feel that they are members of a common public. This matters not just for those who think that community is a good in itself. It also matters because of the sense of commonality, of 'we', that is necessary for the functioning of democratic politics. One is less likely to take another's claims seriously when they are pressed in the public realm if one does not consider the 'other' to be someone to whom one is linked by bonds of identity or common interest. At the same time, it matters to members of isolated groups if they are cut off from easy access to goods and services, either through geographic isolation or through the inaccessibility (which means economic affordability as well as physical presence) of transport.

The community idea points to a third possible influence of form on behaviour, and that is the way that forms act as symbols, anchor points for memories and identities. Why this matters is not often well-spelled out in the literature, but basically the underlying claim is this: physical anchor points of memory help people to think that people like them are taken seriously by the collective, which in turn matters for political efficacy. Ever since the variety of 'argumentative', 'discursive', and 'deliberative' turns, some scholars have analysed political interplay in terms of 'discourse coalitions', which create and nurture a sense of collective identity around shared story lines (Hajer, 2003: 103; Kraus, 2006). One of the ways in which those stories are grounded, anchored, or given a material basis – whichever you prefer – is by association with physical symbols. A symbol acts as a cue that suggests to those who see it elements of a story line and its associated identity (Edelman, 1976: 173). Symbols thus constitute a significant part of the answer to the question about identity posed by MacIntyre (1984), 'of what story or stories do I find myself a part?'. The connection with political efficacy is that efficacy calculations are not just on the basis of personal capacities for eloquence or a sense of the rightness of one's cause but also on the basis of whether one thinks that 'people like me' get listened to, and whether they are taken seriously in the political realm (Goodin and Dryzek, 1980). For that calculation to be made, 'people like me' have to be *visible* in some way, and the presence of 'my' symbols is something that reinforces a sense of inclusion; their absence can undermine it.

There are numerous examples to draw on here. One of the cities most frequently discussed in this regard is Berlin, in which a clash of competing urges to remember and to forget, to freeze and to move on, is being played out in the built environment (Ladd, 1998; Till, 2005). Berlin has much to move on from – the physical reminders of its Imperial, Nazi, and Communist eras still loom over the city – but it is the attempt to erase symbols of the Cold War division of Germany that is becoming increasingly bitter in Berlin. In the rush to reunify East and West, various national and local governments have tried to erase old divisions, which includes removing the vast majority of the old Berlin Wall and building new roads, office blocks, railway stations, and so on in its place. One can still see some markers – tram tracks, for example, dominate the East of the city but not the West – and others have been successfully fought for, such as the delightfully weird *Ampelmännchen*, the hatted pedestrian traffic lights that remain in the East of the city despite an attempt to replace them with their more staid Western counterparts (Figure 4.2). Nonetheless, the pace of development has been extraordinary, and along the way, some people feel that their city is being taken away from them and that they no longer belong to or identify with the city because they lack anchor points for their memories. Many scenes that greeted them every day on their journeys around the city are just not there any more, except in little isolated pockets maintained for tourists. Still, the Berlin demolitions are nothing compared with the erasure that has occurred in some other cities. Cape Town's District Six is one example: a multi-ethnic community removed and houses demolished under the Group Areas Act, with the survivors struggling to assert their existence, let alone celebrate their identity, nearly three decades later (Field, 2001). At least the ruins of District Six remain. Other cities have been built right over the

Figure 4.2. Ampelmännchen, Berlin
Photo © Ole Begemann, by permission.

top of the physical anchors of memory (e.g. Klein, 1997; Rae, 2003). For example, most of the flat land in Wellington's CBD did not exist before the reclaimers moved in, so the foreshore where the indigenous Te Atiawa people fished simply ceased to exist, buried under rubble, soil, tarmac, and concrete.

An example of active inclusion comes in the shape of the US National Statuary Collection in the Capitol Building, Washington, DC, a collection that depicts two worthies from every state. When I took a tour of the building, American visitors seemed most eager to find out which statues belonged to their home state, and thus gain a sense of their own presence in such august surroundings. What was frankly a rather dull tour for me as an outsider was rich and validating for them as insiders. In many capitals similar efforts are made to help domestic visitors feel present, recognized, and dignified – that the national capital is *theirs* in some way. It is not the case that every member of the state is included equally – native iconography is almost entirely absent in Santiago, for example – but even then some limited efforts are being made in other cities not merely to appropriate indigenous imagery for the ends of the dominant culture, but to reinforce indigenous presence in, impact on, and memory of the landscape through interpretive signs, memorials, artworks, and so on, especially in Canberra and Wellington.

Space, Place, and Behaviour

To summarize thus far, we have three ways in which form might relate to political behaviour: it can be (*a*) absolute, physically preventing, or mandating certain action; (*b*) suggestive, encouraging certain kinds of behaviour at the expense of others; and (*c*) symbolic, triggering a sense of identification or recognition, which in turn impacts on such things as political efficacy. Clearly, physical forms can be both types (*a*) and (*c*), or both (*b*) and (*c*); they cannot be both (*a*) and (*b*), by definition.

However, these points raise a significant question: can we separate the influence of physical form from its social, cultural, and political context? To what extent does behaviour respond to the physical object, and to what extent is it responding to contextual elements? There are several ways of approaching this question. One is to start with the increasingly common sociological distinction between 'space' and 'place'. Gieryn (2000: 465) sets out one version of the distinction, with space meaning geographic location and/or built form, while 'place is space filled up with people, practices, objects, and representations'. Similarly, Agnew (1987: 27–8) distinguishes between settings and 'the social practices and processes that go on continuously' in them, along with the 'feelings' that people have about those spaces and practices.[1] Agnew uses different and occasionally opaque terminology, and adds an insistence on the importance of the impact on local practices of macro social and political forces. Nonetheless, the general idea is the same:

> Locale and sense of place describe, respectively, the objective and subjective dimensions of local social arrangements. Location refers to the impact of the macro-order, to the fact that a single place is one among many and subject to influence from these others, and that the social life of a place is also part of the life of a state and the world-economy. Taken together they constitute the defining elements of a place as a historically constituted social context for political and other forms of social behavior. (Agnew, 1987: 230–1)

Another way into this question is to consider how it is that forms-as-symbols acquire particular meaning. Symbols refer to their referents through a process of building up associations: according to most scholars of representation there is no natural, essential link between a symbol and its referent but only what convention, deliberate design, and consistent use build up over a

---

[1] Incidentally, I was told at a workshop in 2010 hosted by the Gendered Ceremony and Ritual in Parliament group (see http://www2.warwick.ac.uk/fac/soc/pais/research/gcrp/) that it is commonplace in some branches of architectural theory to use 'space' to mean the social construct while 'place' meant the bricks and mortar. This seems unhelpful, and perhaps symptomatic of the disciplinary fragmentation that is bedevilling the humanities and social sciences.

period of time (Pitkin, 1972: 94), an insight that derives ultimately from the linguistics of Saussure (2006).[2] This is not to say that symbols are completely arbitrary in the sense that anyone can apply any meaning that he or she chooses to them. Rather, the process of assigning meaning to a symbol is a social process, and thus can vary according to context, even though within a given context the symbol may appear relatively fixed and communicate a small set of ideas, narratives, and identities. Thus, it is that the swastika in many Western contexts stands for Nazism, fascism, racism, and brutality; while for Hindus, Buddhists, and adherents of Shinto it is a sacred symbol referring to ideas including the cosmic cycle, universal harmony, and the sun. The difference is not in the form of the symbol itself but in the accretion of ideas and actions that have, deliberately or otherwise, been built around it in those very different contexts.

We can apply these insights from sociology and semiotics to argue that elements of the built environment do not have intrinsic meaning: their meaning 'is generated through personalization – through taking possession, completing it, changing it' (Rapaport, 1982: 21). As Sonne (2003: 29) puts it, 'a specific form becomes "charged" with a specific political meaning only by virtue of being employed in a specific political context'. If that is the case, then the meaning that goes to make up a sense of 'place' need have no direct relationship to the form of the space itself. This means that we cannot just read meaning off form (Hirst, 2005: 3).

How does the space/place distinction relate to the three types of behavioural effect discussed above? In instances of the first type – absolute prevention or mandate – one can attribute the effect to the space itself, and not the conglomeration of physical and contextual elements that is place. The Israeli–Palestinian wall is not a mere wall in the mind: it physically stops one crossing except at designated (and heavily guarded) points, no matter how fervently one believes it does not. That seems fairly obvious, so let us consider a trickier example: desire lines (Figure 4.3). Desire lines are the 'informal' paths that people wear through grass instead of following the formal paths laid out for them by building and landscape designers. The clearest examples I know come from Canberra, where the neat and orderly lines of a designed city are frequently matched by a network of informal grooves worn through the patchy, dusty grass. They indicate where people really want to walk, to the fury and frustration of groundskeepers all over the city, and thus appear to be a

---

[2] This is not the place for a detailed discussion of semiotics – a reasonably accessible introduction is Hawkes (2003); one classic statement is Barthes (1981) – but it should be noted that I am dualizing here what, for semioticians, is a triple relationship between signifier, signified, and referent; that the thing pointed to by a sign is itself a construction, not 'the thing itself'. Further distinctions in the concept of *political* representation are made by Saward (2006), drawing on similar intellectual resources.

Figure 4.3. Desire line, Kennington, London
Photo © Stefan Szczelkun, by permission.

countercase to type 1 because they seem to be examples of people ignoring the physical cues laid out for them and following their own whims. However, desire lines are *not* playful and wandering, despite some pronouncements to this effect made by artists who have picked up the phrase. No, desire lines connect gathering and access points in the most direct way possible given the terrain. That is, they link entrances to buildings and access points to squares with the shortest practical line. This is demonstrated by the fact that if one shifts the access points – moving a door, for example – then the desire line shifts too,[3] which suggests something more mandatory after all. That is, the configuration of physical objects in space has a predictable impact on how people move between those objects; that is, it is how the nodes of a network are distributed, which determines how people move. Still, we should not be

---

[3] This happened to a prominent desire line at the Australian National University in the last few years. There was a line that ran diagonally through the middle of Fellows Oval, a playing field in the middle of campus, that persisted for many years despite numerous attempts by staff to re-grow the grass. It has vanished not because the groundskeepers finally won, but because several new buildings went up at its southern end, disrupting the access points and thus reconfiguring what counts as the shortest practical route.

too hasty on this point, because this works given an observed predilection for people to take the shortest practical route. We need to know how universal this predilection is, and there are alternative norms: 'keep off the grass' or 'follow the path' might be more powerful in different contexts. Alas, there is no empirical data to draw on here. Still, in the absence of the absolute restrictions imposed by walls and fences, we need to know what individual and social norms there are for movement and interaction in space before we can say with absolute confidence that it is space that's doing the work, not human motivations, or culture, or other contextual elements.

This leads us to instances of the second, 'suggestive' type of behavioural impact, and here we might think that the relationship between form and culture, say, is more dialectical: that culture shapes form, which in turn shapes culture, repeating Churchill's line about us shaping buildings, which shape us in turn, a general claim about political behaviour made by Hay (2002). However, things can be more unidirectional. Consider the issue of accessible and affordable transport. The absence of public transport does not constitute an absolute barrier to participation in public life for most people – if one does not own a car, one can walk or, if disabled, someone else can drive – but the height of the barrier is nonetheless relative to one's personal resources. The barrier is very, very much higher for those on low incomes, or without willing well-off friends, making it more difficult and costly for some to exercise certain freedoms than others, a problem long recognized by various liberal theorists as well as adherents of the new 'capabilities' framework (e.g. Sen, 1985; Raz, 1986). These kinds of barriers affect people on low incomes all around the world: in many places, train and bus fares are too high a proportion of their income; and in a political-economic context where public goods like transport are provided on the basis of private profitability, poor neighbourhoods are poorly served unless governments insist. This is the broader context of place that Agnew (1987) insists on: what structures the attributes of places is not merely 'the cultural', but macro political-economic forces as well. In these cases, to return to networking language, it *is* the lines, as well as the nodes, that matter, because certain kinds of pathway may be structurally favoured over others. Proximity makes a difference here, I think. When one is working at the relatively small scale, the lines of access are relatively unimportant, and one can work one's way around barriers or simply ignore the cues laid out by formal pathways. When the scale increases, and access is not a matter of just walking, then the lines of access become much more important.

In instances of the third type, 'place' acts as a symbolic anchor point for political norms. This takes us back to Churchill. I think Churchill's memorable line is not generally applicable, and that one of the places where it does not apply is the very place he was talking about: the House of Commons. In my view, the shape of the chamber came to symbolize elements of British political culture, and it was the culture that led him to insist on maintaining the arrangement of the benches, and not the arrangement of the benches that led to the culture. Otherwise there is no way to explain the lack of correspondence between form and culture that we observe in comparative cases. The form of the seating in a legislative chamber is an arbitrary symbol; it comes to *mean* something that can endure, certainly, and the meaning can exert an independent, normative influence, but it is that richer sense of place more generally that is doing the work, not the oak and leather of the Commons benches. Changing the seating arrangements for South Africa's National Council of Provinces from portrait-straight to landscape-curved may have *symbolized* the government's intention to embed a new parliamentary culture, and may remind members of that aim such that they start to act in accordance with the new expectations, but it cannot *cause* any change on its own. I take this point up in more detail in Chapter five.

Therefore, we are left with a continuum of spatial effects on political behaviour, with more 'mandatory' forms at one end and entirely conventional, symbolic associations at the other, noting that mandatory forms too have symbolic functions. It is only as we move towards the mandatory end that we can say that behaviour responds to the physical object alone, and even at that extreme walls need to be policed, otherwise they can be scaled, or blown up and torn down, or at the very least covered in subversive graffiti. Towards the middle of the continuum what is in play is as much 'place' as 'space', which means that it is norms and practices, as well as macro political forces, that define what goes on in a given location as much as the physical characteristics of the location itself. Thus, inequality, for example, can be 'emplaced' and reinforced by the way that suburbs are developed, sold, and linked, even in cases where there is no absolute barrier to people crossing in or out. Towards the other extreme, space recedes even further, such that physical form has merely conventional associations with certain meanings: there is no necessary link between the form and the action associated with it other than what convention and habit has bestowed in a given social and political context. As the discussion of the visibility of symbols of identity shows, these signals can be powerful, but it is the signal, not the form itself, that matters here, and on that point Churchill and his followers are wrong. British parliamentarians attribute symbolic importance to the arrangement of benches, and that meaning, nested in a richer context of meanings, is what constrains behaviour in the House of Commons, not the benches themselves.

Given all that, it is worth returning to the work of the only political scientist to have seriously studied the shape of debating chambers and political culture, Charles Goodsell (1988*b*). Goodsell is extremely careful to spell out some of the difficulties that I have raised above, especially the problem that, over time, it becomes impossible to separate empirically what he takes to be the original effects of the space from the habits of action that build up in that space over time. He thus stresses the symbolic function of public space, but does go on to argue that there are nonetheless some symbolic universals, namely height, centrality, and placement on the right being associated with high status; lowly, peripheral, and left-hand placement being associated with low status. In addition, domed roofs are associated with the sky; floors with the earth; stairs with honour and aspiration; doorways with changes in values, norms, or status; and canopies with reverence and sanctity (Goodsell, 1988b: 48–9). Alas, however, the search for human symbolic universals has not taken us very far, and these days anthropologists tend to emphasize the cultural particularity of interpreting forms rather than looking for transcendent meaning (Bender, 1993). Thus, I think Goodsell is mistaken when he defends his comparative approach by asserting that the 'concreteness of architectural forms allows us to make comparison in very tangible, even exact, ways' (1988b: 16). The more we move away from the mandatory end of our spatial effects spectrum, the less this assertion is true, because the further away we move the less work is being done by the architectural forms. We might quantify forms – measure chamber dimensions, the height of daises, the proximity of audiences, and so on – yet find that such things do not *mean* the same things in different contexts, and thus we might be comparing the wrong things. Goodsell, like Lehmann-Haupt (1954) before him, makes much of the intimidating effect of the long, monumental walk to Hitler's huge office in the Reich Chancellery. The point that Goodsell does not make is that this effect is related to the fact that it was *Hitler's* office, and not just anyone's. Forcing someone to walk a long way to *my* office would just be seen as petty self-aggrandizement, and likely to diminish my standing in a first-time visitor's eyes, not enhance it. The effect of such space is relative to the power positions and reputations of the people concerned, and the hierarchical or egalitarian norms prevailing in the society or institution concerned. It is not absolute.

Now, I think Goodsell makes too much of universalism claims when he need not. He is, after all, looking at a single type of public space in a relatively homogenous political culture: city council chambers in the United States of America. He could have avoided the universal-particular controversy simply by limiting his remarks to that single context. I, on the other hand, cannot dodge this problem because this book looks at cases across the democratic world, in different[4] cultural settings. Rather than close that debate now, I will leave it as an open question: *can* we see a relationship between a particular

---

[4] Although not very different, as I confessed in Chapter one – my sample is dominated by G8 and colonial capitals.

82

physical form and particular political behaviour? In principle, I have argued that there is a continuum of effects: we should expect such a relationship where there is something mandatory about the space; to a lesser extent where spatial relationships are not mandatory but certainly present barriers or encourage tendencies to certain action; and, in partial concession to Goodsell, when a certain symbolic cue has universal application.

Government, Governance, and the Political Economy of Public Space

Therefore, some kinds of place can, in principle, be associated with some kinds of political behaviour, but those effects may be more or less strongly driven by the form itself. That leaves us with a democratic worry. On the basis of the norms discussed in Chapter two, democrats should generally prefer spatial arrangements that encourage or 'emplace' respect, inclusion and equality, and not their opposites (while noting Sunstein's point that sometimes enclaves may be valuable things for subaltern groups). The question then is, how likely is it that inclusive kinds of places will be provided? This is a big question, and one that I will address as I go along in Part II. For now, what I want to do is to sketch what is at stake conceptually, first by setting out the dominant approach to this question in the urban theory literature, and then by showing how that helps us understand each of the four kinds of public space.

The dominant way of answering this kind of question is to consider the political economy of urban governance, looking at the relationship between the interests of capital and its mode of production, and the kinds of spaces that are thus constructed and the infrastructure that is built to link them. Thus, there has been much talk, especially in the United States, about 'urban regimes' (Elkin, 1987; Stone, 1993), in which networks made up of property developers, architects and engineers, elected and appointed city officials, and large capitalist concerns come together to develop economic activity by building large scale industrial, residential, office, and retail complexes; or by building roads and parking systems which link suburbs and businesses; often at the expense of the environment (because of their land impact and resource use), local communities (which get displaced or simply bulldozed), or local businesses and services (which cannot compete economically with the large chain stores and megamalls). In such settings, elected city governments are relatively 'weak player[s] in a larger system of power', such that the power to determine what happens in a given locality is exercised not just in the town hall but by a terribly varied mix of

airline schedulers, street-corner entrepreneurs, union leaders, neighbourhood po-
tentates, racial spokesmen, bond rating agencies, bankers, public housing tenant
leaders, criminal gangs, real estate developers, insurance underwriters, and government agencies at state and federal levels. Even "forces" as ineffable as popular
culture – from its veneration of green lawns on quiet streets to its hypnotic
fascination with firearms – form part of the power environment in which city
government must operate. (Rae, 2003: x)

There is disagreement over the degree to which American urban regime
theory fits other institutional contexts (see e.g. Davies, 2003), but still it
seems generally accepted to talk of there being a distinction in modern capitalist states between government; the decisions and indecision of state officials
(elected or otherwise) and governance; the networks of agents, institutions,
power relations, norms, and discourses that structure what governments can
do, setting limits on the range of the possible (Rhodes, 1997; Pierre, 2000).
Thus, governance is not just about cooking up conspiracies between self-
interested actors in now-smoke-free back rooms. Governance may include
personal networks, but it also includes broader ideational, and material limits.
Whichever way one thinks of it, urban theory of this kind leads to the view
that, in the absence of regulations to the contrary and the will to enforce
them, space is organized, designed, and built in ways that favour the powerful
over the powerless, economic interests over social interests, private gain over
public good (Lefebvre, 1991), and developers, corporate tenants, and landowners over the owners and users of small corner shops, community centres,
playgrounds, and parks.

Other kinds of theory point to the same general conclusion. Network-based
theories often have the flaw that they seem to require people's beliefs to align
with the outcome of decisions, but beliefs and intentions need not align for a
single outcome to emerge nonetheless. Instead, the structure of institutions
and incentives can help to align individual decisions in the same general
direction, regardless of what the individual actors might prefer if they stood
back and looked at the system as a whole. This is a commonplace point,
familiar to scholars of social choice, new institutionalists, and discourse theorists alike (Olson, 1965; Hajer, 1993; Peters, 1999). The implication is that
public space of the 'public goods' types – openly accessible space and space for
making public claims – is less likely to be provided under a system where
individuals can do better by exploiting spatial resources for their own gain.
Where space *is* held in common as a public good, the fact that some individuals can do better for themselves by refusing to cooperate leads to a collapse
of the provision of the good, to be replaced by individualized, private ownership and private service provision. This is the classic 'tragedy of the commons'
(Hardin, 1968). Therefore, whether one is a theorist who believes in the power
of conspiracies, networks, economic incentives, institutions, or discourses, the

same conclusion is indicated: space is more likely to be provided in ways that favour powerful private interests, especially economic interests, and less likely to be provided in ways that favour public goods, local communities, relatively powerless businesses, and the environment.

The dominance of large commercial interests in the production of space is linked with an important discursive shift in recent decades, and that is a shift from constructing the public as citizen to the public as consumer, as if shopping were all there is to public life. This shift has been remarked on in various contexts – in the public policy literature it is used to analyse things like the shifting of social welfare resources away from people at the margins of society towards people in the more profitable mainstream (e.g. Barnes, 1997) – and in the urbanism literature the focus has been very much on privately controlled and policed shopping malls as people's only collective space (Barber, 2001; Southworth, 2005). In such spaces, what counts as public activity is shopping; or sitting and chatting so long as it is done while eating or drinking something bought from a mall-authorized vendor. What is not allowed is 'political' activity, unless it is by a politician glad-handing and baby-kissing before an election. Security guards outside Melbourne's riverfront casino will manhandle people handing out political leaflets, but not people handing out commercial advertising; the same applies in the skyways of Minneapolis and in numerous other settings where the only available public space is space to consume together, not space to debate together. Given that, Liverpool City Council in the UK caused nowhere near enough outrage, in my view, when it revealed in 2003 that it was effectively handing control of forty-two acres of the central city to the Duke of Westminster on a 250-year lease as part of a regeneration plan that would focus not on providing a forum, but providing a market place patrolled and controlled by private contractors. Along the way, the project demolished community centres, a Friend's Meeting House, and small businesses, and actively excluded anyone who did not fit the middle-class shopper mould (Russell, 2008).

Three important points emerge from this discussion. The first is that, given the political economy of the production of space and an associated discourse that constructs 'public' in a limited, commercial sense, public space in senses 1 and 4 are less likely to be built than either private spaces or spaces that are public in senses 2 and 3. And yet it is openly accessible space and space for making public claims that are the important ones when it comes to democratic performance. Therefore, we have reasons to think that democracy itself is put at risk by the individualist, capitalist political economy of space. This is discussed further in Chapter eight.

The second point relates to a challenge presented by the governance concept to the normative claims emerging from Chapter three. If formal, elected institutions are not the primary locus of power, then why think that democracy is best advanced by encouraging open public engagement with that locus? Why worry about demonstrations in plazas and central squares when the decision-makers are not located in or near those spaces? There are two responses to make. The first is that we should be careful not to think that governments everywhere are powerless, nor even as powerless as they make out. Not only is it the case, as Davies (2003) argues, that urban regime theory underplays the role that actors in the formal institutions of government play in non-US contexts, it is also argued that the limits on government action are the subject of rhetorical contestation as governments use them to claim or deny responsibility for conditions (Hay, 2002). In other words, some governments may be more powerful than they themselves claim, because pretending otherwise helps them avoid responsibility for economic failure and failure to address inequality and exclusion (see also Flinders and Buller, 2006). It is, suggest Hay, Flinders, Buller, and others, still within the power of governments to take up the reins and direct policy more actively, and therefore worth insisting on a norm that they be held accountable.

Not only are some governments more powerful than they like to pretend, but there are countermovements as well. Two deserve a brief mention here: the community architecture movement (Towers, 1995) and the community gardens movement (Ferris, Norman, and Sempik, 2001). Common to both is the ideal of taking control of neighbourhood environments and giving it back to local communities by buying up empty plots and buildings as they come on the market and developing them using participatory design and planning processes; or converting empty spaces into vegetable and flower gardens. Sometimes these things are organized by local cooperatives, sometimes by a wealthy benefactor, and sometimes land is just commandeered with no one person or group coordinating things. Sometimes a purchase is made; sometimes space is simply occupied with no formal transfer of ownership. Urban gardens have sprung up in inner city plots in the United States, Germany, Japan, and many other countries, and while their record of fighting redevelopment plans or owners is patchy, it shows that there are alternatives to the standard urban regime model.

Thus, the third point that emerges from the governance/government distinction is that formal public space is not all there is to politics. At the same time, as Stevens (2007) rightly insists, the purposes of public space are not just political. So, while I focus on the formal public sphere in Chapters five and six, and the informal public sphere in Chapters seven and eight, I also examine the more diffuse arenas of collective action and the more playful uses of public space in Chapter eight. Government is not all there is to politics: politics is not all there is to public life.

Conclusion: An Interpretive Framework

All the conceptual tools for analysing the empirical examples are now in place. I want to conclude this chapter by restating them briefly, for ease of reference later on.

The first set of tools concerns the concept of democracy, which I have defined as decisive public reasoning on common issues among all affected interests. Democracy is not mere freedom, and political conflict is not itself a sign of democratic failure. Indeed, some of those conflicts are themselves internal to democratic ideals, and cannot be resolved simply by appealing to 'democracy'. These include conflicts over who counts as the relevant 'we', conflicts over how many of us should agree with something before it should be decisive, and conflicts over the rightful scope of subjects that the collective can peer into. On all of these controversies I tend to err on the expansive side: 'all those affected' rather than more limited groups of people in particular territories; large numbers rather than small numbers; and broad scope rather than limited scope. As will be seen, these same controversies arise in conflicts over public space.

Democracy is an ongoing performance, not a periodic or one-shot affair. I have distinguished between five primary democratic roles that actors play in a democracy: narrating, claiming, deciding, scrutinizing, and representing. All of these five have their own proper stages of action: almost limitless for narrating (but not quite, thanks to norms about safe and unsafe topics); highly visible stages for making public claims; single, dignified stages for decision-making and scrutinizing. Representing takes place in different modes across these four kinds of stages.

The concept of democracy is intimately connected with the concept of 'the public' in three different ways: the sense of public as that body of people comprising the *demos*, as that set of issues of common concern, and as that set of things that have collective impacts. These things collectively form the public sphere, and I work throughout with Habermas's distinctions between a formal public sphere of government; the informal public sphere of free citizens engaging in debate and opinion formation; the economic sphere of private business transactions; the 'sphere of the intimate' (using Held's terms); and the complex transmission (or, indeed, exclusion) mechanisms of governance that include policy networks and discourse coalitions and the impersonal coordination provided by discourses, state institutions, and the capitalist political economy.

I use the term 'public space' to mean the physical subset of the public sphere, and include in it those spaces that are freely accessible, that use common resources, that have common effects, and are used for the performance of democratic roles. I specifically exclude ownership from my definition, because it does not track actual political practice. I have insisted that such physical spaces matter for the performance of democracy, especially the scrutiny function. One can still have a kind of democracy without physical stages, just as a human being can still function without the use of his or her limbs; however, democratic life becomes a great deal harder without them, and thus I think they are worthy of evaluation and academic scrutiny. I have also argued that when it comes to explaining political behaviour, clearly political space is not all there is: 'place' matters just as much, and even more, in some settings. Place is defined as the agglomeration of people and practices, symbolic and normative associations, as well as the power relations that drive spatial production and reproduction. There are clearly some settings where it really is 'space' that is doing the work, and others where it is all the habits of conventional association. However, there is no contradiction here. The norms and associations, I think, require physical anchor points: you cannot have place without space.

Looking at the political economy of space, however, suggests that it is also less likely that three of the four types of public space will get built, including the two most democratically valuable types. In the face of environments built for private profit, and the associated reconstruction of the public from *demos* to shopper, we have reason to be concerned about the ongoing availability of spaces for the performance of democratic roles, including limits to the ability of some sections of the public to access collective arenas and resources. Not only that, but spaces for the enjoyment of other public goods may be threatened too – not just political goods, but learning, health, socializing, and good old-fashioned fun spaces. However, governments may be more powerful than they care to admit in the face of governance challenges, while groups in the informal public sphere are offering alternatives to the large-developer-led model of the provision of space.

There are numerous empirical questions that could arise from this analytic framework, but in what follows the primary question is this: how do various cities cater for the performance of the five democratic roles – narration, claim-making, deciding, scrutinizing, and representing? I answer this question by first looking at the roles that the buildings of the formal public sphere – especially legislative assemblies – play and the various ways in which they meet the criteria for public space. I then turn to spaces for the informal public sphere, starting with spaces for direct engagement between the formal and the informal, and then moving on to the broader public spaces of democratic cities where members of the *demos* can go to meet, or get away from, each other. Along the way, several secondary questions arise:

- Which of the kinds of space are recognized in official and popular discourse, and which ones are ignored?
- What kinds of public, of *demos*, are recognized or excluded?
- Which democratic roles are played out in which spaces?
- Which roles receive recognition, and which do not?
- Do the symbolic associations of spaces line up with their theoretically ideal purposes, or official purposes, or their actual use?
- What conflicts arise over the use of public space, and how are they dealt with?

Let me reiterate at this point that my focus is on the spatial requirements of a particular account of democracy; it is not a survey of all the nooks and crannies of cities or of the complete variety of ways in which city spaces can be public spaces. This is very clearly a *political* account, a liberal deliberative account at that, and not a more general sociological or geographical account. The empirical work is far too broad-brush, encompassing too many cities to answer 'nooks and crannies' kinds of questions, and anyway, that is work that has already been done in a variety of contexts. Instead, what has *not* been done, at least not to the satisfaction of someone in a mainstream Politics department, is connecting ideas of space with a political conception of democracy.

It is time to turn to the analysis. In Part II, I examine these issues in three distinct but related contexts. The first is assemblies, the single, dignified seats of the formal public sphere where decisions are taken and scrutinized, and some of the work of representation goes on. The second is the streets and squares where people come to engage with their leaders, not only to press public claims on them but also to share in public rituals. The third is more diffuse: those arenas of collective life that are not strictly for political purposes but that nonetheless matter to people: parks, leisure spaces, shopping, and dining areas, many of the places that go to make up quality of life in a city. In Part III, I bring all that together to describe some criteria for measuring the quality of public space in a democracy, before offering a tentative evaluation of the cities under study.

Part II
Public Space and Democratic Performance

5

Assemblies I: Performing Democratic Roles

Of all the spaces for democracy, it is only the assembly where every one of the democratic roles is performed. They are places where representatives make proposals for the spending of public resources and narrate the experiences of those they represent, where many actors scrutinize the actions of those in power, and where decisions that are binding on all the people present in a given territory are made. Assemblies entail public claims themselves: all embody claims about who the rightful decision-makers are; many have design elements that tell stories about who 'the people' are; and all are, or come to be, symbols of national politics and national culture.

Assemblies are thus public spaces in sense 4 – spaces for the performance of public roles – par excellence. They are also public spaces in senses 2 and 3, because they consume public resources and have public impacts, being expensive to run and often having significant impacts on their built environments. Their publicness in sense 1 is more limited and much more variable: some are fairly open and welcoming; others are closed and kept that way.

This chapter and the next analyse each of these ways that assemblies function as public space. I start by setting out a general account of the purposes of assemblies, specifying why it is that we should want a legislative assembly rather than any other kind of public space to play those roles. In this chapter, I then focus on two major purposes: their symbolic functions and their working spaces. The two are dialectically linked, I argue. The fact that the work that goes on in them affects everyone in a given territory gives the buildings their tremendous status and power as symbols; the symbolism of the buildings provides cues to onlookers that they should take that work seriously. I then move into the buildings and consider the major variations in their working spaces, noting which variations in layout seem to make a difference to political behaviour and which do not – and some of the most talked-about variations do not. I finish with a consideration of the other working spaces of assembly buildings, and argue that maintaining the work of democracy in these locations is extremely valuable both from a working efficiency and from a democratic scrutiny point of view. That scrutiny depends on access, however, which is the subject of Chapter six.

Assembly Purposes

Why have a legislative assembly? One answer seems rather obvious and trivial: like all buildings, assemblies' primary purpose is to meet representatives' basic need for shelter and temperature control while working; bringing in and controlling air, light and water; providing social and personal space; and taking out waste (Allen, 2005). However, there is nothing trivial about it when it comes to counting the cost. In Washington, DC, the 2009 budget of the Architect of the Capitol was US$540 million, just over 9 per cent of the overall expenditure on the Legislative Branch. The point about shelter also helps us avoid romanticizing outdoor settings. It seems marvellous to a demo-crat of a participatory bent to witness the *Landsgemeinde* of Appenzell Inner-rhodes on a sunny spring morning; it is not quite so much fun when rain threatens, especially for the *Ratschreiber* and his or her staff having to manage papers, computers, public address systems and so on; and the gathered citizens who are only able to see as far as the umbrella in front of them. Buildings are not merely symbolic entities but meet basic human needs, keeping us and our papers and electrical equipment comfortable and dry.

If we try to answer the 'why have assemblies?' question by looking at the four democratic roles – inclusive narration, claim-making, decision-making and scrutiny – it is immediately obvious that those roles are played in many kinds of public space. What is special about legislative assemblies? Drawing on the claims made in Part I, they are special in four ways. First, having a 'dignified' site helps cue citizens and their representatives into taking seriously the deliberation and decision-making that goes on in them, which is impor-tant because those decisions affect very large numbers of people.

The second reason is that such sites are useful for face-to-face deliberation and decision-making. Historically, the need for such assemblies was over-whelming: if people were expected to work together then they had no choice but to meet in person. Now that imperative has been loosened by information technology, yet still many scholars of democracy and decision-making argue that face-to-face engagement remains important because it makes communi-cation easier and dissembling harder (see Chapter three, page 64); and even when the opportunities for teleworking from constituencies seem obvious, there is a lot of work of a representative that cannot easily be done by remote, especially legislative committee work.

The third reason concerns assemblies' role as political spaces where the public is made present in various forms, something I focus on more in the next chapter. That public presence is essential for the publicity principle to work (Chapter two, p. 28) – it is having to make arguments and defend proposals in public that forces claim-makers to put forward proposals in terms that others can accept. It also matters for public claim-making: as I argued elsewhere in Chapter two (p. 41), the 'act of making public claims requires that the rest of the public is paying attention somehow'. Having a *single* site for this work helps attentive publics, especially the media, evaluate claims and decisions, and scrutinize claim- and decision-makers. If the sites of collective decision-making are too dispersed – and some argue that this is the case in many democracies now – then it becomes too difficult to ensure publicity, too difficult to demand accountability, and we lose democratic control. In turn, the presence of attentive publics helps decision-makers by presenting a channel through which they can disseminate information about the problems they think the public faces; give their assessments of, and solutions to, those problems; and talk up their successes and their opponents' failures.

The fourth and final reason concerns the need to civilize conflict. As the risk of conflict rises, we are less inclined to leave interaction to chance, and more inclined to ritualize it and control it in some way, perhaps by surrounding it with formal procedures. Placing it in a designated physical space helps cue the appropriate procedures and appropriate behaviour, although there is a long-standing concern from difference theorists in particular that 'civilizing' is merely another way of privileging the norms and habits of traditional power holders, excluding others and their perfectly reasonable, defensible demands on the grounds of their allegedly unreasonable behaviour. 'Merely' is, I think, going too far – ask those who study conflict and conflict resolution about the importance of formalizing procedures as a means of lowering the temperature of conflict so that real differences can be discussed without weapons being drawn.

Those are, I think, the reasons why assemblies are necessary, the functions that only they perform. But those reasons do not exhaust the list of functions they usefully perform, and among those is the function of symbolic representation of things including the people, the nation, and the democratic process itself.

Symbolic Intent

To the extent this is thought about at all, the standard way of thinking about political buildings is to look at the messages of power they send. Thus, typically, Sudjic (2001, 2005) talks about neoclassical architecture sending messages of hierarchy, tradition, deference, and exclusivity; and about more modern buildings like the Australian Parliament as sending more egalitarian messages. Sometimes these messages are unintended consequences, but often are part of the design brief, especially from the eighteenth and nineteenth centuries when new assemblies were built to magnify and dignify nations, and were often addressed as much to foreign as domestic audiences.

The United States Capitol was specifically designed to convey American values, American strength, and American unity both at the large scale and in the small details. Indeed, George Washington and Thomas Jefferson put enormous effort into symbolic design for the new republic, from appropriating the Roman fasces as a symbol of strength through unity to the combination of Roman and Masonic symbolism that makes the Great Seal of the United States. The overall classical style of the building is something that Jefferson insisted on in order to cloak the republic in what he and others accepted as the symbols of a high-status antiquity (Scott, 1995: 23). By contrast, classical symbolism was explicitly rejected in Britain when it came to rebuilding the Palace of Westminster after the disastrous fire of 1834. As Cannadine (2000: 15) argues, the classical 'had become associated in the popular patriotic mind with the rootless anarchy and national enmity of revolutionary France' with the result that an allegedly national style, a version of late Gothic, was chosen to 'articulate a hierarchical image of the social and political order, stressing venerable authority, providential subordination and true conservative principles'. The importance of France as a role model for the new American republic is well-documented (e.g. Field et al., 2007), as is the pointed rejection of both France and 'North America' and the embrace of British heritage in the choice of a modernized Gothic for the Canadian parliament buildings in Ottawa later in the nineteenth century (Young, 1995). The point is that these styles do not mean one thing, universally, or in isolation. They have meaning in particular contexts, and in contrast to each other.

Similar considerations drove the design of the National Diet building in Tokyo, formally opened in December 1936 (Figure 5.1). Proposed by the Meiji Emperor in the 1880s, the building is not merely a deliberative assembly or an office building. Instead, it was built, along with numerous other public buildings, in the context of a massive programme driven by the Emperor and the ruling oligarchy to modernize, industrialize and compete with Western powers (Reynolds, 1996). There was nothing democratic going on here – these were 'authoritarian modernizers' after all (Feldman, 1996: 659). Instead, the motivation was to place Japan symbolically alongside the 'great' nations by providing built symbols of equality with those nations. Stylistically, therefore, the building seems more legible to foreigners than Japanese, using a 'denuded' neoclassical monumentalism that looks broadly familiar to anyone from Washington or Berlin (Reynolds, 1996: 46); along with a Victorian sensibility for the interior (heavy, dark woods richly carved; heavy patterned

Figure 5.1. The National Diet, Tokyo
Photo by 'zoonabar', licensed by Creative Commons.

wallpaper; heavy, deep carpets; overstuffed, plush velvet upholstery). Japanese native design elements are almost entirely absent because 'Japanese' was a highly ambiguous label at the time, associated with 'feudal' and 'undeveloped' in public discourse. Thus, it was that in the various design competitions held from the Meiji period onwards it was almost exclusively foreigners who came up with designs that reflected local aesthetics and traditions, albeit in romanticized versions. While the Treasury Commission running the project decided that it should be built from Japanese materials to a Japanese design, Japanese architects for the most part reproduced variations on the Reichstag or the Capitol in their proposals (Reynolds, 1996).

Still, the fact that a building was constructed for a given symbolic purpose tells us relatively little about how it is actually seen and used, especially if the designers and the users have been long separated in time. Context is what determines how a symbol is received. Therefore, the purposes of the builders are not set in stone, as it were; as politics evolves in a place, so the building evolves with it, with buildings constructed for one political purpose often coming to serve another. Thus, while the Diet had very little power and very little popular regard in its early years, the self-same building now houses an institution that is a great deal more powerful following the Second World War and more recent electoral reform (Shiratori, 1995). Likewise, in the case of the

Palace of Westminster, Cannadine (2000: 19) argues that while Charles Barry and AWN Pugin may have had profoundly conservative, hierarchical and anti-democratic intentions, and attempted to set those in stone, the reality is that the building was opened at a time of rapid constitutional change in the shape of the three major Reform Acts and repeal of the Corn Laws, and evidently failed to derail them. Even Queen Victoria failed to act out the part that Barry and Pugin had written for her, 'turning her back on those accoutrements of majesty' (Cannadine, 2000: 19) by appearing only briefly at the opening, dressed simply, having her speech read by the Lord Chancellor and then not even turning up after the 1870s. Therefore, right from the start, any alleged cueing effects of the new Houses of Parliament were weak at best when even the most regal of beholders chose not to be moved in the ways the designers expected. The buildings took on more democratic overtones as more democracy was enacted within them. A wider franchise, a more varied membership, a more dominant Commons and less relevant Lords have all served to change the symbolism of the building ever since, such that it now means something quite different – including but not limited to majoritarian government – than it once did. To repeat a point made in Chapter four, buildings take on meaning by being owned and used; their meaning is not intrinsic.

This is not to say that buildings cannot work as symbols, but just that what they symbolize is a function of the values and meanings of a specific time and place, and that because times change, so do symbols. Even hated symbols of a hated past can have their meanings altered by new owners, guided by new values and acting in new ways. Thus, while the rebuilding and reoccupation of the Reichstag building in Berlin caused enormous controversy in the 1990s – 'a bombastic, war-scarred fossil, the scene of Germany's darkest hours, an unwelcome symbol of democracy's failure to grow deep roots under either the monarchy or the succeeding Weimar republic' (Wise, 1998: 121) – it is rather taken for granted now. Even the old Imperial name has been retained without attracting much comment, despite the fact that for more than sixty years Germany has not been a *Reich* but a *Bund*,[1] governed in part by the *Bundestag*.

Given all that, it is easy to have sympathy for the new majority government of South Africa whose members felt repelled by the monochromatic, dark, wooden interior of the apartheid-era parliamentary chamber. To them it symbolized oppression by evoking memories of oppressors standing in that very chamber and giving speeches that condemned their people to stunted lives (interview, SA Parliament Public Relations). However, the above analysis

---

[1] That is, not an empire but a union, a federation.

98

suggests there was no *need* to build a new parliamentary chamber to exorcize those ghosts. A great deal would have been achieved simply by taking ownership and working in new ways in the old space, perhaps bringing in new rituals, new procedures, and new symbols, just as the balcony of Cape Town City Hall is remembered not so much because it overlooks a military parade ground but because Nelson Mandela gave his first post-release address to the nation standing at its railings. Perhaps therein lies hope for the Northern Irish Assembly too – its occupation of Parliament Buildings at Stormont has been a sore point for Sinn Féin who see the building not just as filled with unionist symbols but as constituting a symbol of division in its own right (see e.g. Anonymous, 2002), but opposition is waning as use, habit, and the deliberate effort to create new symbols within the old take root.

So, context is king. Within specific contexts, however, assemblies can have very powerful cueing effects indeed, and so let us now turn to the use of those buildings in the rituals of democracy.

Stages for the Rituals of Democracy

For anyone who doubts the importance of the physical occupation of public space, events in Washington, DC, on 20 January 2009 tell us that sometimes very, very large numbers of people think it *does* matter. The inauguration of Barack Obama as 44th President of the United States saw as many as 1.8 million people[2] turning out on a freezing cold January day to witness the event in person (Figure 5.2). In the words of one attendee,

> This is just such an incredible time in our history where you can see the unity of people of different nationalities, different language barriers, socioeconomic status. It's incredible. It's really great to see so many underrepresented groups participate in the political process. You see the mobilization of youth, minorities, women. It's incredible. It's incredible. And I'm just excited to be a part of it. (CNN, 2009)

Journalists covering the event frequently asked the same question – why have you come? – and people in the crowd gave very similar answers. Some African Americans focused on the joy of seeing a black man installed as president, identifying with him, and interpreting the event in the context of a long civil rights struggle. Others focused on themes of unity in diversity. Still others reported a general desire to be part of something momentous, to have a story to tell their children and thus, presumably, to grow in esteem by being able to

---

[2] There is no official estimate of attendance, but the US National Parks Service, which administers the National Mall, supported the *Washington Post's* upper-end count of 1.8 million, which made the crowd the largest ever to gather in Washington, DC (Ruane and Davis, 2009).

Figure 5.2. Inauguration of President Barack Obama, 2009
Photo by 'klipsch_soundman', licensed by Creative Commons.

identify themselves with something positive and significant in national history. Yet others wanted to mark a transition from a despised leadership to one that offered them more hope (BBC, 2009). They turned out to be part of an event that was meaningful in their lives, and, importantly, to share that experience with others. It is noteworthy that the vast majority of those people could only see the president on TV screens and could only hear his voice through loudspeakers, yet gathering together in that particular space at that particular time with everyone else was much more important than seeing the self-same pictures at home. It was the crowd and the shared experience that people came for as much as anything else, but the crowd was drawn and given focus by the inauguration event itself – they would not have all turned up to see a videotape a few days later. And they all showed great fortitude in doing so, having to start in the pre-dawn chill of a day that never rose above freezing in order to claim a small patch of grass to stand and see and hear their new president take office.

As a stage, the site is equally impressive. For the inauguration, the West front of the Capitol is transformed into something approaching a classical amphitheatre, with the main platform near the base of the West steps, embraced on three sides by tall, steep stands for invited guests and VIPs, and with the neoclassical Capitol building itself providing an almost overwhelming backdrop, a perfect *skene*, rising hundreds of feet behind the speakers' proscenium. The big difference between the Capitol as *theatron* and the classical originals, apart from sheer scale, is the fact that the seating is reversed, forming part of the *skene* itself, and facing outwards down the 1.2 miles of the National Mall to the Washington Memorial and beyond.

The presence of a stage and an audience requires some sort of performance, and indeed there is: while the oath of office and inaugural speech are the main events in terms of media coverage, they are scenes seven and eight of an eleven-scene drama that includes music and poetry, anthems and invocations, the vice-presidential oath, and more. The presidential oath and speech aim to cement in symbolic terms a set of associations both with the office of the president and its particular holder. Those functions include legitimation of the office and the office holder through repetition of traditional forms of words; and through reaffirmation of official culture, especially what Bellah (1967) called America's 'civil religion' (Toolin, 1983). But they also help each new president build on that foundation a set of particular, personal associations with norms, values, ideas, and plans that he himself wishes to see embedded in the legal and normative framework of the country. As Emrich et al. (2001) put it, the inaugural speech is *the* opportunity for the president 'to establish a vision and to persuade the people to work with him to enact this vision', and successful communication of that vision through concrete, sense-based imagery has a direct effect both on how much charisma people endow that president with, and how 'great' he is rated by historians (Tulis, 1988). On almost no other occasion does the president have the attention of such a great proportion of the American people, let alone the hundreds of millions of television and Internet viewers around the world.

The key is that it is the full sense of place that endows the president with charisma: the energies and expectations of the nation are focused on that platform at that moment. The anthropologist Clifford Geertz (1985: 14), quoting Edward Shils (1965), puts it especially eloquently when he describes charisma as emerging from

> ...the connection between the symbolic value individuals possess and their relation to the active centers of the social order. Such centers, which have "nothing to do with geometry and little with geography," are essentially concentrated loci of serious acts; they consist in the point or points in a society where its leading ideas come together with its leading institutions to create an arena in which the events that most vitally affect its members' lives take place. It is involvement, even oppositional involvement, with such arenas and with the momentous events that occur in them that confers charisma. It is a sign, not of popular appeal or inventive craziness, but of being near the heart of things.

Geertz pushes his point too far, of course, in two ways. In his paper, he makes much of the idea that 'a woman is not a duchess a hundred yards from a carriage', but not everyone who sits in a carriage is instantly seen as a duchess either – Geertz perhaps needed to see a production of Shaw's *Pygmalion*. Anyway, if his assertion *were* true, it would undermine the claim that perceptions of status and charisma have nothing do with geometry and geography. The more defensible point is that simply placing a specific person at a focal point through the repeated rituals of inauguration on a hallowed site, using all the symbols of national power and performance, creates an extraordinary opportunity for that individual both to legitimate their rule, and to establish a set of norms and expectation for years to come. Not everyone grasps that opportunity, but it is created by the ritual of inauguration. The setting is an important part of that ritual, as is the crowd, just as a play requires a stage and an audience before it can be transformed from a script into a performance (Sauter, 2000).

Other democracies have rites of passage aimed at legitimating the state and its executive office holders (Wilentz, 1985; Barker, 2001), and while they tend not to attract crowds at anything like the scale that Barack Obama did, this is at least in part because most of the other states under study here separate the roles of head of state and head of government. In those systems, it is usually the case that more pomp and ceremony – and crowds – attend the head of state than the chief executive. There are several possible interpretations of this fact. One is that the ceremonies are primarily about identity. They repeat original myths, tell pioneer stories, and narrate more or less exclusive tales of membership and belonging; and that is why they focus on the person who symbolically represents the nation as a whole, the person who represents common values and thus who, it is supposed, transcends politics and mere majorities. Thus it is that the major parliamentary ceremonies in constitutional monarchies focus on the monarch and the opening of the assembly, not on the Prime Minister. This is as true in Japan as it is in Britain and the Commonwealth: the Emperor remains a symbol of the nation as a whole, of things that are lasting, transcendent, and greatly venerable, while Prime Ministers, especially since the end of the Liberal Democratic Party's hegemony, reflect more transitory, partial, and earthly concerns.

Now, of course, the symbols of the one are frequently appropriated by the other – the Emperor's throne and symbols dominate both chambers and many other rooms of the Diet building not simply to remind us of the Emperor but to cloak the assembled councillors with his aura, his legitimacy, and his reverence. Similarly, the monarch's throne symbolically dominates the Upper House of Westminster-style assemblies. Few people these days are fooled by these attempted appropriations into thinking that somehow the government serves the monarch and the nation nobly and purely. If that were the case, leaders would not have fallen as far as they have done in popular esteem. There is another sense, however, in which people *are* fooled. Another interpretation is that the purpose of the office of presidents is 'not to wield power but to attract attention away from it' (Adams, 1979: 35), and that the ceremonial is a deliberate construct to deceive onlookers, or at the very least one that makes for 'heightened sensitivity and easier conviction in onlookers' (Edelman, 1976: 96), primed as they are by the cues of power, significance, and historicity that come with the setting. The degree to which we worry about this interpretation depends on two things: first, whether the context we are talking about separates executive and head of state roles; and second, whether onlookers are educated enough to review the performance critically, going back to an earlier discussion about the place of rhetoric in deliberative accounts of democracy in Chapter two.

It is also worth highlighting the fact that political cues are far from determinative. The Capitol building does not just symbolize the power and dignity of the United States. Depending on the audience, it can also symbolize bickering partisanship, venality, and all the other things that 'politics' can mean. This is a crucial point. It is my view that if those 'grubby' associations come to overwhelm all the other associations, then an assembly building will fail to serve as a grand legitimating stage any longer, and will instead come to confer 'grubby' associations even on members who are otherwise beacons of public service and probity. To repeat, it is the associations that do the communicative work, not the building itself. That is why the meaning of buildings can change.

Some other countries use their assemblies as grand public stages, just not always for the executive installation purpose that so dominates in the United States. Thus, for example, the Canadian Parliament is *the* focal point of Canada Day celebrations, with thousands and thousands of people – especially so-called 'new Canadians', perhaps wishing to affirm their new identity – joining in concerts and fireworks displays in front of the Peace Tower. But other assemblies do not function so well in this regard. As I will discuss further in coming chapters, the Palace of Westminster lacks large, open, accessible public space surrounding it; so New Years' and other celebrations have their focal point at the other end of Whitehall, in Trafalgar Square, or across the River Thames on the South Bank; the South African Parliament is too fenced off, and the Parade Ground much more conducive to large-scale celebration. Clearly, one of the reasons why the Capitol works so well as a space for large-scale public ritual is that it faces the National Mall.[3] I will

---

[3] The use of the West Terrace only dates from Reagan's first inauguration in 1981; from Jackson in 1829 until Carter in 1977, the East portico was used, facing the much smaller but more unified and less cluttered East Gardens, the Library of Congress and the Supreme Court (Library of

discuss further uses of the buildings as backdrops later in this chapter, and again when discussing protest action in Chapter six.

The final point worth noting in this section is connected with the curious yet never-remarked-on fact that the President of the United States of America is inaugurated on the steps of a building that he cannot enter without an invitation. Why, given the American insistence on separation of powers, does the most important act of the inauguration not happen at the White House where the president lives and works? I can find no scholarly discussion of this point, but can suggest some answers. The obvious one is that Congress has a constitutional role supervising and certifying the election of the President and Vice-President (Article II.1 and Amendment XII); it is, as it were, the board of directors to whom the chief executive reports and this is why every presidential inauguration since Washington's second has been either inside or outside the Congressional building. But in the context of the present discussion of assembly buildings as symbols, it is clear too that it has been used as a symbol of the same long-term principles and verities that, in other systems, are symbolized by a separate head of state. The building itself has become the anchor point of traditional ideas of American democracy, liberty, history, endurance, and strength to a degree that other buildings in the group under study simply do not. This is not, I repeat, because those or equivalent values are not symbolized at all in other countries, but because they are often symbolized by different entities, persons, and buildings.

In sum, the points to emphasize are that assembly buildings are not merely symbols of power, although they certainly are that, but are also settings for the performance of grand national rituals, rituals which in some cases attract thousands, even millions, of people who come to witness the event. Their reasons for doing so are to do with the markers of identity: the psychological payoffs one gets from a sense of belonging, of vindication perhaps, of heritage and tradition. These events also provide leaders with opportunities to set their own symbolic associations – associations with visions, aspirations, inheritances, lineages, and so forth. They are certainly expressions of power – but they are not *just* that.

Debating Chambers

To turn from the lofty heights of the symbols of nationhood to the work on the assembly chamber floor will, I am afraid, be an unpleasant change. Common labels do not help here: it is difficult to speak loftily of the floor. Still, the

---

Congress, n.d.). Perhaps it is no coincidence that the dramatic possibilities offered by the building's west elevation were first exploited by a former actor.

vast majority of the work of formal, representative democracy goes on inside the building, not outside, so we must turn inwards. Nonetheless, I think that there is an important relationship between the work that goes on inside the assembly building and the symbolic associations of its exterior, and that is one of the major themes to be explored next.

Debating chambers are built to three broad templates:

- The oppositional, based on the Westminster model, with rows of opposed benches or seats and desks facing each other across an aisle, the Chair at one end, and sometimes with the seats at the far end curved round to join, or nearly join, each other. Speeches are either made at the seat, or from a table between the rows of seats close to the Chair.

- The fan, based on the French Estates General model (Goodsell, 1988a: 296), which comes in pure semi-circular form, a 'chunkier' horseshoe shape, or a broad, open curve, all facing a rostrum where speeches are made and behind which the Chair sits.

- The theatre style, using rows of seats all facing the chair in a long, narrow room, the opposite of the open curve's wide, short room.

There are also a few mixed types, and the Isle of Man Tynwald Court chamber in Douglas is one of these. The Tynwald is the only current parliament in the world to have three chambers, with the Court used for plenary sittings of all the members of the other two houses. It features oppositional benches for the House of Keys members in the 'pit', and behind it a curved bench of seats in a slightly raised gallery for the Legislative Council members. Finally, there are the outdoor assemblies – again, Tynwald Court when it gathers at Tynwald Hill in St Johns in every 5 July,[4] and the *Landsgemeinden* of Cantons Glarus and Appenzell Inner-rhodes.

It is on the topic of debating chamber shape that a degree of myth-making goes on. The myths often start with Churchill's infamous insistence in 1943 that the House of Commons be rebuilt exactly as it was before it was demolished in a bombing raid – too small, oppositional, and with poor acoustics – because he held it responsible for the British adversarial political culture he found so valuable. However, it is many years since Peschel (1960) demolished Churchill with a very obvious observation: that majoritarian, two-party systems thrive in the utterly different chambers of Westminster and the US Capitol. More recently, the South African parliament reconfigured its old

---

[4] Unless 5 July falls on a weekend, in which case Tynwald Day is observed the following Monday. The Tynwald building in Douglas is also the only current assembly building I know where the terms 'upper' and 'lower' house are literally true: the Legislative Council chamber is upstairs, the House of Keys is downstairs, with Tynwald Court in between. Everywhere else, the chambers are on the same level or in entirely separate buildings (Goodsell, 1988a: 293).

upper chamber for the post-apartheid National Council of the Provinces, moving away from the old theatre style to the new broad curve, and seating members not by party but by geography, specifically in order to encourage more cross-party dialogue. It has signally failed to achieve this goal: members are now seen to prefer sitting in silence rather than talk to a neighbour from another party (interview, SA Parliament Public Relations).[5] Still, the existence of evidence to the contrary has never been a terribly effective killer of myths.

In the academic literature, it is Goodsell (1988a) who is most often associated with claims that there is some link between assembly chamber form and political culture, although he does so with a great deal of caution, because he himself realizes that he can provide no systematic evidence, but just a series of selective anecdotes. If we try to be systematic, we end up in a great deal of difficulty. Let me illustrate this by using one reasonably common proxy for political culture, the number of women in the legislature. It has been argued by many feminist scholars that once women reach a 'critical mass' in a legislature, generally reckoned to lie somewhere between 25 and 30 per cent, then debate tends to become more respectful, more courteous, with fewer interjections (for a critical discussion, see Childs and Krook, 2008). If we are generous and take 25 per cent as our benchmark, then the more 'feminine' chambers are much more likely to be oppositional ones than fan-shaped ones in my sample. In Table 5.1, the ratio of chambers with 25 per cent or more women to those with fewer is 7:15 overall; but it is 5:4 in the case of oppositional chambers and only 3:13 in the case of fan-shaped ones. That is, 23 per cent of the sample is both oppositional and has a critical mass of women, but only 13 per cent of the sample is both fan-shaped and feminine. Now, my sample is too small for statistical analysis and skewed towards Commonwealth parliaments, but nonetheless if the form-behaviour nexus had any causal features we would expect to see the opposite, even in my skewed sample. We have other evidence that leads in a similarly unsatisfying direction. Parliamentary punch-ups, for example, do not happen in oppositional chambers but only in fan-shaped ones, including those in Ecuador, Russia, Pakistan, South Korea and – the chamber with by far the most, according to a Google search – Taiwan.

The bigger point is that I think it makes no sense to calculate these or other ratios for every parliament we have data for because a little reflection on the basics of political science would lead us to suspect that we are

---

[5] When New Zealand Parliament House was earthquake-strengthened and refurbished in 1991–6, similar ideas were floated but not given much active consideration, largely because heritage preservation loomed largest in the planning process (interview, Speaker of the House of Representatives).

Table 5.1. Chamber shape and presence of women

Chamber type	Subtype	Examples	% women
Oppositional	Pure oppositional	Canada House of Commons	22.08
		Canada Senate	34.41
		Isle of Man House of Keys	7.69
		UK House of Commons	22.00
		UK House of Lords	20.05
	Closed oppositional	Australia House of Representatives	27.33
		Australia Senate	35.53
		New Zealand House of Representatives	33.61
		South Africa National Assembly	44.50
Fan-shaped	Semi-circular	Chile Senate	13.16
		Germany Bundestag	32.80
		Isle of Man Legislative Council	10.00
		Japan House of Representatives	11.25
		Japan House of Councillors	17.36
		Mexico Chamber of Deputies	26.20
		US Senate	15.31
	Horseshoe	Chile Chamber of Deputies	14.17
		Germany Bundesrat	21.74
	Broad Curve	Greece Hellenic Parliament	17.33
		South Africa National Council of Provinces	29.63
		US House of Representatives	16.78
Theatre		Mexico Senate	19.53

Source: For all except Isle of Man, Inter-parliamentary Union 'Parline' database, http://www.ipu.org/parline-e/parlinesearch.asp For Isle of Man, The Parliament of the Isle of Man, http://www.tynwald.org.im/ Percentages accurate as at 24 June 2010.

extraordinarily unlikely to find what we are looking for. In order to make this a worthwhile pursuit, we would need to convince ourselves, despite all the other influences we know are brought to bear on political behaviour – party affiliation, political place-seeking and interests, institutional structures, the structure of power relations in the society concerned, constituents' expectations of representatives, ideology and discourse, and so on – that the arrangement of the seats is going to be the decisive factor that turns parliamentarians from party political hacks into consensus seekers, or something approximating that. As one of my Canadian parliamentary interviewees puts it, 'If you have a party system it's going to be a blood sport, no matter what the shape [of the room] is.'

And indeed, a closer reading of the sources that Goodsell quotes in support of his more general claims reveals that they support my reading of the situation, not his. When it comes to assemblies, Goodsell (1988a) cites R. G. Barker's behaviour setting theory (1968) in support of the idea that architecture 'helps to channel and regularize behaviour', but what he does not say is that the patterns Barker and other environmental psychologists identify are not to do with particular spatial arrangements on their own but with the associations between a given setting *type* and the behaviours that are culturally linked with that setting type.[6] In other words, behaviour setting theory tells us something about how people are likely to behave in parliamentary chambers in parliamentary democracies, not in particular chambers; courts in general, not particular courtrooms; and that any behaviour observed is a result not just of the setting but of that plus its 'attached standing pattern of behavior' (Scott, 2005: 298); *place*, in other words, as much as space. Therefore, as I argued in Chapter four, there is no evidence that merely changing the seating arrangement within a given assembly space will have an effect on behaviour in that space.[7]

What is much more likely is that different chambers emplace or symbolize political relationships in different ways, and here Goodsell is surely right to highlight the following features:

- *legislative–executive relationship*, with the executive absent from the US Congress, given the emphasis on separation of powers;[8] clustered around the dispatch boxes in Westminster-style parliaments; and seated separately from, and facing, the rest of the assembly in Germany.

- *relationship to head of state*, with the monarch's throne set high and dominant over both chambers of the Japanese Diet, or behind and slightly above the speakers' chair in the upper house only in the United Kingdom, Canada and Australia; absent in the United States (with the executive and head of state roles being combined); and not particularly distinguished in my other cases.

- *relationship to outsiders*, with public galleries in some assemblies, always above the main chamber floor with separate access routes from the members; a lack of public galleries but seating for dignitaries in the Greek, Mexican, and Chilean assemblies; space for the media, sometimes as an extension of the public gallery, sometimes quite separate; and television cameras and microphones either integrated into the design of the space in the case of new or rebuilt chambers, or bolted on in more or less happy ways in the old.[9]

---

[6] This is a stance that has drawn criticism from within psychology; but the fact that that stance dominates the field means that we lack more fine-grained empirical evidence of the kind that would support Goodsell's more specific claims. Barker could well be wrong; but we just do not know.

[7] That some assembly managers should even think that such transformation might be possible is, it seems to me, associated with the rise in hostility to politics and attempts to replace it with some form of rational 'management'. For a further discussion of the idea of management as an allegedly rational, value-neutral activity, see Forester (1984), Fischer (1990), Pollitt (1993), and Hood (1998), among others.

[8] Although this overlooks the role of the Vice-President as presiding officer of the Senate.

[9] One of the most striking features of the UK House of Commons when first one sees it in person is the inverted forest of small black microphones hanging just above head-height from the ceiling. They are almost invisible on video; in the room itself, one can see almost nothing else. Other chambers have microphones in desks, or at a speakers' rostrum, but the Commons lacks either of these conveniences.

Goodsell (1988*a*: 294) says 'In the Westminster tradition, there is very little overt physical expression of the executive', but that is not quite right – even in Westminster, which has only benches and not fixed desks, the Prime Minister sits directly in front of the dispatch box on the right of the chamber from the Speaker's point of view; the Leader of the Opposition directly opposite him or her; and other members of the cabinet and shadow cabinet on the 'front bench' (a synonym for 'cabinet') in a flexible but carefully thought-out order depending on the particular issue being debated. Proximity to the PM and being on the front bench certainly comes with status, but it also comes with benefits of visibility and ability to interact effectively in debates and with leaders. Thus, in the Australian House of Representatives, with its unique mix of desks for back-benchers but open benches without desks for front-benchers, there is a great deal to be gained from sitting in close proximity to what Clerk of the House Ian Harris (2003) calls the 'prime parliamentary triangle' of Speaker, Prime Minister and Leader of the Opposition. This is not just so that one can grab the leader's ear or the Speaker's eye more easily; it is also the case that these are the places that the television cameras focus on, being the main locations from which speeches are made.

Again, however, the seating arrangement is not doing all the work here. For one, the party and electoral systems add a layer of complexity to these arrangements. In a unitary state with a plurality system and two dominant parties like the United Kingdom, the oppositional seating style means that climbing the greasy pole of the main party hierarchies also means getting ever closer to that prime triangle; and because seating tends to be organized in party blocs, climbing a smaller party's pole does not translate into visibility to the Speaker and the television cameras. Thus, before joining a coalition government, the leader of the Liberal Democrats, the third largest party in the UK House of Commons, often looked like a peripheral figure, just another MP, because his or her speeches were given from a peripheral position in the House. Likewise, in the New Zealand context, where every member shares an identical semi-detached desk with one other member and speaks from that, nonetheless there are cues that give away status: again, proximity to the Prime Minister and Leader of the Opposition, being paired with a high status figure, sitting on the front row rather than further back, and sitting on one of the straight rows of seats rather than the lower status curved rows furthest from the Speaker. Even when television cameras crop a shot fairly tightly, it is nonetheless possible to pick up those cues and thus make judgements about the status of the speaker. However, where plurality elections are combined with federalism to create more parties of varying but similar status, and where speeches are not given from a dispatch box but from the seats, as in Canada, there is no 'prime triangle'. There have been four major parties for many years in Canada, with the leaders of each well-known figures and proximity to each

Figure 5.3. The plenary chamber of the German Bundestag, Berlin
Photo © Deutscher Bundestag/Lichtblick/Achim Melde, by permission.

of those figures mattering at least as much as simple proximity to the Prime Minister (interview, Office of the Clerk of the House, Ottawa).

The big difference that a fan-shaped chamber makes is not more consensual behaviour or anything like that, but to the means of signalling status. This is because speakers do not generally speak from their seats but from a central rostrum. Regardless of party system, electoral system and the federal/unitary dimension, every speaker occupies a high-status, dignified position in the chamber and in video presentations of the chamber. Does this mean that status cues are not given? Not at all: they just emerge in different ways. Thus, for example, in the German Bundestag (Figure 5.3), one can tell a great deal about the status of a speaker on the basis of whether he or she is being listened to or ignored, whether a minister responsible for a bill has bothered to turn up for the debate, whether the speaker is a 'single-issue fighter' or a higher-status generalist who appears in many debates, and so on (Beyme, 1998: 69–71).

This matters because perceptions of speaker status make a difference to the reception of what he or she says, and thus have an impact on a particular legislator's ability to communicate his or her arguments not just within the chamber but, because of the focus of the media *on* the chamber, to wider attentive publics as well – and I will come back to those attentive publics in a moment.

The other element that does seem to make a real difference is absolute chamber size. Goodsell (1988*a*: 298), again following Churchill, remarks that smaller chambers tend to be more 'intimate' affairs. Intimacy can refer to speaking style: larger, more resonant rooms require a slower, more stentorious delivery, whereas smaller rooms can permit a more conversational style (Black, 1961), although sound amplification can do away with some of that, such that relatively intimate, even 'quietly menacing', tones can be adopted in relatively large spaces. There is also the 'whites of their eyes' interpretation, which comes from Australian MP Barry Jones who remarked on the differences between the old and new chambers when the Australian parliament moved to its new location in 1988. Referring to the new, he wrote that it did not have 'a good debating chamber. Members are too remote to see the whites of their opponents' eyes' (*The Age*, 25 October 1988, quoted in McIntyre, 2008: 43). There is an intensity to the party battle that is dissipated in larger chambers, and this is one of the features that Churchill was trying to maintain. Whether we celebrate that fact or not is another matter, and is associated with whether one values party identity and conflict or more deliberative, consensus-seeking values. It has been remarked that this preference is associated with gender, women preferring a more deliberative style, men preferring a more combative approach (Childs, 2004), although the (female) Speaker of the House in New Zealand thought this was more an age- and experience-related matter: that older members, steeped in a two-party tradition, got a lot of their enjoyment of politics from the partisan cut and thrust of Question Time, while newer members, brought up in an environment that increasingly reviled such behaviour, and trained in the coalition-building arts of the post-1996 electoral system, were more likely to dislike 'whites of their eyes' approaches.

Now, all of this matters for reasons that are connected with why we have chambers in the first place. For one, recall their representative functions, as set out in my account of democracy in Chapter two – they are the places where particular experiences and perspectives are 'made present', where claims on public resources are made, and where decisions on the allocation of those resources are made by members who are elected for those purposes. They are also places where parties compete to win public confidence. All those purposes can conflict, of course, depending on the particular party and electoral system in place: in some systems, party demands overwhelm all others, and members are held responsible for promoting or defending party views that conflict with the views and preferences of constituents or their own conscience; in others, party loyalties and constituents' claims and experiences are in tension with each other, while the deliberative vision of democracy would have us value the representation of constituents' views more highly. The point is that, even if the procedures of a given assembly and electoral system are changed such that proportionality is enhanced and party discipline relaxed, nonetheless some chamber features seem better suited to expressing that normative vision than others. The first is the use of a speakers' rostrum. Allowing all speakers to operate from the same spot removes many of the obvious status cues that come with speaking from desks, and thus allows those who would speak against the government line, or articulate an unpopular or marginal view, more persuasive space in which to operate. It thus emplaces equality and respect more effectively than alternatives, rather than merely symbolizing it. While it is fan-shaped chambers that generally use the rostrum, there is no reason why oppositional chambers could not do the same thing with some minor alterations in front of the Speakers' chair. In other words, while it may seem that fan-shaped chambers impose fewer structural barriers to marginal voices, this is *not because they are fan shaped* but because they are much more likely to be focused on a rostrum. The second feature is chamber size, and here the very limited evidence available suggests reasons to think that both small and large chambers have strengths from an inclusion point of view. While smaller chambers are traditionally thought to encourage a less declamatory, more conversational style of interaction (Bessette, 1994: 221), sound amplification has removed the necessity for stentoriousness in large chambers, and small chambers might actually be *more* aggressive because more 'in your face', more 'whites of the eyes', and thus more likely to shut down marginalized voices.

I want to push this point a little further. Why might we care that minority voices are heard in the debating chamber, when there are other sites where such voices might be more effectively heard? The answer goes back to why chambers are important in the first place: these are the dignified spaces, the spaces which send (or should send) cues that 'this matters'. If certain voices and perspectives are never heard in that dignified space, then it is my contention that they are not *seen to matter*, and thus have less impact on the political agenda or the outcome of public deliberation.

That is not to say that debating chambers are effective chambers for every role. One of the implications of the analysis so far is that it is unlikely that good deliberative quality will be achieved in a chamber of 100, 200, even 600 and more members. Good deliberation – respectful, mutual, rational – emerges in groups that are very much smaller, as small as five to seven members (Parkinson, 2006a: 6). Plenary chambers remain sites for broad contestation and claim-making, not detailed narration, deliberation, and hammering out agreements. For that kind of role, we need much smaller groups and very much smaller rooms, and to those we now turn.

112

Committee Rooms and Other Public Spaces

As Norton (1997) has argued in the case of Britain and others have argued elsewhere, the main debating chamber has long since ceased to be the only important political space inside assembly buildings. At least as important are the committee rooms in which the details of laws, regulations, appointments, and political context are scrutinized in much more detail and in which, according to Norton, members have the opportunity to act more as independent policy entrepreneurs and less as cogs in the party machine. This has, perhaps, always been the case in the United States where committee chairs dominate legislative proceedings to a much greater degree than elsewhere.

Committee rooms are sometimes fairly utilitarian affairs, and sometimes quite grandiose, even in the same context. In the United States, for example, Senate committees that wish to honour particular witnesses, or dignify the proceedings in some way, might use the Caucus Room with its carved columns, oak panelling, and all the other fittings and fixtures that go with 'dignity' in the US context; other committee rooms in the Senate office buildings have a more workaday style. Sometimes the size of committee influences what space is required: the full House Ways and Means Committee is a sizeable beast with forty-one members and thus requires the large[10] assembly room in the Longworth building for its hearings. Regardless of whether the room is more or less upmarket, however, each shares a common format: committee members seated behind a bench (or two) on a raised dais; witnesses at a table or bench facing the panel but at a lower level; photographers huddled on the floor between them; television cameras in niches above and to the side; and behind the witnesses rows of seating for the witnesses' staff, interested public, media, and so on. Contrast this with the UK parliament. There, committee room layout is superficially similar – a curved table for members, behind whom sit their advisers; facing them a straight table for witnesses; behind the witnesses the public 'gallery' – but with the big differences that all the furniture is generally on the same level and the rooms are generally very much smaller, relatively intimate affairs, because committee membership rarely exceeds eleven in total. Even the relatively small US congressional committee rooms are much more intimidating for the uninitiated because of the closed frontages to the benches and their raised position, which means that only the head and shoulders of members are visible. Indeed, the layout sends 'courtroom' cues and thus cues feelings of guilt, crime, and punishment. The British rooms, on the contrary, send cues of a business meeting, thanks to the open-fronted tables all on the same level, and while that hardly makes the neophyte

---

[10] And frankly rather ugly: it has all the ambience of a state-planned dining room in Moscow, circa 1980.

completely relaxed – there is a little too much dark wallpaper, wood panelling, and massive oil-on-canvas portraiture for that – it does not feel like an inquisition either.

There is little that the average committee member can do about this in the US context – the furniture is fixed in place. In Canada, a decision was taken following the *Building the Future* report (House of Commons, 1999) to reorganize committee rooms away from the standard model described above towards a more flexible model that recognized the changes in the ways committees worked. The report noted that committees had multiplied in number but had also shrunk dramatically in size and that they no longer just operated along traditional 'inquiry' lines but increasingly held round-table discussions, workshops, and 'town-hall' format meetings (1999: 16). Members had become more insistent on openness to the public, which meant that some hearings demanded lots of room for the audience and invited witnesses, while others needed much smaller space to encourage conversations. Add that to the hardware demands of broadcasting and the security demands of the Royal Canadian Mounted Police and the twenty-four, 1920-designed committee rooms were no longer up to the job. Therefore, the report recommended, and the parliamentary authorities have implemented, a plan that includes a variety of committee spaces, with large, small, and medium rooms to accommodate different sized groups; some rectangular rooms to accommodate traditional 'inquiry' style hearings; and diamond-shaped rooms to accommodate more circular seating patterns for workshops and discussions; all with flexible furniture that can be shifted around as need be, and information technology wired into every room. Thus, these rooms come with a very different set of cues from their US counterparts: they are work spaces, business spaces, discussion spaces, and deliberative spaces, rather than inquisitorial courtroom spaces.

In interview, the former New Zealand Speaker said that working in Parliament House was 'like working in a museum', given the urge to preserve the past rather than using it as a living, working building. This echoes a major shift between the 1950s and 1990s in attitudes to the US Capitol: 'From being a structure capable of extension and remodeling, it took on a new character as a venerable historical landmark that must be preserved' (Wilson, 2000: 135). In Westminster they have got around this by building new committee rooms in Portcullis House;[11] in Ottawa they have radically redesigned the interior spaces; but in the United States, even the congressional office buildings are taking on an 'untouchable' aura that means publicly accessible committee

---

[11] The new Portcullis House rooms tend to be a little larger and use flexible seating, permitting flexible usage. However, some rooms, like the Boothroyd Room, are just that little bit larger, and just beyond the limits of what this observer felt was 'intimate'.

work remains stuck in spaces that come with a set of intimidating court-room cues. Now, Wilson (2000: 139) claims that this preservation instinct has had the unintended consequence of making the work of Congress disappear into the background. The more that the Capitol is seen purely in symbolic terms, and preserved as a museum, the less it is seen as an active workspace. I think that Wilson's observation is important, but he has cause and effect round the wrong way here: as Congress has receded in political importance relative to the President, it has become easier to treat it purely as a heritage space and less as a space for democracy. This then makes it easier to think of the building in terms of tourism and less in terms of democratic citizenship, which in turn makes the securitization of the building easier. The fact that the Canadians have strongly resisted some proposals to enhance the security of Parliament Hill is, I suspect, related to the fact that while *some* parts of the precinct are preserved in aspic – parts of the East Block are maintained as a fascinating museum of Victorian parliamentary office space – the rest of it is seen primarily as work space, *and* that that work is still seen as being crucially tied up with public access and public engagement. The US Congress, on the other hand, has a long tradition of keeping itself away from public gaze, and this has gradually allowed its buildings to become packaged as artefacts, which further obscures their role as providing working, democratic, public spaces. I will return to the themes of security and access in the next chapter.

The cause-and-effect point is reinforced strongly by the example of the Australian Parliament House. In Canberra, parliamentarians did not merely reconfigure their building when it became too cramped and too hostile to technology; they abandoned it and built a brand new Parliament House further up Capitol Hill where, incidentally, the city's designer had intended the building to be in the first place. I will discuss aspects of the external design in the next chapter, but internally open spaces were created to encourage casual interactions between ministers and back-benchers, between Senators and MPs. Now, much was made in the design brief and in the following years about the way in which the design would create a new way of working (Giurgola in Fewtrell et al., 2008: 22–4). Fewtrell (1985) collated and published those predictions, and three years after the building opened went back to see what had happened. What he found (Fewtrell, 1991) was that there had indeed been some changes in behaviour and procedure, but they (*a*) were fewer, and of less magnitude, than expected; (*b*) were not uniformly 'democratic' in the way the designers imagined; and (*c*) *had largely been occurring before the move.* For example, many commentators have remarked on how the new building gives greater prominence to the executive over backbenchers and opposition members by providing a separate entrance and internal 'escape routes' through the building that only ministers can use. In the old building, there was one entrance and no escape routes, and so ministers and backbenchers, journalists and, sometimes, ordinary members of the public encountered each other in the King's Hall and corridors, the accidental encounters increasing backbenchers' and others' opportunities to engage with senior decision-makers. In the new building, these opportunities vanished, despite the deliberate design by Giurgola and his team of meeting points (Beck, 1988), especially the broad open space of the reflective pool. It is open to public gaze from above, and because it lacks nooks and crannies, is hardly used even as a transit point, let alone a place for accidental encounters (see Chapter three, page 55). Still, the point that Fewtrell makes is that while it is easy to attribute the change to the building alone, moves to greater executive dominance and ministerial privacy, separation from the press and public, and so on had started happening in the old building well before the move to the new. In other words, Australian parliamentary decision-makers emplaced their changing norms, values, and power relations; those things did not change merely by virtue of being in the new building (see also McIntyre, 1997).

One final aspect of committee rooms that is a little more unusual is a symbolically representative and inclusive role. While many assemblies include such details, the New Zealand parliament has recently gone further than any other in my sample. It started with the Māori Affairs Select Committee room, named after the demi-god and ancestor Māui Tikitiki-a-Taranga, which was moved during renovations in 1995 to a prominent and culturally meaningful position next to the main entrance of the building, and filled inside and out with carved and woven panels that depict stories and symbols connected with the room's location in Wellington (*Te Whanganui a Tara*, the Harbour of Tara), stories of ancestors and all the New Zealand tribes (*iwi*), of migration and deities, in styles from across the country. For the carvers,

> It was their view that a person standing within the completed room should feel the four winds blowing, and not just feel or sense the symbolism of one iwi (tribe). Through this approach, all Māori people would be represented in the room. The stories and symbols that have relevance to all iwi would be on its ceiling and walls. (NZ House of Representatives, n.d.)

The layout of the rooms in New Zealand are more of the business meeting style than the inquiry style – a long table with seats arranged either side and microphones for recording purposes. Since then, several other committee rooms have been designated to represent specific people and purposes, notably the Rainbow Room in September 2008 to 'recognise gay, lesbian and transgender New Zealanders and their contribution to society and Parliament'; as well as a Pacific Room, an Asia Room, and a Suffrage Room. While easily sneered at, these were not empty gestures in the New Zealand context:

116

the Suffrage Room celebrates the fact that New Zealand was the first country to grant women the vote, in 1893;[12] and while New Zealand was a laggard on gay rights, it was the first to welcome a transgender MP and has had several openly-gay cabinet ministers. Still, none of these carry the same status or are treated quite as seriously as Māui Tikitiki-a-Taranga, given the unique constitutional position Māori hold in New Zealand. Here, then, we have another example of the difference between making symbolic gestures alone, and using symbols to anchor real political commitments – and perhaps a set of counter-examples to the Speaker's somewhat gloomy 'working in a museum' remark.

There are several other kinds of public space in assembly buildings. Often, but not always, these buildings have large reception or banqueting rooms that are often used for a mixture of state occasions and sometimes even quite private celebrations where the organizers want to give their event a dignified air. Rooms in the Canadian Centre Block are frequently used for wedding receptions and such like, and while staff seemed a little uncomfortable with some uses, they clearly thought of the building as 'public' in more than just the ownership sense, and thus were willing to allow it to be used as the public required, so long as such uses were consistent with the 'dignity' of the building.[13] What constitutes public and private are slightly more restrictively defined in New Zealand – the purposes have to be 'community-related' in the words of the Speaker, cannot be charged for, and must have a sitting Member of Parliament sponsoring the occasion – which means that events tend to be celebrations of anniversaries like ANZAC Day, or the annual congresses of public bodies like the Council of Trade Unions, and range in scale from large state banquets in the irritatingly curved Banqueting Hall in the Beehive – people at the ends of the hall cannot see the top table, let alone the opposite end – to slightly less formal occasions in the old Legislative Council chamber. Public events are slightly more openly defined in some respects in Britain, where charging for attendance *is* allowed but sponsorship by a member still required. Other assembly buildings – Athens, Cape Town, Valparaíso – are largely off limits for such purposes.

---

[12] Although what constitutes an independent country at this time is highly debatable. New Zealand gained independence from Britain in incremental steps between 1856 and 1947, and while effective self-government can be dated from the start of that period (King, 2003), it could be argued that several other places have prior claims to being first on womens' suffrage.

[13] One could, of course, argue that weddings are highly public occasions, in the sense that they are rituals that are both legally and culturally defined and prescribed, no matter how much individuals would prefer them not to be, or liberal theorists would say they should not be. Individual marriage ceremonies are not public, however, in the political sense that I am using through the book; that is, they have nothing to do with making claims on public resources. Both of these points are separate from questions about the institution of marriage – who should be able to do it, what role the state should have, and so on – questions, which *are* public ones in the relevant sense, and therefore whose appropriate site *is* the assembly.

117

Beyond these large gathering spaces are those that are reserved for members only, and some that are in between. Thus, there are members' dining rooms, members-only bars, often the libraries (although not, in the best known case, the Library of Congress in Washington, DC), the corridors and intersection points throughout the buildings in which members sit, read, chat, muse, deliberate, and machinate. These spaces can be very important to building working relationships between members, not just between parties but within parties too. These are in addition to spaces where, say, the media have access but the general public do not, including the Members' Lobby and some of the bars in Westminster. There are two points to be made about these spaces concerning the conflicting values of privacy and publicity. On the positive side, there is deliberative value in privacy because it helps representatives with commitments to competing courses of action to hammer out agreements (Parkinson, 2006a: 137), or to allow arguments to be assessed on their own merits rather than in terms of who made them – 'Chatham House rules' and the doctrine of cabinet collective responsibility are related to these ideas. There is also the matter of working time and space: while it might be tempting to insist that the powerful should be on display all the time and to all people, two consequences would ensue: representatives would spend all their time talking about what to do and little time doing it; and their time would be monopolized by those already well-endowed with time themselves; that is, those paid to engage (professional lobbyists); those with independent means (the rich); and highly motivated cranks. The negatives are obvious: if too much discussion goes on behind closed doors, then the scrutiny function, the part that disciplines democratic representatives, is undermined. Part of the solution is that arguments made in private should be presented for public testing by the executive, and do not become decisive until so tested; and that members of all parties use the same back rooms, so that each keeps an eye on the potential dodgy-dealing of their competitors.

One final point on these more casual, accidental spaces in assembly buildings: it is important not to overlook the impact of information and communication technology. In many assembly contexts it has been noticed that members spend a great deal more time in their offices and less time in the chamber, corridors, libraries, bars, and restaurants than they once did, and one of the members of the Australian Parliament architectural team observed an interesting reason for this during a symposium on assembly design:

> Hansard[14] always had the rushes of the evening that members had to go and read them. They had to walk from their office to the Hansard. We had a special

---

[14] For non-Commonwealth readers, 'Hansard' is the semi-official name for the record of debates in the chamber, as well as for the parliamentary office that produces it.

118

requirement in the brief and a special place in the building where they checked the rushes to make sure that they were correct. The members had a specific reading area in the library. Once the computer went on the desk, that was changed and eliminated. So things that brought members and their staff out to intermix and talk, discuss, whatever, bump into each other, were changed because of the technology.... We see that impact of the computer on the desk being the most significant. (Hal Guida in Fewtrell et al., 2008: 32–3)

This is important because, like the contextual details about changes in chamber procedures and institutional relationships, it reminds us not to be too quick in linking every change in assembly behaviour to changes in the physical setting. There may be, and frequently are, other variables in play that a focus on the physical settings of assembly life does not reveal. These points should remind us that chambers are not static entities that can be examined in isolation from the work that goes on in them.[15] They are settings that facilitate certain kinds of political behaviour, but that influence is a great deal less than architects would have us believe, and act more as a mediator of other political and social forces than a direct variable.

Conclusions

In this chapter, we have begun the work of detailed analysis of the sites of democracy. Thus far, the key points are as follows.

First, democrats should value assembly buildings for four main reasons, but the first of these is their role in providing a 'dignified' setting that cues us to take the work within it seriously. There is a two-way relationship here: in common with behaviour setting theory, I have argued that the setting is dignified in part because of the work that goes on in it, not just because it has been clothed in the symbols of dignity. Settings can send powerful cues, and the example of the inauguration of US presidents shows how they can be directed to generating a sense of shared identity, a 'we', among onlookers; charismatic legitimacy for those who hold centre-stage in such settings; and an extraordinary opportunity for those office holders to nudge the values and ideas associated with that setting and their person for their term in office. Other settings send other kinds of cues: I have claimed that US committee

---

[15] It is a pity that so often chambers are presented and analysed empty, and not as stages for political debate and action. For example, most of the chamber photographs on the Inter-parliamentary Union's Parline database (http://www.ipu.org/parline-e/parlinesearch.asp) are of empty rows of seats; few feature parliamentarians at work. Likewise, school groups in many countries get to see the chamber only in recess, and so while it might be fun for some to sit in a member's chair or give a mini speech from the rostrum, one gets little sense of the life of the chamber unless one sees it in action.

Figure 5.4. Doorway to the Māori Affairs Committee Room, Wellington, New Zealand
Photo © New Zealand Parliament, by permission.

rooms send inquisitorial cues whereas modern British ones send cues more appropriate to a business meeting; the New Zealand Māori Affairs Committee Room sends cues of welcome, belonging and centrality to the traditional owners in the colonial seat of power, all of which has an impact on the behaviour of people in those rooms and sets expectations about citizenship and participation for those outside (Figure 5.4). However, these examples also tell us that what counts as a symbol of dignity is more variable than a list of standard neoclassical design elements: marble, columns, ornate backdrops, a raised proscenium, and a pit for the plebs. 'Dignity' is context dependent, and it is malleable. This fact tells us three things. It means that whatever the designers of a given building intended, and whoever their intended audience, interpretation of an assembly's symbolic language is never entirely in the designer's control, and gets less so the more the designers and audiences are separated in time and space. It gives us reason to hope that reviled settings can be transformed by new occupants or expressions of new values. And it leads to disappointment when systems ossify: the tendency to see assemblies in purely symbolic or heritage terms can lead to them losing value as working buildings, which, as I will argue in the next chapter, has a discernible impact on whether citizens engage with the buildings as citizens or tourists, or not at all.

The second major point is that some kinds of variation in room layout seem to have effects on political behaviour while others do not. The sorts of differences that do seem to matter include (*a*) scale, because a large room is not only a less deliberative room than a small one but also one in which all relevant perspectives can be included and thus more likely to be transmitted in the public sphere; and (*b*) speaking position, because speaking from a central rostrum means that while status cues do not disappear, they become controllable, especially in broadcasting terms. Sound amplification can moderate some of the effects of scale. Seating layout seems to matter more at the small scale than at the large: party political imperatives and other elements of political culture overwhelm any effects that tinkering with seating plans might have in the main chamber; but in the more intimate, less declamatory environment of a committee room, room layout can have a significant impact on whether proceedings are business-like, exploratory, or inquisitorial. Even then, however, the dominant presence of the media can turn any committee meeting, regardless of layout, into an opportunity to play to the gallery rather than seriously engage with one's interlocutors (Parkinson, 2006*a*: ch. 5). Television cameras in particular are a more powerful behavioural cue to a political actor than any seating arrangement.

The third point is that assemblies still matter as work spaces, because the roles of representation and scrutiny are enhanced to the extent that members work out of one, readily-identifiable building or group of buildings. This is so for the members themselves: proximity between senior and junior colleagues, between government and opposition members, helps grease the deliberative wheels, encouraging perspectives to be heard that might not otherwise be heard. This is also so for attentive publics: it helps avoid the politics of the backroom deal, although the way that is done is to ensure that arguments for a given proposal are presented in public, not necessarily that all the *argumentation* is done in public. There is deliberative value in moments of privacy too.

The issue of assemblies as work spaces turns out to have implications well beyond the 'good management' of the assembly itself, however. In some countries, it is used as a foil not just to 'intrusive' access but democratically useful access to the formal public sphere. It is to those big issues of public access, to public space in the first sense, that I turn in the next chapter.

6

Assemblies II: The Public and Accessibility

Most democratic assembly buildings are described and justified in terms of some account of 'the public'. They are the buildings where public servants work, where public concerns are raised, where public money is spent and, sometimes, where the public themselves can come and scrutinize what representatives are doing with that money.

That last function is critically important in the account of democracy I have presented. The presence of an attentive public is what disciplines arguments in the public sphere, forcing claim makers to put their claims in terms that others can accept. However, it is increasingly unusual for members of the public to turn up and watch assembly proceedings, the public being more represented – by assembly members, the media and lobbyists – than actually present themselves. This chapter asks how much that matters. Should democrats be concerned if 'the public' is only ever an abstract entity, invoked in parliamentary speeches but not physically present; or if 'attentive publics' are there watching the work of government on behalf of the rest of us?

I start by considering the particular constructions of 'the public' that assembly members and managers use, focusing on five different categories: citizen, worker, student, tourist, and threat. These are important because different constructions of the public legitimate different kinds of access to and action in the assembly, which in turn serve to legitimate and sometimes obscure important exclusions. I address these inclusions and exclusions through the lens of security arrangements in and around assembly buildings, and argue that, especially since the 'war on terror', changes to access have significant and deleterious impacts on democratic quality in some countries, much less so in others. The reasons for those differences come back to different concepts of the public and public space in operation in those settings.

122

Halls of the People

New parliamentary designers make much of the values of accessibility. The design brief for the National Assembly for Wales, for example, emphasized the importance of generating 'a sense of open government and public accessibility' (National Assembly for Wales, 2009b), to which the architects responded with a design that they describe like this:

> Architecturally, the Assembly Building seeks to embody democratic values of openness and participation. . . . The idea of openness is exemplified by the transparent form of the building. Public spaces are elevated on a slate-clad plinth stepping up from the water level and cut away to allow daylight to penetrate the administrative spaces at lower level. A lightweight, gently undulating roof shelters both internal and external spaces, pierced by the protruding extension of the 60-seat Debating Chamber.
>
> A large, circular space at the heart of the building, the Chamber is defined by the dramatic roof form which is drawn down from the roof above to form the enclosure. . . .
>
> The Debating Chamber is the physical and metaphorical centre of the design, and is surrounded by public space so that it is open and accessible to all.
>
> (Rogers Stirk Harbour and Partners, 2007)

Similarly, the new Australian Parliament opened in 1988 had democratic values written into the competition brief and the designed response (Parliament of Australia, 1980). Members of the public are allowed to penetrate quite deep into the core of the building, although not into the working spaces that occupy the wings and rear of the building: indeed, the accessible corridors barely intersect with the exclusive ones, with two sets of pathways overlying each other. The most obvious symbol of accessibility is the way that the building appears to be set into the top of Capitol Hill, with grassy banks curving over the top of the edifice, allowing citizens to walk over their representatives' heads and remind them just who is boss. This is the same function that is said to be performed by the new dome that rises once more over the refurbished Reichstag in Berlin – the spiral walkway and roof terrace allow a view directly down into the Bundestag chamber below – although the fact that one has to queue for hours and submit to security before enjoying the privilege does diminish the feeling of ownership and accessibility somewhat (Figure 6.1).

These design impulses are not new, but the degree to which citizens can access assembly buildings has varied enormously over the centuries. In particular, access to modern democratic assemblies is often more symbolic than authentic: one can stand over the heads of members of the German Bundestag, or stand behind members of the Welsh Assembly, but is cut off from the actual debating chamber by thick layers of impenetrable glass,

Figure 6.1. The rebuilt Reichstag, Berlin

This shot clearly shows the degree to which the new building has been inserted into the old shell. Photo by Matthew Field, GNU Free Documentation License, Version 1.2, via Wikimedia Commons.

isolated from the unreachable members below. This is completely different from the early days of the United States Capitol, for example. When Washington and Jefferson worked on the plans, one of their primary requirements was that the building be directly accessible to the public. Of course, their idea of the public was a highly exclusive one, based on a very limited conception of those – lawyers, planters and landowners; educated, enlightenment men (Pasley, 2004) – who were seen to have the capacity for self-government. In addition, the purpose of access was not that this limited *demos* could influence or scrutinize the deliberations, but that the deliberations would influence and educate *them*, growing their capacity for autonomy by allowing them to attend to the debates of their betters (see Bessette, 1994: 3; Kohn, 2008). The educational function is important, and I will return to it in the next section. Still, the point is that exclusivity was a social, normative matter, not one of physical barriers. While citizens and representatives were kept separate inside the chamber, there were large antechambers or lobbies (Jefferson used both terms for the same space) immediately outside where both could mix. The space under the giant dome was intended to be a 'Hall of the People', while even the crypt, the inner sanctum, was to be publicly accessible and large enough so that several hundred people could gather (Scott, 1995: 68). Not only that, but Representatives and Senators did not have permanent offices in the first Congress building. Instead, they worked from their desks in the chamber, listening to debates but conducting conversations of their own, holding ad hoc committee meetings in corners, catching up with constituents

124

in the lobbies; while all around them clerks and messengers hurried in and out, booted feet clumping on wooden floors, and vendors wandered around the building selling food and souvenirs to visitors (Freeman, 2004; Office of the Clerk, 2009). Thus, the Capitol was more like eighteenth century theatres or assembly rooms: rumbustious by modern standards, with attention not focused on the rostrum but diffused both inside the chamber and out.

While its evolutionary path was very different, a similar kind of publicness and accessibility could be seen in Westminster in the seventeenth and eighteenth centuries. While the Commons and Lords chambers themselves were not particularly open, nonetheless the courts that took place in the conglomeration of buildings and spaces we now call Parliament were very open affairs in large, open spaces. Multiple hearings took place in any one hall, with observers – genteel observers to be sure – wandering from hearing to hearing, and merchants of various kinds hawking their wares in between (Kyle and Peacey, 2002; Mulcahy, 2009). And so while the Palace of Westminster could hardly be described as democratic space until well into the twentieth century with the eventual grant of universal suffrage, it has a much longer tradition of public accessibility. Therefore, either by design or by historical use, democratic and proto-democratic assemblies were multi-centred hives of activity that were open to the public, albeit a public defined in limited ways. They had more in common with the Athenian *agora* – a rambling market place with a multiplicity of social, deliberative, economic, and devotional spaces – than with the assembly ground of the Pnyx, focused as the latter was on a speakers' dais.

Nowadays things are a little different. In the case of the United States Capitol, much is made by writers on its architectural history of the numerous changes to the building that helped accommodate new representatives created by the rapid westward expansion of the United States. The reconstruction completed in 1857 left the building with two new wings and chambers much more widely separated, which created new ceremonial and symbolic space in the Rotunda and the National Statuary Collection (most of which is in the Old House Chamber), but which worked to lower the intensity of interaction in the space between the two chambers, and provided representatives with new routes into the building such that they could avoid having to mix with the hoi polloi. However, I suspect that what was more significant was the construction of six dedicated office buildings for senators and representatives on Independence and Constitution Avenues, the first of which, now known as the Cannon Building, opened in 1908 (Office of the Clerk, 2009). This allowed much of the day-to-day work of representatives to move not just out of the chambers but out of the Capitol building entirely. Therefore, when constituents and lobbyists want to meet representatives in their DC offices, they very rarely do so in the Capitol building itself. This is now largely occupied by those officials who run the building: the Speaker of the House and staff, the President of the Senate and staff, the Architect of the Capitol and staff, among others.

Over time, the shift in emphasis away from the chambers and towards office space has rendered the Capitol building a great deal less busy, and removed the imperative to permit public access to the building on the grounds of allowing constituents access to members. This shift laid the ground for some further developments in the 1950s onwards, especially what R. G. Wilson calls the 'historicization' of the Capitol.

> From being a structure capable of extension and remodeling, it took on a new character as a venerable historical landmark that must be preserved. . . . The reorientation is important since the building now tends to be treated as an artifact and to disappear from public view. (Wilson, 2000: 135, 139)

By 'disappear from public view', Wilson means that while the edifice looms large as a symbolic entity, the *work* that goes on in it disappears. This move was partly to do, Wilson argues, with a belief held by congressional leaders that their interests were best served by treating the building primarily as a symbol of power. This allowed them to deflect attention from the cosy, cooperative, and closed environment that reinforced the power of committee chairs over the chambers as a whole, and the influence of the Speaker of the House and President of the Senate over the committee system (Ritchie, 2004; Schudson, 2004). A succession of Speakers were hostile to direct, public oversight of congressional work, including broadcast media, right up until the crises in confidence of the 1970s which opened the chamber to broadcast media and ushered in a new era of public scrutiny. Still, as Schudson (2004: 659) argues, Congress has continued to slide in media airtime, with the President taking more and more of the attention and the democratic work of Congress slipping further from view. This means that the historicization of the Capitol building continues – it is now seen more as a piece of American heritage than a living, breathing, *democratic* building.

We can see the effects of this kind of historicization by looking at the information materials of the new Capitol Visitor Center. The homepage of its website distinguishes between three broad kinds of purpose: a 'visit', involvement in the workings of the Senate and House, and art appreciation. However, the 'involvement' purpose is otherwise absent from the site except in the form of one brief mention of 'official business appointments' on the 'Plan a visit' page.[1] That page starts with a remarkably revealing paragraph:

---

[1] http://www.visitthecapitol.gov/

The United States Capitol is a monument, a working office building, and one of the most recognizable symbols of representative democracy in the world. Visitors are welcome to enter the building through the Capitol Visitor Center, located underground on the east side of the Capitol. You can begin your Capitol experience at the Visitor Center by visiting the Exhibition Hall, perusing our Gift Shops or dining in our Restaurant. (US Capitol Visitor Center, 2009)

So, it is a 'monument' first and foremost; then a 'working office building'; and only then does democracy get a mention – and even then, according to its own publicists the building is a *symbol*, not a site, of representative democracy. A visitor's experience of the building starts not with the debating chambers, but with an exhibition and things to consume. It is a tourism experience, with 'work' well down the list of priorities and active citizenship and involvement in democracy barely rating a mention.

The same criticism has been made of one feature of the Australian Parliament: a room at the front of the building that the architects had intended to be a meeting room for use by constituents and their MPs was turned, at the last minute, into a shop (Giurgola in Fewtrell et al., 2008: 33); and one that, like Duty Free stores at many airports, visitors are forced to walk through in order to get out of the building. By contrast, at least in Ottawa one can choose either the tourist route or, if one has an appointment, one that goes straight to the heavily securitized reception in the Centre Block, although again, physically it is the tourism infrastructure in the shape of a temporary visitors' tent that dominated this visitor's first experience of the site.

Publicity and the Galleries

Before conceding too much to these other constructions of the purposes of assembly buildings, it is worth spending a moment considering the places where ordinary members of the public have a democratic role to play, and that is the chamber galleries, often divided into public, VIP, and media galleries. Every chamber I visited has one or more of these, and their alleged purpose is both informational and deliberative: the former to ensure that the public knows what is being debated so that they can make their wishes known to representatives (House of Commons, 1999: 53); the latter, to ensure that arguments and proposals are disciplined by being presented in public. For example, in the early US Congress, Quaker campaigners against slavery have been neatly described by Pasley (2004: 49) as 'looming over the proceedings like the spectres of a guilty national conscience' whenever they sat in the House gallery watching debates. Sometimes the public galleries might still perform this function. In Australia, for example, there are frequently queues to get into the galleries for Prime Ministers' question time, and the Australian galleries are large, seating several hundred observers. Assembly galleries are often full for the final votes on controversial bills, with active campaigners and more generally concerned citizens alike coming to see their hopes fulfilled or dashed.

However, the most frequent users of many public galleries are organized groups of school children learning about the legislative process, often outside sitting hours, and tourists. School children and tourists are given a very different experience, especially when the chamber is in recess. Besides giving talks about assembly procedure, symbolism, and history, some assemblies encourage school groups to come right into the chamber and sit in the leader or speaker's chair, imagining themselves taking an active part one day. Others have encouraged the growth of Youth Parliaments, where young people debate real issues in the chamber. Tourists, however – and for the most part, I observed that tourist groups were dominated by locals, not foreigners – tend to get a more attenuated experience. For the most part, they are given an account of the chamber by official tour guides who focus on 'facts and figures': heights, weights and costs; the number of trees it took to furnish the Japanese House of Councillors; the symbolism of the particular shades of green and red in the two Australian chambers; and the height of the ceiling covering the US House of Representatives. My South African guide made a point of showing me the seat in the disused apartheid-era chamber where Prime Minister Verwoerd was assassinated; and the Australian guides make an effort to tell stories about particular characters and amusing incidents. The end result of all this is a little like learning about a country's politics through the peculiar combination of a quantity survey and a gossip magazine. Yet for the most part, this seemed to be what many visitors wanted to hear. For example, in the tour of Congress I joined, American visitors seemed most eager to find out which statues in the National Statuary Collection belonged to their home state, and thus gain a sense of their own presence in such august surroundings. What was frankly a rather dull tour for me as an outsider was more rich and validating for them as insiders, because it was aimed at reinforcing their sense of identity with the federation via its symbols.

Public galleries have rather strict rules of behaviour when the assembly is in session – no talking, no cameras or recording devices, no taking jackets on and off, dressing 'with respect for the dignity of Parliament' (New Zealand Parliament, 2009), and so on (Figure 6.2). These strictures are relaxed slightly, in New Zealand, for Māori for whom a celebratory song or *haka* performance might be considered essential to mark the passage of a bill that directly affects them, but otherwise Speakers and gallery security guards impose a strict emphasis on observing debates, not participating in them. There might be

Figure 6.2. House Armed Services Committee in session, 2011

Note the hierarchy of levels and closed benches typical of many US committee rooms. Photo by Specialist Kevin S. O'Brien, US Navy, public domain via Wikimedia Commons.

good reasons for this, of course, to do with protecting the quality of the proceedings, but it conflicts with a desire I have observed on many occasions where people in galleries are busting to intervene, or find themselves sternly cautioned or even removed for letting a comment slip. What is interesting from a staging point of view is that all assembly galleries occupy what, if we followed Goodsell, would be seen as a dignified position above the main chamber floor; but if we think of theatre cues instead, the raised gallery has more in common with 'the Gods', the top tier of seats with a restricted view and a low price for the lower classes. In any case, it is not surprising to me that gallery audiences seem sometimes frustrated about the behavioural strictures placed on them. The members are their representatives, paid out of their taxes; yet the staging of the chamber sends ambiguous cues of both supremacy over the cock-pit below, and being in 'the cheap seats'; with the lower status cues reinforced by the strict access and behaviour controls enforced by guards, physical barriers, more subtle design elements, or all three. In a world of declining public deference to authority, the cues of public galleries are deeply off-putting.

Some governments are not responding to these pressures well. In Britain, the government drew flak in 2004 when it responded to an extremely rare example of direct action in the chamber – a Fathers for Justice[2] protest that took the form of a condom filled with dyed flour hitting the Prime Minister during a speech – by ramping up security screening for visitors. What is ironic about this instance, however, is that the parliamentary authorities had already cut the gallery in two with VIPs (ambassadors, etc.) and guests of Lords and Members seated in the front two rows, the rest of the public quarantined away from the chamber behind thick, bullet-proof glass. Therefore, the overriding impression in the House of Commons is that, as an ordinary member of the public, one is 'common' indeed; a contagion that needs to be isolated behind glass.

Still, in more countries than not, the idea that an ordinary member of the public would wander up to the chamber just to watch a debate struck many of my guides, guards, and interviewees as behaviour only exhibited by those with something not quite right upstairs. The exception was if there were some very significant piece of legislation being passed, and even then, those who turned up would be doing so to *celebrate* or condemn its passage, not to exercise a publicity function that disciplined the arguments being made along the way, and certainly not to make their feelings known to those on the chamber floor below. When pressed on this point, interviewees tended to refer to the major alternative means of achieving publicity, via the other gallery occupied by the media. Many Westminster-based systems use the term 'gallery' in a metaphorical sense not just to refer to the physical seating above the chamber floor but to the body of parliamentary journalists, whether they work directly in the building or not, and it is *this* gallery that has taken on the deliberative publicity role on behalf of the citizenry more generally. This is more than a matter of practical necessity, given that only a tiny proportion of the *demos* can be present in any public gallery at any one time. From a liberal point of view, the fact that an 'attentive public' like the media actually attends parliament and reports on significant activities is a positive strength, and means that the rest of the public can get on with their own lives and their own projects, trusting the professionals to spot things that they would not, and to alert them when something goes on that affects their interests or threatens the system (Schudson, 1999; Zaller, 2003).

Given that, we might worry less that people can only access assemblies in their role as tourist or student, and only in a truncated sense as citizen. Instead, we should look at the degree to which the media is able to access decision makers, and in some places that access is quite considerable. For example, while journalists in the New Zealand Parliament cannot just wander

---

[2] A sometimes-controversial campaigning group that focuses on divorce settlements and child access rights for separated fathers. See http://www.fathers-4-justice.org/f4j/ for critical discussion, see Collier (2005).

130

into members' offices, and complain constantly to the Speaker about limited access, they nonetheless have access to Executive Wing lift lobbies, which means that ministers and other members face a media scrum whenever they are in the spotlight. The fact that the toilets are in the lobbies makes the media even harder to avoid, although the Prime Ministerial levels have connecting stairs inside the protected office zone. In Westminster, journalists are more restricted in where they can roam. They have access to the Members' lobby and some of the bars in a way that ordinary members of the public do not (Rogers and Walters, 2006: 177), but they have very restricted access to the corridors and lobbies outside members' offices, either in the Palace of Westminster itself or in Portcullis House, the main parliamentary office building across Bridge Street. Access to ministers is even harder, because ministers work in their departmental buildings: Richmond House for the Department of Health, and the Treasury building on Horse Guards Parade, for example. Media 'scrums', therefore, are a rare sight on UK television: interviews are usually more controlled affairs, either staged on a scrap of lawn opposite the Victoria Tower or, for members of the government, outside Downing Street. Still, the fact that the primary 'attentive public' has a great deal more access than everyone else might speak against any concern that everyone else has very limited access rights indeed.

That conclusion is a little too quick, in my view. First, there are all the reasons why the media are limited channels of information, including limited constructors of what counts as news in the first place; the strong tendency, driven by narrative conventions, to focus on people doing things to other people rather than capturing more impersonal forces; limited resources, attention and 'news holes'; and so on. This means that only certain aspects of complex stories get told, rendering it problematic to rely on the media as the sole channel between the chamber and the rest of the public sphere (Parkinson, 2006b). Second, when the media and those they scrutinize occupy the same space over many, many years, accusations of excessive cosiness and manipulation emerge (Schudson, 2004; Rogers and Walters, 2006: 178), although crises like Watergate have occasionally prompted clear-outs and revisions to rules of engagement, both by assembly authorities and news editors. Third, if the media concentrate on the hurly-burly of main debating chamber engagement – and they do – then they miss a lot of the substantive argument for and against proposals, ending up transmitting just the cock-fight and not the business that is transacted around the pit. This, it has been argued (Stoker, 1996: 129), is one of the reasons why people in many stable democracies are increasingly turned off politics, because they equate it with playground name-calling and other antics, instead of narrating, claim-making, deliberation, and decision-making.

131

This does not mean that plenary sessions are of no importance. Traditional mud-slinging sessions like Question Time 'are all about confidence': generating it, keeping it, or attempting to undermine it in the government or opposition, in particular ministers or other members, in one or other political party, or in the Speaker and the institutions of representative democracy as a whole.[3] In the US context, a period of extreme committee control between the 1910s and 1960s was gradually pared back following the Watergate scandal and the ensuing crisis of confidence in the then-inscrutable and very powerful House and Senate committees (Zelizer, 2004: 312) such that more emphasis was placed once more on plenary sessions, facilitated by rule changes to open up media coverage of congressional debate (Schudson, 2004). Nonetheless, detailed scrutiny of public claims, proposals, and actions is not primarily done in the main chamber, but in committee rooms and other space in assembly buildings, and in these spaces similar restrictions on public access apply. Committee rooms generally have a small number of seats for public observers; people occupying those seats are forbidden from speaking themselves, with speaking rights reserved for committee members and witnesses. At least outside the United States, committee rooms do not send quite the same disempowering signals as the main chamber does – member of the public are on the same level as everyone else, and the rooms are on a more intimate, familiar scale – yet nonetheless, these are not spaces that welcome outsiders. They are places for insiders and those they invite; they are not spaces for the people themselves to stand up and be heard in.

The most important exceptions to all this are found in the *Landsgemeinden* of the Swiss cantons of Appenzell Inner-rhodes and Glarus (Barber, 1988; Reinisch and Parkinson, 2007). As semi-direct democracies, the assemblies are, in theory at least, assemblies of all the citizens of the cantons, not assemblies of representatives, although both cantons have elected office holders who meet in council chambers as well. Both *Landsgemeinden* feature opportunities for citizens to address their fellow citizens, with people who feel strongly enough able to queue up to speak from the rostrum (in Glarus) or put their hands up and wait to be chosen to speak by the chief elected official, the *Landammann*, who runs proceedings. The distinction between 'floor' and 'gallery' in the assembly is very different in these contexts: in both, citizens are on the 'floor', facing a raised rostrum for the *Landammann* and speakers; there is tiered seating for the media and VIP guests at the back and one side of the 'ring' in which the citizens stand; others sit perched in the windows of houses and other buildings surrounding the square, while other visitors – German tourists enjoying what they see as funny local dialects and customs,

---

[3] The quote is from the Speaker of the House of Representatives, New Zealand. See also Uhr (1998: 198) for a similar point on Question Time in the Australian parliament.

132

plus the odd academic with recording equipment – stand outside the ring looking on. In all this, the ordinary citizen is at the centre of proceedings; non-citizen VIPs are kept at the back in the cheap seats; outsiders look on from the wings. I have only speculative evidence on this, not having been able to conduct much in the way of non-elite interviews, but the citizens of both Appenzell Inner-rhodes and Glarus are said to gain a tremendous amount of satisfaction from their central role as co-creators of canton politics – and thus it has become an emblem of their membership of these societies, and is protected despite all the pressures to abandon these seemingly anachronistic ways of deciding public affairs (Reinisch and Parkinson, 2007: 5).

To summarize, then, the galleries in modern assemblies are enormously ambiguous places. While they could be interpreted to serve a deliberative publicity function, and do to the extent that the members below are conscious of them, most assemblies do all they can to ensure that members are *not* aware of the galleries, protecting them from the public by lifting them up and out of eyeshot, smothering them with behavioural injunctions and, as a last resort, sealing them off behind glass partitions. The media gallery plays this delibera-tive scrutiny role instead, and while there are reasons to think that it cannot play this role perfectly, democracy is undoubtedly better for having them there – to have the scrutiny role played solely by the public gallery would mean that a very attenuated form of scrutiny would survive. Instead, the public galleries are used occasionally to mark the passage of significant legisla-tion; by some people to witness the argy-bargy of general debates; but for the most part by school groups and tour groups, the first as part of their civics lessons, the second out of some need to reinforce identities and group mem-berships. I will reflect more in the final section on whether this is a state of affairs to be lamented or not, but the example of the Swiss *Landsgemeinden* suggests that there is, in relatively local politics at least, an alternative way of running things that reverses the more common order and encourages a very different kind of identification, one that focuses on the institutions of democ-racy themselves rather than the symbols of state power engraved in the marble of assembly buildings.

Securing the Assembly

In the discussion of assembly galleries, I mentioned several times the role that assembly guards play keeping the public in line. This raises the issue of security more generally, and in the last decade assembly security matters have caused an amount of public disquiet. Whereas once visitors to the US Congress could walk up the Rotunda steps and into the central hall itself, they are now forced to enter through the new Capitol Visitor Center, opened in

2008, and where, if they have an appointment, they pass through metal detectors and are personally escorted to the relevant office. Citizens can also get tickets to the public galleries from their representatives, but if they are with a tour group they have to pre-book their arrival, are screened, and herded around a small number of rooms by a variety of guides and guards before finally being released. On the day I visited – before the new Center was open, but using the new visit procedures – there was a heavily armed Capitol Police officer barking orders at visitors from behind a wire fence as if they were inmates in a prison camp rather than citizens wanting to see where their money is spent (see Warden, 1995, on the Australian Parliament's likeness to a prison). Where once visitors wandered in and out of their building through the main entrance at their leisure, and interacted relatively freely with their representatives, they are now herded, hectored, and quarantined. Perhaps many Americans are used to that now – it is how they are treated at airports too – but for me at least the entire experience was deeply unpleasant as a result.

With variations depending on the precise arrangements of the buildings in space, security restrictions have been ramped up at all the national assembly buildings in my sample. As much as possible, rather than just rely on security personnel within a building or patrolling the streets, security advisers have for many years emphasized the value of 'perimeter security': stopping bad guys getting close enough to damage a target in the first place. This approach soared up the US policy agenda following the 1995 bombing of a federal government office building in Oklahoma City, and accelerated dramatically following the 11 September 2001 attacks on New York and Washington.[4] The same applies to assembly buildings now: security perimeters enforced by street closures and Jersey barriers at first, and by more subtle design elements like high kerbs and 'designed' bollards more recently; closing or moving underground car parks; plus screening all visitors as close to the perimeter as possible (National Capital Authority, 2003). While this makes a certain kind of sense from a security point of view, there are well-known lines of critique, including the now-famous line from Benjamin Franklin, that 'They who can give up essential liberty to purchase a little

---

[4] The approach goes back further. The standard plan for US embassies and military facilities around the world changed dramatically after the 1983 truck-bombing of the US Marines' barracks at Beirut Airport, with demands for large set-backs from the street and heavy fortifications. Governments that host US – and increasingly British – embassies in older, street-fronting buildings are pressured to close city streets and erect barriers to prevent vehicles getting close enough to cause damage. Thus, the Land of the Free is represented abroad by the architecture of bunker and prison camp. For limited detail, see the State Department's Bureau of Overseas Buildings Operations, www.state.gov/obo/ for more detailed discussion of the contrasts between Canada's new embassy in Washington, DC, and the United States' new embassy in Ottawa, see Gournay and Loeffler (2002).

temporary safety, deserve neither liberty nor safety' (Franklin and Franklin, 1818: 270). In other words, security is not the only value, yet in the environment of the 'war on terror', it is elevated to a supreme value to which all others – democracy, accessibility, accountability, urban amenity, and just plain fun – are subordinated. Perimeter security approaches stop pedestrians getting near, creating a 'barren environment' in which access is firmly discouraged, not warmly welcomed (Flint, 2005: 9).

So, my one-time regular walk as a research student from my home in Canberra's inner south over the top of the grassy slopes of the Australian Parliament to the Australian National University campus is now impossible. In 2001, red and white plastic Jersey barriers went up at the foot of the four access points up the parliament hills, patrolled by Australian Protective Service officers who had once stayed fairly unobtrusive at their posts near the flagpole at the top. The Jersey barriers have now gone, but a new kerb has been installed, fixed metal fences are now in place, more CCTV has gone up and the officers are zealous in their pursuit of any of those who look like they might breach the perimeter except through the approved, northern public entrance. One can no longer use the space as the designers intended; and even though there was something slightly tokenistic about that freedom when one's ability to penetrate the working corridors of the building was close to zero, nonetheless it was a freedom that mattered to many Canberrans, and its removal greeted with ambivalence by people walking past Parliament to work, by children who loved to roll down the slopes, and by other Australians who valued its symbolism of citizens in charge (Anonymous, 2003; Malone, 2004).

In the case of the National Assembly for Wales, access has been somewhat tokenistic from the start. It was the intention of the designers to allow – invite, even – members of the public to walk up the front steps and into the main body of the building where, almost immediately, they would find themselves looking down into the debating chamber from the public gallery. Perimeter security is subtle but nonetheless present – the plaza is bollarded, the plinth is difficult to drive up or under, and visitors are screened once inside the main doors – but once through that screen people are fairly free to wander about as they choose through roughly 70 per cent of the building (National Assembly for Wales, 2009a). However, the 70 per cent figure has to be seen in the context of the fact that there is very little office space in the Assembly building in the first place, and a strict separation maintained between work space and visitor space. Furthermore, the galleries themselves are glassed off from the chamber below, with committee room galleries similarly glassed off from proceedings. The result is one of separation, not inclusion, a clear signalling of who is in charge and who is not.

At least a member of the public can get into the Capitol Building, the Australian Parliament and the National Assembly for Wales in the role of observer, tourist or student; in many other countries, public access is not permitted at all, in any role. In my own sample of cities, there were three assemblies that were completely off limits to citizens without a specific piece of business to conduct: the Chilean *Congreso Nacional* in Valparaíso; the *Congreso de la Unión* in Mexico City; and the Hellenic Parliament in the centre of Athens. It is the Mexican building that is most forbidding: built in red, white, and green stone to mirror the national flag and represent the nation, yet sealed off behind an astonishing perimeter wall of thick steel pillars designed, it seems, to repel tanks rather than mere citizens bearing claims. The barrier is pierced on the northern side by a couple of heavily guarded gates, at which one guard stared at me with naked astonishment when I had the temerity to ask whether I, as a visiting academic, could come in and see the building. No appointment, no entry, and efforts to gain an appointment were fruitless.[5] The road outside the entrance, 10 de Mayo, was bustling with people; across the road were cafes and hairdressers and shops selling all kinds of goods; the nearby San Lorenzo metro station was a busy one; yet all this seemed set up to serve those who worked in the building, not for visitors. The idea that a citizen might want to visit the place had clearly not occurred to them. It was not even as if those working in the building were locals – the building is next to the working-class suburb of Candelaria but separated from it by a heavily fenced railway line and a multi-lane highway, crossed by a single, narrow footbridge that keeps the poorer locals very much on the wrong side of the tracks. Congress workers use the San Lorenzo metro station further east of the building, not the slightly closer but harder to access (and more forbidding) Candelaria. In Valparaíso, similarly, there is no means of casual access to the Congress building, although the fence is much more modest, and there was only one puzzled rather than hostile guard on duty at the gate (admittedly on a weekend). In Athens, the barriers are more of low-slung stone than steel, but the reception was the same, and there was a similar lack of clarity about how one might overcome the barriers.

Now, in all three places the assembly matters much less than in others. Mexico, Chile, and Greece are all fairly strong presidential systems (Linz, 1994; Philip, 2003), especially Chile whose legislature has been seen as almost irrelevant from 1973 onwards, despite reforms in 2005 (Siavelis, 2000; Nogueira Alcala, 2008). The fact that the legislature is not in the capital, Santiago, but 120 kilometres away on the coast at 'Valpo' – shifted there to a hideous lump of a building erected during the Pinochet dictatorship – merely adds to its sense of marginality. This meant that Chileans' puzzlement about why

---

[5] I am sure with more time and working of contacts it could have been arranged; it just was not possible in the short time I had available, and certainly not possible on the casual, walk-up basis that is taken for granted in other cities.

136

I would want to go there, despite the city's real charm, was well-founded. Instead, I was constantly directed to the Presidential Palace, La Moneda, in Santiago, and told stories about President Allende attempting to defend it against the coup – those are the narratives that the site anchors. Likewise, in Mexico City the centre of attention is the Presidential Palace that forms one side of the massive Zócalo square, and the City government offices that run at right angles to it. These buildings *are* relatively open and accessible, especially the Mexican Presidential Palace: all one needs to do is present some ID – a local identity card for Mexicans, a passport for foreigners – walk through a metal detector, and then one is free to wander about the front half of the building at least with very few restrictions and with guards relatively unobtrusive. Guarding around La Moneda was much more visible, but not so intimidating that local visitors hesitated to ask soldiers to pose for photos with them, particularly, and somewhat ironically in my view, in front of the statue of Salvador Allende, killed in a soldiers' coup. Thus, in these countries where presidential power carries normative weight (Philip, 2003), openness seemed to go with perceived political importance; the legislatures are not open, but nor are they seen to matter very much, and no one that I spoke to seemed terribly bothered about that fact. This is unlike the presidentialism of the United States where all three branches of government are seen to matter more, and where securitization has been hotly contested.

Close to the opposite end of the spectrum is the New Zealand Parliament in Wellington. Again, the main steps at the front of the Edwardian central building used to be the main entrance and pretty much anyone could – and did – wander up them and inside, although now one has to enter through doors in the link between Parliament House and the Executive Wing, the Beehive. That entrance is not easy to find: the main steps provide the only obvious entrance cue, but a sign at the top says 'no entrance' and directs one back down to sliding glass doors that otherwise look like a blank wall and not an obvious entry-way at all, at least from a distance. But once one *has* found the entrance, the guards are warm and friendly; the scan brief; and if one does not have an appointment in the buildings one can wander around the lobbies, the banqueting hall, the shop, and the public gallery when the House is sitting without much bother and with security unobtrusive; until one wants to enter the public gallery, that is, when the behavioural restrictions and guarding become more obtrusive. Tourism, it seems, is fairly free and easy in the New Zealand Parliament; active democratic engagement treated with a degree of suspicion. When asked about security and access, the Speaker at the time was very keen to emphasize the importance of maintaining security but keeping it unobtrusive, and of allowing as much public access as possible. 'It's the people's building' she said, although she contradicted herself shortly after-wards by insisting that first and foremost it was a 'working building', and that

137

nothing would be allowed that compromised that. These points lend some support to Vale's view (2005: 41) that '"securing public space" means securing space from the public, rather than for it'. Vale puts things too bluntly: public space is not secured from the public *tout court*, but from particular kinds of public. This issue will come up again in the next chapter, but one of my key claims is that people and groups of people with public purposes – *purposive* publics for short – are now systematically excluded from a great many political domains, while *incidental* publics – those made up of people pursuing more private, individual ends, and thus only a group in an aggregative sense – are privileged. In the next chapter, I will show how this division is reinforced by the way that squares and plazas are constructed and managed. But in the context of assemblies, this particular impetus takes the form of a tendency to grant access to groups of tourists and school children over almost any other form of public.

The issue of 'entrance cues' deserves a brief discussion. This came up in discussions with the Clerk of the Senate in Ottawa, in which it was pointed out that the Peace Tower acts as a magnet, a massive architectural cue that does not just say 'here we are' but also 'enter here', and that this entrance point has been maintained by parliament's managers and members in the face of opposition from security advisers and despite the presence of a visitor reception tent to the west of the Centre Block (Figure 6.3). Likewise, St Stephen's Tower and to a lesser extent the Victoria Tower at the Houses of Parliament in Westminster give a very similar and equally strong cue – 'this way in'. The St Stephen's Tower entrance, however, is the Members' Entrance, which causes no end of consternation to puzzled tourists who think that they too should be wandering in that way, and no end of bother to the police officers who have to redirect them to the real visitors' entrance further along past Cromwell Green.[6] In Washington, DC, Capitol Police officers are constantly stopping visitors trying to get into the Capitol up the Rotunda steps; after all, visitors *used* to be able to do so, and it *is* the obviously cued thing to do. No such confusion strikes visitors to the Australian Parliament. While it has four entrances – one public, one for ministers, one for senators, and one for MPs – it is so clearly signalled by the broad, open arms of the plaza on the north side that *this* is where one goes in.

The siting presents further complications. I have already mentioned the difficulties of accessing the Mexican and Chilean parliaments, but then no one expects them to be accessible. In London, while the exact doorway to use

---

[6] Just to add to the confusion, there are seven main entrances to the Palace of Westminster, all serving different groups of people; and while the 'business' entrance is called the St Stephen's Entrance, it is not under St Stephen's Tower. This obscurantism is just one of the myriad ways by which the British signal their status to each other.

138

Figure 6.3. The Centre Block and Peace Tower, Ottawa
Photo by Steven Dengler, edited by Jeffrey Nichols, licensed by Creative Commons.

is not at all obvious, getting to the building is easy, with a very central and easily walkable location, with an Underground station and Thames riverboat pier just a short walk away. Westminster station is one of the few on the tube network to be wheelchair accessible, so it is even relatively inclusive in that regard. In Wellington, Cape Town, and Ottawa, the parliaments are all quite central; in Tokyo it is easily reachable by metro. In Canberra, however, the drama of the site has come at the expense of accessibility. Canberra is a city designed for grand vistas. Covering a quarter of the area of metropolitan London but with less than 5 per cent of its population, it is not a city that works for pedestrians or lovers of public transport, and the walk from Civic to Parliament is just over 3 kilometres along Commonwealth Avenue, a long and irritating slog in the summer heat. When one gets to the Parliament end, if one has been stubborn enough to walk, it is not at all obvious how to proceed – four of the six lanes of Commonwealth Ave turn into the semi-motorway of State Circle with no pedestrian access; and the two-lane ramp up the hill to Parliament is not easily accessible on foot. The good pedestrian access is up Federation Mall, but that is not obvious from the far end of Commonwealth Ave; it is not obvious even from the lakefront, because the paths around Old Parliament House seem well hidden. The buses are good but take confusingly circuitous routes, so the option that most visitors take is the car – although the car park is under the entrance plaza, making where to park a confusing puzzle for some motorists. The building itself is then set back from the perimeter road, which pleases the Australian Protective Service, although not so much that they did not attempt to close the perimeter road completely to traffic. All of this enhances a sense of the Australian Parliament as somewhat remote and isolated (cf. Warden, 1995); easily legible in terms of its access points once you are there, but not a journey that many people would take in their lunch break or because they just happened to be passing; because of its siting, almost no one just happens upon the Australian Parliament. I will talk more about why this matters in the concluding section and the next chapter, but for now, I think this has an impact on how purposive publics engage with decision makers and the rest of the public sphere – the whole building is at arm's length, and thus risks fading into the background, becoming more a symbolic entity like the US Capitol than an active site for the performance of democracy.

Let me return from that brief detour to sum up the points on security. The new security agenda in the first decade of the twenty-first century has fundamentally altered the relationship between citizens and assembly buildings in many countries. Where once assembly buildings symbolized openness and accessibility, most are now protected by heavy perimeter security in the form of large set-backs from the road – and when the building cannot be moved away from a road, attempts are made to close the road instead – with fences and barriers that create barren zones around buildings, decreasing the likelihood that citizens will interact with them accidentally. At the same time, certain kinds of purposive citizen – those who are not 'accidental' at all, but who have active, democratic purposes in coming to the building – are treated with suspicion not only by parliamentary officers but also by the very design of the chamber. Visitors to the public galleries are set apart in the cheap seats unable to interact, sometimes even held behind thick plate glass. The kinds of visitors who are welcomed at many assemblies are tourists and school children; the former are given gossip and quantity surveys; the latter are taught about democratic citizenship in a building that strictly curtails their ability to express that citizenship. Some assemblies are not even open to tourists and students, but that is at least partly to do with the strong presidentialism of those systems, in which the assembly is seen as a relatively unimportant entity not worth bothering about.

140

Democratic Implications and Conclusions

Why do these observations about public access matter? Does democracy fail if the public cannot access their representatives in the representatives' building? Ric Thorp, co-designer of the Australian Parliament, put the issue this way:

> ...on the point of senators and members meeting with the public. In one sense, it doesn't make sense because...all senators and members in fact expect to meet with their constituents in their local area. It would be quite unusual for me to come and lobby my member for Wentworth[7] in Canberra, I guess. I would more likely show up at his place down the road from where I live. (Fewtrell et al., 2008: 32)

The same objection applies in Britain, in New Zealand, and in the United States: no one sees their representatives in their offices in the assembly complex; everyone sees them either by appointment or in first-come-first-served 'surgeries', as the British call them, in their constituency offices or other public spaces like Council offices, library meeting rooms, and so on. This is much more convenient for the constituent than having to traipse to the capital. And while members generally meet their constituents in their role as local representative, not as cabinet minister or committee chair, say, they nonetheless often take constituent concerns to responsible ministers, acting as a conduit to government and the legislature.

Similarly, there are other, monitorial citizens in the shape of the media who get access. Despite all their imperfections, media representatives access and scrutinize the assembly far more effectively than the average citizen can, transmitting their findings to the rest of us, ringing the alarms when things are going wrong. Therefore, to worry about access to galleries that at best seat only a few hundred observers could seem peculiar, to say the least, when those few hundred can more actively engage representatives in constituency offices, and when the media is watching for the rest of us anyway.

One way to think about whether direct access matters after all is to consider the one city in my sample where members *do* meet constituents at the assembly, and that is Ottawa. There are rooms set aside for this purpose in parliament's Centre Block, and they are used fairly regularly while parliament is in session, sometimes because a constituent or group of constituents has come all the way to Ottawa specifically to meet their MP, sometimes because they happen to be in town for other reasons and make an appointment to discuss something with their representative while they are there. This is an interesting

---

[7] A generally conservative lower house electorate in Sydney, including some of Sydney's most affluent harbour-side suburbs, but also including more bohemian inner-city and Eastern Bays territory. See http://www.aec.gov.au/Elections/federal_elections/2007/Profiles/w/Wentworth.htm

sign of a somewhat different attitude to the relationship between representatives and the represented in Canada, and one that makes a real difference to issues of access at the Canadian Parliament. It was the one place I visited where the defenders of public access to parliament did so not primarily for reasons of education, heritage, or tourism but specifically to protect citizens' access to parliamentarians. While there was acknowledged to be a 'built-in tension' between parliament as a place of work, a site for celebrations, a democratic space and a securitized space, the Clerk of the Senate said that she had had Senators objecting to certain perimeter security proposals by saying, 'But it's Canadians' Parliament, I want them to have access'. Other interviewees supported this: it is members who have been the most vociferous defenders of citizens' rights to access them, whereas in the United States and Australia, representatives have been seen to be too-readily accepting security recommendations, and criticized for locking themselves away from citizens behind security perimeters (e.g. Longstreth, 2006: 17–18).

The reason why I think this matters is to do with the symbolic cues that such openness sends, both to citizens more broadly and to representatives working in the building. Within the chamber, public access should cue representatives to frame their arguments in publicly defensible ways, although this may require some changes to the way that galleries are arranged, to maximize, rather than minimize, lines of sight between the floor and the gallery. Access can also remind representatives that the public is in charge. Representatives who are seen to think of their constituents at least as much as their own comfort and security by providing public access and meeting points, whether they are widely used or not, are likely to be more responsive to those people's preferences – recalling our definition of democracy – than those who are not. Likewise, the cue to the public is, 'they work for us'. A lack of public accessibility sends a symbolic message that politicians are inaccessible and unresponsive, regardless of how accessible they really are in their districts.

Not many people take up the opportunity to watch their representatives in present assemblies. That is not an argument to say that they would never take up the opportunity, given different structures. The fact would remain, however, that only a limited number of people could take up an opportunity at any given moment – a few hundred at best. This does not matter so long as *some* can take up the opportunity, and that the opportunity is relatively evenly distributed. It matters that people in the gallery are visible to other members of the public. That is not to say that access to the assembly is the be-all-and-end-all of democratic responsiveness; rather, it is a phrase in the symbolic narrative of assemblies, one that can either reinforce or undermine the credibility of other democratic symbolism, other democratic pronouncements and procedures.

To encourage symbolic and procedural harmony, I want to conclude with a modest proposal for the reform of assemblies: Public Question Time. Versions of this are already common in local government in Britain, where dozens of local authorities – town and county councils, police and national park authorities, among others – set aside 20–30 minutes at a variety of full council and committee meetings for questions from the public. In Australia too this is common practice in local government, especially in the states of Tasmania, Victoria, and Western Australia. But imagine this implemented in national assemblies, extending the Westminster tradition of Prime Minister's Question Time, and creating a parallel institution that is open to members of the public. One could hold a 1-hour session every week that the assembly is in session in which registered voters[8] can ask questions of party leaders, committee chairs, cabinet ministers, minority leaders, and so on. Questions would need to be submitted in advance to the Speaker or some other neutral arbiter, because almost certainly there would be more questions proposed than time to ask them, and the Speaker would need some procedure for choosing questions – perhaps on the basis of connection to the current legislative programme; or put the choice to an online or television poll every week. Advance submission would also ensure that the chosen questioner could make arrangements to get to the assembly – with travel expenses paid by the government to ensure equity of access – and to ensure that the politician to whom the question was addressed was in the chamber to answer. Those who wished to ask questions themselves could do so from the public gallery, if it were open and visible enough, or from a lectern in the chamber; or, if that was felt too intimidating or was otherwise difficult for them, they could elect to have the Speaker ask the question on their behalf, so long as they were physically present in the chamber to act as a signifier of real public accessibility to decision-making. Opposition or minority party members would have the opportunity to press supplementary questions in a session immediately afterwards.

Would people turn up? If we answer that purely by looking at current practice in local authorities then the answer is mixed. In Britain, such facilities are not well advertized and browsing council minutes suggests that few people take up the opportunity, although that depends on whether there are any particularly salient issues at the time. On the other hand, in the Swiss *Landsgemeinden*, there are always many more citizens wanting to speak than

---

[8] I say 'registered voters' here because I mean to include permanent resident non-citizens who have the right to vote in the country's elections. Few countries extend the vote in this way: New Zealand is one, which gives the vote to all citizens plus those who have been granted permanent resident status; Britain is another, which gives the vote to EU and Commonwealth citizens who are also permanent residents (but not to other permanent residents like US citizens, for example). Following the 'all affected' principle, this is a rule I prefer over restricting voting to citizens only. The registered voters restriction might be an additional encouragement, albeit a small one, to register in those places where voter registration is optional and low.

there is time available for speakers. In Britain, there is a national radio show called *Any Questions?*,[9] which for decades now has seen people pack village halls and city council chambers to put questions about topical issues to travelling and changing panels of politicians, journalists, and pundits. It is followed up by a programme called *Any Answers?* in which listeners respond to the questions and have their answers heard. Both shows attract high rates of participation and listening, so clearly there is an appetite for political engagement of this kind.

Public Question Time would have several points, in terms of achieving democratic goods like opening up the agenda setting and scrutiny functions. But in terms of public space, the end I am most concerned with here is to ensure that more of the symbolic language of assemblies lines up with democratic values; in particular, that symbols of openness are not undermined by realities of closure and isolation. In that regard, therefore, the thick glass screens that some assemblies have installed in public galleries have got to go as well, with Franklin's words ringing in the ears of managers, members, and security advisers as they are taken down. Perimeter security approaches should be scaled back at the same time, in favour of more human – less 'secure', yes, but more democratic – alternatives. The same principles can be applied to committee hearings, but this analysis does *not* imply the complete opening of assembly buildings to access by the general public. They should be, in my view, working buildings, and for reasons of working efficiency as well as deliberative effectiveness, some privacy, some retreats are essential. An unintended consequence of opening assembly buildings too far would be, I suspect, to push assembly members further and further out of them, encouraging the 'historicization' of the buildings such that they functioned purely in symbolic terms and less as sites for the everyday performance of democracy. There is a balance to be achieved here between encouraging the public into the workings of the building, while protecting it as an effective workspace, and the idea of Public Question Time helps achieve that.

At the same time, as we saw in the previous chapter, it can be healthy to encourage the use of the building for national celebrations too. In this regard, the grand theatre of US presidential inaugurations is one way to go, but using Parliament as the site for Canada Day celebrations gives us another vision that is more about connecting the people with the assembly site, less about legitimating the authority of a powerful individual and a powerful set of institutions. This should not be carried so far as to lead to a loss of dignity of the site. That dignity is important for signalling to people that the decisions taken in this place are collective decisions that affect everyone in a given country. But

---

[9] http://www.bbc.co.uk/programmes/b006qgvj

nor *does* it go too far, it seems to me, in the Canadian case, because the Canadian authorities are well aware of the dangers of what they called 'Disneyfication', and the balance that needs to be struck between popular celebration and controlled ceremonial.

In conclusion, therefore, assemblies can more effectively perform their roles as public space in the fourth, public claims sense if they are made more public in the first, accessibility sense; but that opening needs to be done with sensitivity to the wider role of the building as a site of national, collective decision-making, both as a workplace and as a symbolic cue. This should be done with an eye on the dangers of historicization, securitization, and Disneyfication, so that people can engage with the site in their roles as democratic citizens, not merely as tourists, learners, and consumers. At present, assembly authorities the world over are privileging tourists over citizens, and attenuating democracy in the process.

7

Protest and the Plaza: Engaging the Formal Public Sphere

In Chapter five, we saw how the presence of a mass audience is an essential ingredient of national rituals: the crowd legitimates the ritual, and at the same time reinforces individuals' sense of themselves as a people, sharing symbols and experiences to transmit to each other and to future generations.

Some kinds of purposive, political crowds are embraced by political leaders; others are not. The former include crowds that gather for officially sanctioned or organized celebrations. The latter include crowds that gather to challenge the official line, to undermine the state's self-celebration, or simply to demand official action on collective problems – that is, space for members of the *demos* itself to make public claims directly, rather than through their representatives. At times it has been taken for granted that the right to assemble as the latter kind of public is something that is essential to democracy; right now, in a state of official paranoia, that right is being denied and abrogated around the world. In Chapter four, I argued that a right to protest physically matters in a world in which the public sphere is a great deal more than physical, because the physical occupation of space sends signals that are harder to ignore. If we accept that claim, however, it is not at all clear what we should do about it. In this chapter, I show that while some cities lack space for mass public protest, or have space that is too 'arm's-length' to have much impact on important audiences, in cities *with* good space available protest can easily become ritualized and regularized to the point where it no longer matters very much. While this dilemma is inescapable, its implications can be managed; although, for reasons that may already be obvious, I suggest that this should be more a matter of tactical choice by protest organizers than official planning and sanction.

I start by comparing those cities that have traditional spaces and routes for protest, looking at what happens when those spaces are close to or separated from the assembly building sites considered in the last two chapters, as well as

146

what happens where there is no traditional or effective site. I also note some differences between cities that have traditions of mobile protest – marching – and those that have more static traditions. These sections reveal an interesting tension between the need for direct confrontation with the powerful, and the need to avoid predictability and ritualization, something that can greatly diminish the impact of protest. I then turn to consider the way in which space for protest is being constricted by two forces: privatization and changes in policing. While both of these topics have extensive literatures behind them, I concentrate on one particular issue in both: the way in which control mechanisms are predicated on recognizing the public only in its role as shopper and consumer; and an associated deligitimization of the public as active citizens. I conclude that the public provision of sites for engagement comes with strong positives and strong negatives, but that the only way at present to manage the negatives is for protest groups to (a) use mixed methods and (b) only use the large scale sites when they can demonstrate the scale of their support base, or when they can use a space persistently, visibly, irritatingly. In this, I set my face against current trends in the design of large, public, city spaces, which emphasize breaking up flat, featureless plains with furniture, trees and other 'breaks' to encourage casual, accidental encounters between individuals, but which thus make them useless for large, purposive, democratic publics.

The Ritual Spaces of Public Protest

Let's start by comparing the space available for protest in the cities under study. I argued back in Chapter four that these spaces matter for four main reasons: presence, attention, membership, and dignity. The first concerns making physically explicit the range of 'people, perspectives, and problems' that make up the public and the public sphere (Bickford, 2000: 356), making one's claims visible. The second is about attracting the attention of fellow citizens, decision-makers, attentive publics, and other onlookers to those public narratives and claims. The third is both about attracting and encouraging new claim-makers to join in and, from the individual protestors' point of view, to demonstrate their membership of the *demos*, their dignity in dignified spaces, especially when they feel their views ignored or even existence overlooked. The fourth is about cloaking those claims in the symbols of authority (Hajer, 2009), making them more readily understood and accepted by the target audiences.

In some cities, that space is so obvious to locals and visitors alike that it hardly needs pointing out: Mexico City's Plaza de la Constitución, universally known as the Zócalo, and Washington's National Mall, for example. There are plenty of other examples from Bucharest to Buenos Aires, Bangkok to Beijing. All these spaces are full of the symbols of nation and authority. Standing in them, one is surrounded by the facades of presidential palaces and town halls; there are national flags flying from gigantic central flagpoles or from the roofs and balconies of the surrounding buildings, bowsprits of the ships of national enterprise. In some – Mexico most obviously – traffic circulates so that, standing in the middle of the square, one is at the centre of a maelstrom of activity. The traffic helps define these squares as the hub around which the nation revolves. They are not so much a 'still point of the turning world' but bustling places with no restrictions on access, full of tourists sometimes, but plenty of locals too, and are used as centres of protest so that people can cloak themselves and their claims with the same symbols and dignity that the powerful do when claiming the symbols and status of high office.

In London, Parliament Square is often derided as a mere roundabout, but that is because it is small and almost completely cut off for pedestrians: there are no crossings to it, and no easy ways past the safety barriers. Even more restricted are Hong Kong's Chater Gardens and Statue Square, so small and so full of seats and tables, arcades and planters, and fountains and pools that only around 5,000 people can use the pair of them at any one time (Figure 7.1). While under colonial rule, Statue Square fulfilled some symbolic, ritual functions; these days it is not expected to fulfil any particular symbolic role – it is a picnic and meeting spot for domestic workers, and while that gives it a role in the collective identity-building of *those* people, it says little to other Hong

Figure 7.1. Chater Gardens, Hong Kong, showing the largest open space
Author photo.

Kongers about their collective narratives. Thus, size matters – the number of people we can get into a square has an impact on the degree to which organizers can show the scale of popular displeasure with a government, and in London's Parliament Square that scale can only ever be relatively small, making it easier to dismiss even those demonstrations that manage to pack the square as unrepresentative of popular opinion. In Hong Kong, one could pack Chater Gardens to the gunwales yet the crowd would barely be noticed through the thickets of vegetation and covered seating.[1] By contrast, filling the Zócalo in Mexico is a much, much more impressive achievement.

In several cities, there is a single traditional space for protest that is somehow divorced from the sites of the public sphere. This divorce can be thanks to scale: in London, most protests gather not at Parliament Square but a mile eastwards in the larger and more accessible Trafalgar Square. Many very large protests in London occupy Hyde Park rather than the much smaller inner-Westminster spaces. Other divorces have happened gradually over time. In Santiago, the traditional centre for civic activity of all kinds is the Plaza de Armas, which once was *the* hub of government and military power, with the cathedral, town hall, army barracks, courts, governor's residence and city jails all clustered around the square – the legislature was one block to the west. Now only the church and the city authorities still occupy their old buildings, while other elements of the formal public sphere have drifted away from the plaza – as near as a few blocks or as far as Valpo on the coast. Nonetheless, the Armas remains the hub of civic activity, as it always has been, because, along with the presidential palace, it remains the symbolic centre of the Chilean public sphere.

Other divorces occur for mixed reasons of practicality, history and the convenience of the powerful. In Cape Town, for instance, the gathering place for protest is the old military parade ground, now market place and car park, in front of the old City Hall building. Parliament is a few kilometres further up the hill, behind walls and fenced-off streets, with the only accessible footpaths at the upper end of the complex accommodating only a few hundred people at best. The only reasonably sized public space nearby is Corporation Gardens, but that is a lush, densely vegetated space, more botanic garden that open plaza. Parliament Buildings have their backs to the Gardens rather than facing them, rendering the Gardens unconducive to the symbolic politics of confrontation and protest.

---

[1] With apologies for intruding with a personal note, this has particular resonance for me. In the 1970s, my brother and I played in Billy Tingle's Saturday Morning sports on what is now Chater Gardens but what was then the open, grassy field of the Hong Kong Cricket Club. Hong Kongers of a certain age will know what I mean. A peculiar relic of a colonial past has gone, but so has a useful public space.

In Athens, we find yet another pattern, with two traditional protest routes, one of which has multiple gathering points. Large, non-party rallies tend to gather on Alexandras Avenue then down Patission (aka 28th October Avenue) to Omonia Square. The second route is more associated with political parties. It features a single marching circuit – down Stadiou Avenue and back up Panepistimiou[2] – but multiple gathering points and termini, each of which has particular associations with a given political party. Therefore, traditionally the socialist party, PASOK, gathers at Klafthmonos Square; the communists at Kotzia Square; the New Democrats at Syntagma and the left–green coalition Synaspismos at the University. Either way, political demonstration takes a highly predictable, ritualized form which emphasizes not just national symbols and concerns but partisan ones as well.

All this ritualization has clearly positive and negative effects. I have already mentioned some of the positives: directly confronting the powerful in the places where they work; dignifying one's claims by linking them visually with the symbols of the state and nation, or reinforcing more particular partisan identities. Regularity also has benefits when it comes to people joining in. Organizers do not need to give Mexicans detailed explanations of where exactly to gather – all that needs to be said is 'El Ángel' and everyone knows what to do. It can have benefits for onlookers too: as if banners and slogans were not enough, Athenians simply know that if there is a large group mustering at Kotzia Square they must be communists. However, therein too lies one of the problems, and it is a big one. Because of the ritualization, it is easy to pay no attention to the actual claims being made – 'There go the communists again', rather than 'Oh, a protest about wages' – or to greet the umpteenth protest march down La Reforma this month with a shrug, or not even have it register because one sees the same sight every other day of the week. A protest march in Mexico City, unless it really snarls up the traffic, is as much a part of La Reforma as the trees, the buildings, the roadway and the traffic lights.

In response, many protest organizers try to turn to new sites or new methods (Maddison and Scalmer, 2006) – scaling a building and draping it with banners, say – although whether local law and policing *allows* organizers to break out of traditional routes is something else again, and a point I will take up again later in this chapter. However, some organizers positively encourage a degree of ritualization. Unexpectedly, I found this in Washington, DC, where anti-war protestors reported that while the regular transgression of rules controlling protests meant the whole encounter between activists and the

---

[2] This is one of several examples in this chapter and the next of a street or locale having both an official name that no one uses, and a common-usage name. Panepistimiou Avenue was renamed Eleftherios Venizelos Avenue after a former Prime Minister, but no one, not even many map-makers, uses the new name. 'Panepistimiou' means 'university', after the main University of Athens site half way along its length.

state had become ritualized and thus lost some of its impact as a media and public spectacle; nonetheless, it served a purpose in that forcing police to arrest people for these infractions 'jams up the court system' and thus helps maintain public protest as an irritant to the state.

The one place I visited where protest is both ritualized and not (yet) problematic in the 'fail to register' sense is Hong Kong. The territory's citizens have long been seen by internal and external observers as particularly apathetic (most notably by Lau, 1982), and yet Lam (2004) shows a more complex picture in which a succession of rulers have deployed a set of depoliticization tactics to dampen down the public expression of what is otherwise a highly active civil society. She gives a number of examples since the Second World War of activism bursting forth onto the streets, but since 1989 most of that activity has been focused on two days every year: 4 June and 1 July. The first commemorates the Tiananmen Square massacre, and a march and candle-lit vigil has been held in Victoria Park on or about that date every year since then. The 1 July marches began in 1997 with the return of Hong Kong to PRC control, and while every year they emphasize some different, particular claim, they are all focused on the relationship between Hong Kongers, their more-or-less-elected leaders, and the PRC leadership in Beijing. The march that really put 1 July on the calendar, as it were, was the 2003 event which attracted an estimated half-million people protesting the 'anti-sedition' Article 23 of the Hong Kong Basic Law. The protest was, almost unbelievably, successful in forcing the abrogation of the law, and since then the 'apathetic Hong Kong' cliché has become harder to sustain (Cheng, 2005). But the important point here is, I think, that while the protests have become ritualized in the sense that they happen in the same places on the same days every year, they are not *daily* occurrences, and thus do not become part of the landscape. On the contrary, they become more like a public festival, things that happen just a few times a year, things that are looked forward to, that are written into journalists' diaries and thus generate column-inches in the press for weeks before and afterwards. They are regular, ritual reminders to liberal Hong Kongers of the dangers of an overwhelming state. Their very regularity keeps them in the news and in people's minds, but they are not so frequent as to become ignored.

Site-Less Cities

In other cities, space for protest is not at all obvious and its performance not ritualized in the same way. This can be for several reasons. For one, it can be that the buildings of the formal public sphere and the symbols of national significance are not all gathered together in one central location. Tokyo, for

151

example, has no obvious centre. Guide books often use Tokyo Station as a starting point, or label the surrounding district of Marunouchi, or the Imperial Palace, as the 'centre', but these are more for the convenience of visitors than categories that Tokyo's citizens recognize. Likewise, the sites of the formal public sphere are relatively dispersed, and so demonstrations tend to gather around whatever ministry or symbol seems appropriate at the time. Marchers sometimes gather in Hibiya Park but this is not so much because it is handy to the Imperial Palace – heavens forbid – but because of its proximity to the broad avenues of the Ginza. It is by no means the regular gathering place, and is not terribly big. There is no particular tradition of gathering near the National Diet building either: the nearby park is too hilly, too full of nooks and crannies, without any large open space. Among Tokyo's large parks, Ueno and Yoyogi parks are commonly used, and while they are both redolent with symbolic associations – Yoyogi hosts the Meiji Shrine, Ueno was Tokyo's first public park and the site of a nineteenth-century battle between Meiji and shogunate loyalists – they cannot be said to be the symbolic centres of the city. The end result is rather more pragmatism than tradition. With the odd exception like Yoyogi Park for May Day demonstrations, protestors choose whatever site suits their immediate purpose.

In Canberra, there is a different set of problems. While on the face of it there is abundant space for protest and eyeballing the powerful, in practice that space is strictly controlled and limited. In part, this is through policing and a permit system, to which I will return shortly. In part, it is due to the physical layout of the city, discussed in Chapter six, which means that activists face a dilemma in choosing whether to engage with fellow Canberrans and attract local media, which implies demonstrating in the commercial district of Civic; or whether to confront the powerful in their 'citadels' (Warden, 1995), which implies demonstrating 3 kilometres further south outside Parliament, the Prime Minister's residence and, often, the US Embassy.[3] Another issue arises from the fact that Canberra has a small population – 350,000 people compared with the roughly four million each in Sydney and Melbourne – and so if the aim is to attract the national media or directly engage a large number of fellow Australians then one holds one's protest in those cities, 292 and 656 kilometres away, respectively.[4] But even on the doorstep of Parliament itself,

---

[3] Note here the importance that sometimes *other countries'* formal institutions play in a particular deliberative system. With respect to Iraq War protests, it was frequently the case in the cities under study that protests focused on United States embassies and trade missions, as much as that was possible given the security regimes in place.

[4] The Australian media is quite regionalized, not to the same extent as in the United States, but much more so than in Britain. There are some genuinely national news programmes and one national newspaper, but even then they vary the offering, sometimes markedly, from state to state. The major media are largely headquartered in Sydney, with some broadcast national news delivered from Melbourne. Canberra offices are small, peripheral, and in some cases only staffed

Figure 7.2. Old and new Parliament House, Canberra
The Authorised Assembly Area is a small strip at the top of the largest grassed area between the two buildings. Photo by Nicholas Brown, licensed by Creative Commons.

protest is controlled through the very layout of the available space. Within the Parliamentary Precinct, protest is usually only allowed within the 'Authorized Assembly Area', a 27×87 metre strip of grass at the top of the Federation Mall Parade Ground (Figure 7.2). It is separated from the main, public entrance to Parliament by a full 150 metres, including the forecourt, a raised area of grass and shrubbery, and the circum-parliamentary road, and is set a good metre and a half below road level on ground that slopes firmly back down towards the lake (for regulations governing the space, see Parliament of Australia, 2007). Protestors are kept within those boundaries by thickets of police officers and parliamentary security. All this has important effects on protestors and their audiences. For both, protest can seem somewhat farcical – except for the flagpole, the low-slung Parliament House is not a dominant physical presence when seen from the Authorized Assembly Area, while the area itself is hardly visible from the building. There is little sense of taking one's claims to

part-time. Thus, events in Canberra do not automatically make it onto Australian national news in the same way that events in London set the UK news agenda.

153

the powers that be, not least because members and senators rarely use the front of the building anyway; they use either the House or Senate entrances at the sides of the building or the Ministerial Entrance at the back, and are driven up to the doors through guarded barriers in limousines so that the chances of an encounter with a member of the public are slim. Protest organizers report that the sense of having an impact, of being taken seriously in the dignified spaces of collective decision-making, is simply not achievable under such conditions. For a protestor, the overwhelming sense is a strange combination of suspicion, surveillance, containment, and threat on the one hand, and pointlessness on the other. From inside the building, the impact of protest is similar – the tiny, distant space available makes protest groups seem small, and thus their claims small and unimportant too. Those who bother to turn up are clearly, to insiders, the lunatic fringe; rational, sensible people are inside the building wearing suits.

This makes quite a contrast between the old and new Parliament buildings. In the old, everyone used the same colonnaded entrance, and so it was frequently the case that one could bump into a minister – even the Prime Minister – coming through the doors. Although still separated from the building by a two-lane road, verge, car parks, and driveway, the broad, open grass between the portico and lake was both closer to the building – 35 metres instead of 150 – and flatter than the new arrangements, which gave protest much more of a sense of purposive confrontation than the new. As with the ability of backbenchers to encounter ministers noted in Chapter five, this ability to encounter the powerful easily was celebrated by some Australian politicians when plans for the new building were unveiled, plans that so obviously segregated the powerful and the powerless (Fewtrell, 1991).

Indeed, there is something mendacious about the new building. While its design is all, allegedly, about openness and the dominance of the people over their rulers (Giurgola in Fewtrell et al., 2008), the reality is one where the people and rulers are kept strictly separate, and the people clearly subordinate when they attempt to switch role from tourist to engaged citizen. As tourists, they can walk on top of the building and penetrate into its centre, but that centre is a blank space where no democratic work takes place. As citizens, those same people are confined to a small – humiliating, even – rectangle of grass, barely in eyeshot.

Static and Mobile Protest

Some places have static protest traditions while others have more mobile ones. In Ottawa, for example, people tend to gather at Parliament Hill and conduct their demonstration there; while there have been exceptions, they do

Figure 7.3. Anti-prorogation protestors, Parliament Hill, Ottawa
Note the steps to the bottom right are the main steps into the building, proximity that contrasts strongly with Canberra. Photo by Michelle Tribe, licensed by Creative Commons.

not tend to gather somewhere else first (Confederation Park, say) and then march, en masse, to the Hill (Figure 7.3). In other cities, it is not the gathering that matters so much as the getting there, and in those places there are often traditional marshalling points and marching routes as well. In some places, this is simply because there is no obvious terminus. Hong Kong has a good, although still-tight gathering point at Victoria Park; it has a marvellously broad and direct route from there down Hennessy Road to the Legislative Council chambers in Central; it just has nowhere for the crowd to gather at the other end, and this is one reason why in Hong Kong the protests are less about direct confrontation with the powerful, more about mobilization and making visible the dissatisfaction of the people in a state that would prefer such discontent remain invisible.[5] Santiago faces a similar problem: Plaza de Armas is also a somewhat 'programmed' space, with trees and other plantings, benches and café seating, merry-go-rounds and donkey rides, and street artists and tourists all jostling for space, among which protestors have only relatively small patches of open ground in which to make themselves visible. Thus, protest becomes mobile, often gathering at Plaza Italia and sweeping down the

---

[5] For a discussion of this and other reasons for the middle class preference for protest marches in Hong Kong, see Cheung (2005).

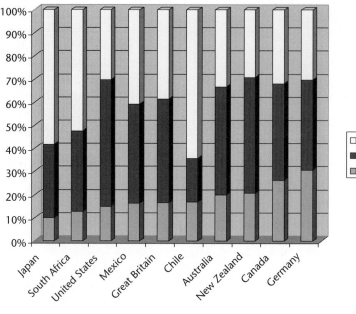

Graph 7.1. Willingness to attend lawful/peaceful demonstrations
Source: World Values Survey, question V98, www.worldvaluessurvey.org

broad avenue known on the maps as Avenida Libertador Bernardo O'Higgins but to everyone else as the Alameda, ending at the presidential palace of La Moneda, or wherever the police choose to intervene. For some issues and some people in Santiago, as in Athens, the running battle remains a key way of enacting public claim-making!

A different kind of mobility tradition is found in Wellington. There, standing still in Parliament grounds and yelling slogans at politicians has a long history but not a particularly respectable one. While it is a right that is respected by the powers that be,[6] New Zealanders tend to have a cultural suspicion of the political, and confine their confrontations to the sporting field. Marching, on the other hand, is a bit more respectable, and something undertaken by young and old, progressive and conservative alike. Indeed, World Values Survey comparisons between the countries under study here show that New Zealanders are among the more willing to participate in peaceful demonstrations – see Graph 7.1. With a few

[6] Speakers of the House have long protected the right of people to gather in front of the building against the urge of some security advisers who would rather impose an exclusive perimeter. It often happens that petitions are symbolically received on the steps of Parliament House, and that MPs address demonstrations from the same raised position. Demonstrators are now kept back from the driveway immediately in front of the steps where once they were able to swarm up them, right up to the doors, without anyone bothering too much. This has reduced the sense of proximity to power in Wellington, something that is maintained in Ottawa.

exceptions,[7] political protests in New Zealand tend to be relatively quiet affairs, certainly by Chilean standards. In that context, peacefulness is an entry badge, something that says that is safe to join and show one's support for a claim or viewpoint by parading from Courtenay Place (for a big protest) or Civic Square (for the smaller ones) down Lambton Quay and past all the shoppers and office workers that make up their public. The march usually ends at Parliament, and speeches are made in the grounds, but a lot of marchers wander off before then, having made their point by walking rather than talking.

There is a sense in which protest in Berlin takes this 'demonstration' to more abstract heights. The traditional gathering point for many protests is Lausitzen Park in Kreuzberg, but the first time I visited I was struck by how small and peripheral it felt. It also felt uncared-for space, with buildings covered in graffiti, the grass in a mess and rubbish everywhere. This was not space that would be instantly welcoming to the middle classes of Berlin, regardless of how passionately they felt about a topic. Still, it is important not to dismiss it, because while Lausitzen Park might not attract the bourgeois, it instead serves as a badge of identity for much smaller groups of radicals, activists, alternative life-stylers, and so forth – a home for alternative counterpublics rather than mainstream burgers, and a place where they feel in charge and powerful. Likewise, the modern Athenian district of Exarchia, full of squats, street art, and the flashpoint of the 2008 riots, serves a similar function, although I am starting to get ahead of the narrative here – I will return to Exarchia and Kreuzberg in the next chapter.

New Zealand, Australia, and the United States share another tradition: not so much marching *in* the capital but marching *on* the capital. In Australia, it has been farmers who have most used this tactic; in New Zealand, it has been mainly Māori lands rights campaigners using what is called the *hīkoi* (Harris, 2004). In the United States, the tradition is traced to 'Coxey's Army' in 1894, a 'petition in boots' from Ohio to DC by unemployed workers demanding community facilities and jobs through road building programmes (Barber, 2002). Given 100 years of contrary experience, it is surprising to learn that, before Jacob Coxey, it was illegal for citizens to use the Capitol grounds for political purposes, and that the march was seen as an invasion, a populist mode of action that would fundamentally undermine the principles of the republic (2002: 11–12, 27). Following Coxey, and reinforced by further marches by suffragettes, war veterans, civil rights campaigners, and more, the ceremonial, symbolic spaces of Washington came to be seen as spaces to

---

[7] Most notably some of the protests against the visiting South African rugby team in 1981 (Chapple, 1984), and a number of violent incidents surrounding the 1951 waterfront dispute (Bassett, 1972).

which any member of the American public had a right to use and occupy, setting up a tension between the city's roles as national public space and home for its denizens that lasts to this day. But the point of the march is not just to eyeball the powerful, but to engage with as many people as possible in as many states as possible, gathering supporters along the way; and to generate news coverage that lasts not just for more than the day of a single, static protest, but for the days, weeks, even months of a grand tour.

However, static protests need not just be about a few hours gathered in front of a legislature chanting, waving banners, banging drums, and making speeches. Static protests can last for long periods too, and use a variety of tactics to confront leaders and maintain news coverage. The primary aim of Brian Haw's long-running anti-war protest in London's Parliament Square has been to confront politicians directly with visual images and aural annoyance, 'reminding those in power of the costs of their wars' (www.parliament-square. org.uk). In this Mr Haw and his supporters succeeded spectacularly, filling one side of the square with a huge array of banners and posters and so annoying the government that they tried repeatedly to remove him by a combination of legal instruments, intimidation, and harassment. I will have more to say about those actions later when discussing the policing of protest, and about the sometimes-laudable motivations for wanting to control it, but for now there are two points to make. The first is the degree to which the instruments are targeted at *physical* presence. Part 4 of the Serious Organised Crime and Police Act 2005 (commonly known by its abbreviation, SOCPA) which targeted Mr Haw makes specific mention of 'the number and size of banners or placards used' (Section 134(4)(e)) and largely bans the use of loudspeakers on 'noise nuisance' grounds (Section 137) as ways of controlling the physical impact of his protest. The second point is that while Mr Haw's sprawling protest site was certainly unusual and thus likely to attract media attention in its own right, what has kept it newsworthy has been the astonishingly ham-fisted nature of the attempts to control the scale of protests. As activist Mark Thomas puts it, SOCPA has been a combination of the sinister and the farcical – it has led most famously to a woman being convicted under the act for holding an unauthorized demonstration when she stood next to the war memorial on Whitehall and read out the names of British soldiers killed in Iraq; by failing to act retrospectively, for nearly a year its provisions applied to everyone *except* Mr Haw; it has led to people being threatened with arrest for picnicking with a cake iced with the word 'Peace' (Thomas, 2007); to police not being able to decide whether the wearing of a charity red nose was a demonstration or not.[8] In May 2006, police removed the vast majority of

---

[8] Ireland (2008). See also www.repeal-socpa.info and the Parliament Protest blog at http://parliamentprotest.org.uk

Mr Haw's signs in a pre-dawn raid; in response, artist Mark Wallinger reproduced the display in its entirety and installed it under the title 'State Britain' inside the Tate Britain gallery,[9] such that the raid had the effect of increasing the protest's visibility, not diminishing it. Indeed, the net result of all the efforts to contain Mr Haw's physical occupation of Parliament Square has been to help it spill out of those confines. At the same time, the square has become a focal point for many other interest groups concerned about the erosion of civil liberties in Britain, and to keep it in the news on and off from 2001 until the Labour government was voted out of office in 2010.

One might think that a better strategy, from the state's point of view, would be simply to ignore such long-term, static occupation of public space, and let it fizzle out as familiarity bred popular contempt. For example, consider the Aboriginal Tent Embassy in Canberra. First established by a small group of Northern Territory people in 1972 to protest government inaction on land and resource rights, the Tent Embassy has at various times provoked violent state reaction, broad-based mediation processes, and long stretches of indifference. Despite a few moves, it has been situated for most of its history on a patch of land across the road from the Old Parliament Building (shifted out of the direct line of sight so as not to spoil the view), and comprises a few tents and an old shipping container that served as the main office and reception room until destroyed in an arson attack in 2003. It is now 'part of Canberra's physical and political landscape' (Dow, 2000), but as such has largely lost relevance, something only made worse when parliamentarians moved up the hill to the new building, leaving the embassy to wave its flags in front of what is now a museum and art gallery, a building that is losing its symbolic power. The embassy was never popular with the local Ngunnawal people, some of whom considered it an affront to their standing as traditional custodians of Canberra, and while it has been linked to the successful placement of land rights on the political agenda in Australia, it has gradually lost its significance to white and black Australians following a series of legal decisions and negotiated agreements.

However, ignoring something is not always effective either. Consider the well-known case of the Mothers of Plaza de Mayo who, Torre (1996) argues, were instrumental in undermining the military dictatorship in Argentina because of the persistence of their silent presence in the face of the security forces. Demonstrations were forbidden, so the Mothers did not 'demonstrate' in any standard sense – they quietly walked in pairs around the plaza's central obelisk wearing their distinctive white headscarves, and by doing so every Thursday afternoon for years on end drew local and international attention to

---

[9] http://www.tate.org.uk/britain/exhibitions/wallinger/

their claims. When all other avenues of claim-making were denied them, they used their bodies to occupy public, symbolic space. By walking around that obelisk every week, they 'emplaced' their claims, establishing them among the symbolic associations of that space. Now, there are reasons why the Mothers were successful in that particular context – the symbolic status of the plaza and the norms of respect for motherhood that operated in that time and place came together to make it more difficult for the security forces to intervene – and that should lead us to be wary of generalizations about the effectiveness of silent persistence. The Tiananmen Square occupation of 1989 too was persistent and peaceful, yet the Chinese leadership eventually sent in the tanks and reasserted their dominance not only over the square and protestors' bodies but of the narratives that accumulate around that space. Twenty years on, however, Shanghai protestors are turning to a variety of the same tactic, the 'collective walk', in which large numbers of people simply gather together to occupy space, drawing attention to the scale of their displeasure not by holding a (forbidden) demonstration, but simply by coordinating a stroll in the centre of town (Li, 2009: 79). The particular context of the time and place matters at least as much as the physical constraints of the space.

* * * * *

That last point about tactical flexibility raises the objection that many raise to the thoughts in this chapter: that these variations in the physical spaces of capital cities do not matter very much. Ironically, it is the opposite objection to the one most raise to the thoughts in the other chapters – surely variations in those contexts matter quite a lot! Still, it is not the case that there is substantially less contentious politics in those places that have no single site for protest, or whose major site is somehow divorced from the sites of the formal public sphere. Activists work with the places they have; they do not just give up and go away when unable to find a plaza in front of the presidential palace or a marching route conducive to high visibility. However, it *is* the case that the space available has an impact of which of the tools in their political repertoire activists select (Tilly and Tarrow, 2007: 16–17), and this in turn has an effect on the kinds of impacts they can have on particular audiences. Politicians, for instance, seem not to like being confronted directly; they expend an awful lot of effort keeping protest at arm's length. Everything said so far about symbolic communication[10] would suggest that this is because politicians want to control the messages that their physical settings send, something that is disrupted when activists have the temerity to unfurl their

---

[10] Not only in this work but by Pitkin (1967), Weber et al. (1978), Edelman (1988), Barker (2001), Hajer (2009), and any number of scholars of symbolic politics.

banners on politicians' buildings. Of course, leaders themselves usually make a different claim, to do with protecting the peace and quiet needed for effective working (interviews, parliamentary officers in Ottawa and Wellington); or the dignity of the formal institutions (e.g. Parliament of Australia, 2007). In London, the effort that has gone into removing one man and his extensive construction of tents, banners, and placards has been extraordinary. The mere fact that politicians dislike it so much says that it matters; the people *should* be able to confront their leaders and make them uncomfortable; politicians *should* be forced to deal with the physical manifestation of the distress that people feel over their actions. For that reason alone, my account of democracy puts positive value on cities that have spaces where direct confrontation is possible and permitted. That means in principle positively valuing Ottawa, Mexico City, Washington, Wellington, and Berlin, with their open and accessible spaces closely surrounding the main sites of the formal public sphere; disliking the restricted or fragmented spaces of Tokyo, London, and Canberra (especially given Canberra's isolation from the major population and media centres); and being more ambivalent about Cape Town, Athens, Hong Kong, and Santiago. I will provide more of an evaluation in the final chapter when all the threads are drawn together.

Now, it will be clear from these examples that the pressure on decision-makers comes not just from the direct confrontation preferred by Brian Haw, but from the fact that confrontation attracts the attention of others: fellow citizens, journalists, campaigners, bloggers, and so forth who, if they care about the issue at hand, will start generating their own communication about the subject. It might be that they transmit the claims being made by the protestor; it might be that they disagree with those claims and rather transmit alternative claims, or dismissive gestures, but which, even if they do not advocate the same position on an issue, nonetheless widen the degree to which the issue is discussed. Given that, it is clear that using relatively 'formal' sites of protest, next to the sites of the formal public sphere, is just one means to that particular end, and that there are many other sites that can be used to attract media attention. Commercial centres, major roads, parks, or the workplaces of specifically targeted organizations might all be used, so long as the cameras can get to those sites fairly easily, or so long as citizen-journalists are around and can make their own footage – from mobile phones and iPods more often than traditional cameras – available to mass media. Remember too, however, that attracting media attention is just one of the aims of protest organizers. For some of the other purposes, the symbolic messages of the stage matters, and we will see a few more reasons for that by examining what happens when access is closed off to stages that use the formal public sphere as a backdrop. One of the ways in which that closure happens is through the privatization of public space.

Privatizing Space

The privatization of public space has attracted much discussion in the literature. The major points are these: there is space that *appears* to be public in sense 1 in that it seems to be open and accessible; and that might, because it is often full of fellow citizens, be useful in sense 4 for engaging with those citizens in some kind of public narration or claim-making; but that is really only public in sense 3, having common impacts. In every other way it is private space: privately owned, privately controlled, with only limited kinds of people allowed in and public, political purposes forbidden.

One of the common examples of this kind of space is the shopping mall. Barber (2001) is one of many writers who argue that when shoppers and shopping moved from Main Street to The Mall, what got left behind was public, civic space, space for encountering each other as citizen rather than dodging and competing with each other for goods and services. Shopping, on this account, used to be just one of several things that drew people into spaces that were controlled by publicly accountable authorities; classic plazas with a town square in front of the town hall; with shops side-by-side not just with cafes and barbers but local representatives' offices and libraries; with places to sit and feed the birds, play chess, kick a ball, and talk to the neighbours. Now, goes the argument, shopping and civic encounter have been divorced. Citizen-led political activity is explicitly forbidden in such spaces, and while elected politicians are often allowed to press the flesh in election campaigns, the unelected are usually barred from doing the same. Seating is removed, often to stop allegedly threatening youngsters and homeless people from congregating, but also because sitting people do not shop. Perhaps Barber's 'decline and fall' story is a little romanticized, but the overall point about commercially designed space is still valid. Dovey (1999: 130) describes the result thus:

> The mall is a clean and highly designed place in contrast to a sometimes derelict context. It embodies the signifiers of class – terrazzo paving, brass and glass – and there are no signs of poverty. The mall creates a purified environment, not only physically and climatically, but also socially. The mall offers at least the illusion of a vital public life and harmonious community.... The mall establishes its meaning in opposition to the perceived dereliction, danger, placelessness and alienation of the public realm. Indeed, the more the public places of our cities decline in quality and safety, the greater the relative advantage of the private mall.

The mall is just one example of this particular drive that classifies and stratifies citizens as employees and shoppers. Other features achieve the same end. One such is the 'skyways' of Minneapolis which stratify people into street-class and upper-class (Byers, 1998), with besuited office workers and (certain kinds of) shoppers having privileged access to the intricate network of bridges and first-floor shopping spaces, unmonitored or unhindered by the private security guards employed by the building owners. Other shoppers, politically-active citizens, the down-and-out and otherwise marginal tend to use the city streets, a cold and forbidding prospect in the Minnesota winter, but an alienating experience at any time of year. Even Nicollet Mall, the central, pedestrianized shopping street, has a clear upstairs/downstairs divide that was instantly noticeable to me as an outsider the first time I walked along it. Other means include the use of zoning laws, the private purchase of once-public land, and the gated community movement, which similarly privatizes streets in the name of security (Low, 2006). The point to emphasize is that while cities like Minneapolis certainly possess space of the kind I am advocating here – the streets themselves, and Government Plaza between City Hall and the county government office tower – these spaces have become marginalized, and public claim-making in terms of direct engagement with fellow citizens delegitimized. Dovey (1999: 126) suggests that this may well have been the opposite of the intentions of Victor Gruen, the planner credited with designing the modern mall. Gruen was interested in creating spaces where car-dependent suburbanites could rediscover community; what he delivered was pseudo-community, an anaesthetic, an apolitical therapy (see also Kohn, 2004). The road to this particular hell was paved with good intentions as well as terrazzo.

This situation has not gone uncontested in the United States. Particularly important has been a series of attempts at federal and then state level to designate malls as public forums and thus spaces where First Amendment freedoms of expression and assembly are protected. However, Zick (2009: 145–61) – in an excellent book – tells what is, from the present normative standpoint, the sad tale of how, in 1972, the US Supreme Court upheld a very limited right to picket a specific place of work, but otherwise upheld property rights over first amendment rights, holding that malls were private spaces whose primary purpose was profit-making in a 'controlled, carefree environment' (407 U.S. 553, 1972); that they and many other spaces – transport terminals, for instance – do not have and cannot ever gain the character of 'traditional' or 'immemorial' public forums and thus expression in them cannot be given basic protection under the US constitution. They thus implicitly applied an extremely limited definition of public space, focusing on type 4 space for public claim-making, yet limiting that further by applying an ownership criterion. The result is that one cannot even conduct voter registration drives in most American malls, let alone actively campaign for a candidate or on an issue. This applies to any new kind of space, and to any privatized space. As business consortiums take over the management of many open city

163

spaces in the United States, the spaces available for purposive expression and civic engagement are becoming fewer.

The gradual transformation of people from citizen to consumer is something that is pervading many kinds of public life. One of my interviewees talked about convention centres charging full rates for political purposes that once were free. It used to be something that was considered good corporate citizenship but now is a business opportunity, especially when public engagement itself is seen as a business like any other. Likewise, businesses are taking on the language and symbolism of publicness while providing little of its reality. Take, for example, the promotional campaign for a new shopping and residential development I saw in downtown Minneapolis whose strapline was 'creating community', or the shopping area in the skyways called 'Gaviidae Commons'.

This is not just a US phenomenon. When I visited in 2008, there was a building on the north-west corner of Syntagma Square in Athens which proudly called itself 'The Public', dressed in the orange livery of central and eastern European democracy movements, but basically a music, books, and IT shop with a small espresso bar on one level. There is 'The Forum', a small amphitheatre-type space between two of Hong Kong's World Trade Centre tower blocks, which is really just a place for office workers to eat their lunch; it is certainly *not* a space for public deliberation. Note too the appropriation not just of democratic language but pseudo-classical language, attempting to give the new and commercial an aura of antiquity and civic duty.[11] Similar problems occur in Canada, where one activist reported having to seek permission from local business owners' associations before they could demonstrate outside big hotels, convention centres, or even ordinary city streets, because of the particular extension of property rights onto the sidewalk that is upheld in the Canadian context. Likewise, some Wellingtonians complain about the commercialization and subsequent restrictions on the use of what once was fairly free, unconstrained waterfront space. The same story is heard in Tokyo, in Berlin, in Santiago, and all over the world.

Space for the pressing of public claims is problematic not just because politicians often want to insulate themselves from such claims; not just because suitable spaces might not be large enough or close enough to have an impact; and not just because some spaces' physical features militate against effective, large-scale expression; but because the entire ideal of the citizen as a purposive claim-maker is being undermined, to be replaced by the idealized citizen-shopper, who expresses him or herself purely through his or her purchases and presence in fashionable places, acting as what Benjamin

---

[11] For an entertaining but nonetheless insightful discussion of the appropriation of classical and other high-status symbolism in America, see Eco (1986).

(1999) called the *flâneur*. This is perhaps the more important challenge to space for making public claims; not just that its availability is more limited, but that the very performance of important public roles has become delegitimized in public discourse. Who cares about the public plaza as democratic stage when few value the performances enacted on it? This, I suggest, helps explain why it is that city authorities the world over have embraced forms of public spatial design that discourage the large-scale pressing of public claims, and encourage sitting with a sandwich. This is a movement that some writers on urban design have been complicit in: fixated on an account of the public whose emblem is unscripted encounters with strangers, they have recommended spatial design approaches that play into the delegitimization of scripted, purposive, democratic claim-making.

This is also one reason why those people who *do* occasionally want to press public claims face not just challenges of staging, but of access to those stages. I approach those issues by looking at the policing of politics.

Policing Politics

The policing of protest has rocketed up the media agenda in several nations in the last ten years, first in relation to a series of anti-globalization/anti-capitalist confrontations including the 'Battle of Seattle' in 1999 and the G20 Summit protests in London in 2009; and second in the aftermath of the 11 September 2001 terrorist attacks on New York and Washington, DC and the subsequent anti-war protests. The first set of protests have been seen as particularly significant because they led to a re-evaluation of what had been the dominant mode of policing protest for twenty years, negotiated management, something that has been seen as central to the reduction in violence of police–protestor interactions since the late 1960s (della Porta and Reiter, 1998; Soule and Davenport, 2009). Indeed, Waddington (1994) argues that this approach has allowed for the vast majority of protest to pass off peacefully, in an atmosphere of facilitation, even 'fun', as I witnessed when I visited City Hall in Mexico City and watched as protestors and a wall of police officers protecting the building laughed and joked with each other in between the serious business of slogan-shouting and drum beating.

Still, while negotiation about, even collaborative management of, protest continues, the model presumes the existence of organizations with whom police can negotiate, organizations that can direct and discipline their members (King and Waddington, 2005). This is not the case with many protests – there is no one organizer, no one manager. This is not just a matter of having protests in which there are groups actively hostile to the idea that the police should determine access to and claim-making in supposedly public streets

(Noakes et al., 2005). It is also the case that the lone, occasionally active citizen is not recognized in this model. For example, in Washington, DC, one must apply for permission to hold a protest, but figuring who to apply to, on what form, by what deadline, and with what information can be a daunting task given the sheer number of organizations that have overlapping jurisdiction over public space in the federal capital. Given the nature of the spaces involved, this often includes the National Parks Service, which owns around a quarter of the land in the District of Columbia, rather than the DC government; and one or more of a multitude of overlapping security services, including the Secret Service, the DC Metro Police, the Capitol Police and the Parks Police. While the American Civil Liberties Union produces a guide to managing these processes – although one seemingly not available on the organization's own website, www.aclu.org – it would be very easy for the ordinary citizen to fall foul of them. There are different deadlines by which applications must be filed, for instance; and there is no line on the sidewalk designating this stretch of Pennsylvania Avenue as falling under this jurisdiction, but that stretch falling under another; nor could there be, because the regimes differ not just by physical location but by issue and event type as well (Mitchell and Staeheli, 2005). Other permit regimes make similar presumptions that protest implies the organization, resources, and corporate knowledge required to figure out the sometimes-Byzantine rules and act on them. And this is at least partly why the Metropolitan Police in London tie themselves in knots over what individual actions – wearing a charity red nose, icing a cake – constitute a protest, and thus what requires prior approval from the Commissioner.

Given what police leaders around the world saw as the failure of this model to control violence at Seattle, Genoa, and elsewhere, the policing approach now is characterized by a mix of three elements: (*a*) the old negotiated management model; (*b*) the identification, containment, and isolation of potential troublemakers; and (*c*) pressing the very design of public space into service. The second element has attracted the most attention from the media and, to a certain extent, criminologists and sociologists of policing. The issues here are fairly straightforward. 'Trouble' gets defined in terms of potential threat to officers on the ground (Earl and Soule, 2006), and that threat perception is connected with perceptions of the kinds of people attracted to a given issue, based on experience of prior encounters (King and Waddington, 2005). The resulting judgements are often over-broad caricatures (Gorringe and Rosie, 2008) that can seem blackly humorous – because police forces have encountered deliberately transgressive action (which, *nota bene*, is not necessarily violence) at, say, environmental actions, they are now much more likely to treat any environmental group as a threat and any discussions of protest, or even owning copies of a mainstream political magazine, *The New Statesman*, as evidence of intent to cause trouble.[12] When it comes to protest, this kind of information is used to justify pre-emptive arrest, the creation of heavily fortified 'free speech zones', and what in Britain is called 'kettling' – the surrounding and isolation of troublesome groups, preventing them from reaching and using symbolically useful stages. Because troublemakers are identified the way they are, these tactics are applied to a great deal more people than the rock-and-bomb throwers, and while the death of a bystander at hands of police at the London G20 protests has led to efforts to rework some of these tactics in *some* cities (HMIC, 2009; Rosie and Gorringe, 2009), they, and the intelligence-gathering processes that support them, are still widely applied.

While there are all sorts of fascinating avenues that could be explored here, for my purposes the point to stress is the degree to which this kind of action is about controlling and countering staging, and thus the symbolic messages that are conveyed to attentive audiences. Versteeg and Hajer (2009) use precisely this approach to analyse the G20 events, revealing the lengths that political leaders went to establish themselves on symbolically redolent stages in an attempt to boost the credibility of their claims that a 'new world order' was being fashioned behind the closed doors of the summit. In response, various protest groups tried to commandeer those stages; when they were prevented from doing so, they attempted to 'upstage' the officials, and in this were partly successful. Why 'partly'? Because the policing of protest became the story, not the original claims and counterclaims that brought the G20 leaders and the protestors to the streets of London in the first place. What was emplaced was a set of debates about access to public space and the rights of citizenship. Similar police reactions in other cities have provoked similar debates: the policing of the Republican Party Convention in New York in August 2004, or the Asia-Pacific Economic Cooperation (APEC) meeting in Vancouver in 1997, for example. The official response to attempts to upstage leaders' presentations itself becomes the source of new public claims, although at the expense of the original arguments about globalization, capitalism, and the environment.

This analysis, however, makes the third element of the new approach more troubling. The spaces of cities themselves have become part of the control mechanisms; the streetscape has been 'deputized' (Krieger, 2003). Because it employs indirect means – bollards, building 'set-backs', seemingly natural barriers, lighting, surveillance points, and so on – it is less obvious, less visible, easily taken-for-granted, and thus less likely to provoke a public reaction and a

---

[12] Porter (2009).Video of the seizure of 'political material', including the *New Statesman*, referred to in Porter's column, is available from http://www.guardian.co.uk/environment/video/2009/apr/19/police-activism For a discussion of the impact of state surveillance on campaigning organizations in the United States, see Starr et al. (2008).

set of public claims. While urban geographers, sociologists, and some architectural theorists – but not political scientists, in the main – have noticed and roundly condemned these methods, they have largely gone unremarked in wider public debate except in their crude forms.

The 'crude' forms include things described in Chapter six: concrete or plastic Jersey barriers slapped up hurriedly around US government buildings following the Beirut and Oklahoma City bombings, then in many other cities following 9/11. Benton-Short (2007: 424) neatly sketches the situation and general reaction:

> On 20 January 2005, at his second inauguration, President George W Bush took the oath of office and delivered a speech forcefully enunciating principles of extending democracy, freedom, and liberty throughout the world. This event took place amidst bollards, barriers, sentry boxes, more than 13 000 soldiers and police officers, and miles of security fences. The irony was not hard to miss.

In the public spaces around many of the buildings of the formal public sphere, some of the crudeness has been tidied up, but the key elements remain. The traffic barriers close to the Capitol now fall back into recesses in the roadway; the Jersey barriers along Constitution and Independence Avenues now sport pseudo-classical design features and planters in their tops, the flowers serving to prettify what is still basically an anti-car-bomb device (Figure 7.4). In many cities, roads have been closed, fences made more permanent, and surveillance cameras proliferate.

However, the crude barrier approach is gradually giving way to softer, more subtle means of protecting public buildings. One way of doing this is to disguise barriers not with flowers but as public art – one of the best examples comes from New York where massive bollards in Wall Street are designed as if they were somehow an avant-garde artistic installation than an anti-terrorist device. In Wellington too, there are bollards shaped like fern fronds, the softness of the shape belying the hardness of the barrier. But more subtlety again is found in documents like the National Capital Urban Design and Security Plan for Washington, DC (NCPC, 2005), which sets out a number of tactics for securing public sites without jersey barriers by

- increasing building set-backs from the footpath and roadway;
- using trees, seating, planters, bollards and streetlamps as replacements for barriers; and
- using low retaining walls around monuments in open spaces to prevent car access.

A very similar plan was released almost simultaneously in Australia (National Capital Authority, 2003), which was no coincidence, as there is extensive collaboration between federal zone authorities in Canberra, Ottawa, and

Figure 7.4. Disguised Jersey barriers outside the Smithsonian, Washington, DC
Author photo.

Washington. Other design elements can be used as well – in Seattle, lots of breaks in level, furniture and fountains are used to break up space so that large crowds cannot easily manoeuvre in them, and to provide bastions behind which security forces can protect buildings and businesses.

Now, from a 'pressing public claims' point of view, some of these barriers might not be particularly objectionable on their own. Low retaining walls might stop cars but not protestors on foot, while increasing set-backs could be a positive move if it increased the amount of flat, open space in front of buildings that could be used for demonstrations. This is one of the major problems in Central Hong Kong: land values being what they are, open space is a luxury in which property developers rarely indulge. Thus, the de facto offices of the Beijing administration are in a building in Sheung Wan with a tiny set-back on a busy road with a flyover right outside, and so the area is able to hold no more than a few dozen people in any safety.[13] However, where set-backs are provided, they are *not* made available for claim-making purposes – they are fenced off, patrolled by guards, and overlooked by security cameras – while the other techniques can be used to render space useless for gatherings of more than a few thousand people, and thus useless for some of the reasons that protest organizers still value the mass demonstration.

Conclusions

To conclude, let us go back to the key question that underlies this chapter: why should democrats value public spaces that are both large and next to legislatures? In Chapter four, I argued that there are four answers to that question: presence, attention, membership, and dignity. One needs large spaces to impress upon target audiences – decision-makers, media, other citizens, other states – the scale of public displeasure on an issue. Protests are often dismissed by the powerful when they do not attract people in large numbers or from a broad enough spectrum of society, but in some cities, these dismissive acts are easier than in others, simply because their major forums cannot hold anything like enough people. While 'enough' is clearly a matter of context, filling a large plaza with hundreds of thousands of people is much harder to dismiss than a few hardy souls; although likewise, a persistent few, who occupy space over long, long periods of time, can prove just as effective, especially when the state massively overreacts. But whether it is small scale or large scale, one-off or long-standing, protest in places of national significance is important not just for making claims, but to cloak those claims in the symbols of national importance and dignity, and for reasons of democratic narration. Protest in such sites helps people feel that they are not alone, that others share their views, and that it is OK – even right and just – to express those views in public.

I have also argued that these needs stand in tension with at least one other significant consideration, and that is the dangers of ritualization. Ritualization makes control easier, and can lead to protest losing its impact. Protest can become so commonplace that it either fades into the background, or onlookers simply take in the membership cues and not the substantive points that the protestors are trying to make.

---

[13] A 'Democracy Now!' protest on 1 January 2010 managed around a thousand – estimates varied – but that is an extraordinary number given the tiny space available (*South China Morning Post*, www.scmp.com).

Hong Kong protestors have overcome this to a certain extent by having two shared national days of protest, made easier by the fact that in Hong Kong there is one big issue: the relationship between liberal Hong Kong and a potentially, and sometimes actually, repressive government in Beijing. They also have two days, 4 June and 1 July, that symbolize that relationship because they are the anniversaries of key events that shape that relationship, namely the Tiananmen Square massacre and the 1997 handover. These features make it easier to get otherwise-disparate protest groups to work together and focus their energies on two key moments. But over time, those dates will probably lose some of their power. May Day marches used to be both widespread and huge; nowadays, they are seen as anachronistic in many cities.

Ritualization is not the only danger, however. Privatization and the policing of public space is having significant impacts on people's ability, perhaps propensity, to engage with the public sphere as citizens rather than as shoppers, sports fans, consumers, *flâneurs*. While the *Landsgemeinden* cantons in Switzerland have problems of their own, this is one major benefit of the annual gathering of citizens in the *Landsgemeindeplatz* every year: it shows people, physically and visibly, performing their citizenship role. This, it seems to me, is very important in a mediatized, digitized, and privatized era in which the only other times one encounters crowds is when those crowds are accidental, as in lots of individuals shopping in the same area; or leisurely, when crowds gather at sporting venues or parks for a good fireworks display. Without that, citizenship can easily be shifted online, such that people never *see* each other acting in concert on public, political issues, and that matters because it helps further delegitimize politics, and democratic engagement along with it. This issue of meeting the public is a major theme of the next chapter.

Active citizens are responding to all this in various ways. There are long-standing attempts in the United States to revisit the Supreme Court judgements on political activity in space that is, or should be, public on every one of my criteria (Barber, 2001; Zick, 2009). Protestors themselves are responding by using mixed methods: not just large-scale protests in the usual sites for purposes of visibility, dignity, and membership but also actions that target specific sites in order to upstage the performances of elites (Maddison and Scalmer, 2006; Versteeg and Hajer, 2009). In some cities, counterpublics have tried to set up sanctuaries and no-go areas, with more or less success. In my sample, these include the Exarchia area in central Athens, full of squats and communes and the flashpoint of just about any of the major confrontations that have rocked the city in recent years. Kreuzberg in Berlin fulfils a similar role every May Day. Outside my cases, notable examples include the Haight Ashbury area of San Francisco; The Block in Redfern, Sydney, one of the few aboriginal-dominant urban areas in

Australia, and frequent scene of conflicts between residents and police; and the once-self-governing but increasingly state-managed Christiana in Copenhagen. There are ideas at the other end of the direct confrontation scale, including movements to create new commons through such things as urban gardens and small-scale and small-number experiments with participatory planning and architecture (Towers, 1995; Cybriwsky, 1999).

The aim of these movements is to put residents in the driver's seat when it comes to the built environment rather than urban regimes of planners, developers, businesses, and architects. But what they tend not to do is successfully defend traditional, highly symbolic plazas. That, I think, is a great pity. Democrats should celebrate the Brian Haws of this world, willing to put everything on the line to defend people's right to act not as mere consumers but as active citizens, getting under the skins of the powerful. What we need less of is mendacious public space like the current state of the Australian Parliament House, full of symbolic gestures to openness and the primacy of the people, but too remote from them, and too full of mechanisms that aid the control of citizens with a point to make.

8

The City as Representative Space

There is more to political life than yelling at one's leaders; there is more to life than politics; and yet the distribution of those things that make for a good life is itself a political matter. One of the things that make life in cities more or less pleasant is the presence of public facilities: space to sit and space to run; libraries; trains, buses and trams; and park benches, drinking fountains, and clean public toilets. Another is the degree to which we feel 'home' in a place, and that is not just a function of who we know in that place, but how well we know it, what we experience in it, and the degree to which our memories and narratives are associated with its natural and built environment.

What worries many writers on the urban experience is that the freedom to enjoy the city is more restricted than appearances might suggest. There are places that appear open but in which one meets a much more narrow slice of society than if it really were fully accessible. There are places that are controlled not by their denizens but by much more limited elites, property developers, investors, business associations, and their friends in local government and local police who tear down and rebuild the city to suit their interests, or who sometimes set troubling limits on what kinds of actions are permissible and what are not. There are places whose residents are cutting themselves off from city membership behind gates, walls, and razor-wire fences. All this worries urbanists of a democratic bent for two main reasons. First, it means that the very fabric of cities stratifies people, meeting some needs but not others, often the needs of those who are not democratically accountable to others, and thus not easily changed. Second, urbanists worry that this leads to a fragmentation of the *demos* and a loss of fellow feeling, such that the stratification comes to be seen as justified because 'we' have nothing in common with 'them'; that 'they' need to be controlled and quarantined, not included and engaged; and certainly not deliberated with.

In this chapter, I am going to look at some of those issues of stratification and fragmentation through the particular lens of representation: what kinds of claims are made about the make-up of the *demos* in capital cities? I start by

173

looking at spaces for meeting the public – the major places within cities where people meet, talk, discuss and debate – and also spaces to which people flee in order to escape from each other. I then move on to explore a series of cases of naming and memorializing in the cities under study, something that reveals a great deal more complexity. In both these discussions, the common thread is the idea that a city's residents feel themselves to be not just denizens but empowered citizens when they see others like them being taken seriously in the public realm; and when they recognize and feel themselves to be part of the public narratives that accrete around elements of the built environment.

In Chapter seven the emphasis was on 'external' forces like privatization, bureaucratization and policing, associated with the liberal state, that restrict access to public space. While those forces still matter in the structuring of space and the kinds of activity that can be pursued in it (Stevens, 2007), in this chapter the focus is more 'internal', looking at the competing motivations that city publics bring to public space, and the conflicts that arise as a result.

Meeting the Public

The idea of 'meeting the public' would not have struck an ancient Athenian as a particularly odd one. He (and a member of the Athenian *demos* was invariably male) could see a reasonable proportion – something like 10–30 per cent – of his fellow citizens more than once a month on the hill of the Pnyx for gatherings of the *Ecclesia*, and thus knew a good proportion of them by sight if nothing else (Figure 8.1).[1] For the modern citizen of Appenzell Inner-rhodes, the idea is just as natural: one sees around half of 'the people' every year during the *Landsgemeinde*. But in both cases the *demos* is a fairly homogenous thing. In Athens, there were big class and wealth divisions among citizens, but otherwise the citizenry excluded a great deal more than it included (Sinclair, 1991) – women, slaves, and a fairly expansive category of those who counted as foreigners. The Appenzeller *Volk* is nowhere near as exclusive as that, although women were excluded right up until 1990 when a Federal Supreme Court decision forced a change, while 'foreigners' – small in number but an

---

[1] Estimates of *Ecclesia* attendance are notoriously shaky. Total citizenry figures are best modern estimates rather than contemporary censuses, and vary enormously, from circa 60,000 citizens to perhaps fewer than 20,000, with the vagaries of disease and war. The quorum for some decisions, but by no means all, was 6,000; and this is the estimated *seated* capacity of the Pnyx; which gives my range of 10–30 per cent. Sinclair (1991: 114–19), however, argues that the quorum may have been more conventional than actual; that for many issues, at different seasons, and in different periods the attendance was probably much lower; but that for some decisions the likely *standing* attendance was a great deal higher. The surviving evidence provides little other than hints either way.

Figure 8.1. The Pnyx, from the speakers' platform or *bema*, with the Areopagus in the middle distance and the Acropolis behind
Author photo.

expansive concept in a *ius sanguinis*[2] country like Switzerland – remain excluded.

Political pollsters get to meet random samples occasionally. The convenors of large scale, randomly selected deliberative events often tell tales of how interesting it is to see a random sample in all its diversity (e.g. Fishkin, 1997). But otherwise, the most that the vast majority of citizens of national-scale democracies get to experience is either meeting the public of a relatively small locality, or a mosaic built up of lots of different experiences at different places and times, or very occasional glimpses of the scale and diversity of the public at a particular moment.

For both large-scale occasions and the mosaic of small-scale experiences, it is easy to mistake the presence of some diversity for full representativeness. The crowds at President Obama's inauguration (see Chapter five) were seen as coming close, but there was no demographic survey done and so no way of knowing. Other political events that get closest to full representativeness across a range of physical, cultural, economic, and political attributes have

---

[2] 'Blood law', or citizenship by descent, as opposed to *ius solis*, 'soil law', citizenship by place of birth. For discussion of the historical development and structure of competing citizenship concepts in Europe, see Singer (1996). For discussion of who should make up the *demos*, see Chapter two.

included some of the 2003 protests against the Iraq war, although that depended on the particular context, and even then the better-educated dominated significantly (Walgrave and Verhulst, 2009). While the numbers and diversity of people engaging in protest are increasing, nonetheless it remains the case that on most issues in most contexts, protestors are not going to be a fully representative sample of society, despite what can appear to casual observers and participants themselves as enormous variety in dress, accent, employment, and party political allegiance. Other kinds of events can appear to be highly inclusive, yet mask important exclusions. For example, Canada Day celebrations at Parliament Hill and Confederation Square attract around 70,000 participants with Canadians in all their variety apparently gathered together, yet the National Capital Commission (interview) reported that so-called 'new Canadians' are somewhat over-represented on the day, while First Nations and Québecois are significantly underrepresented. In London, some media observers have remarked on the changes to the Notting Hill Carnival, first set up in 1966 by local West Indian residents in an area that was a by-word for inner-city racial tension (for a detailed description, see Thompsett, 2005). However, the event has gradually become more and more part of the mainstream London events calendar, attracting a global tourist audience; while the demographics of the area have changed dramatically with steady gentrification, to the point that 'Notting Hill' no longer denotes edgy immigrant territory but romantic comedy actors and the Conservative Party leadership.

Apart from those large-scale events, the mosaics of impressions of the public are developed in ways that are many and varied. In Tokyo, one of the public spaces where communities gather for all sorts of purposes is the local shrine. This is not just a religious centre; indeed, applying the term 'religion' to Shinto and popular spiritual practice is problematic in itself. Rather, it is a centre for community life, a blend of an English village hall, shop and local church, because the sacred permeates Japanese life in a way that it does not for most Westerners (Grapard, 1982). It is a place where one goes to perform rituals and to pray, certainly, but also where the retired go for art classes, where mothers and nannies sit and talk while the children tear around in the outer courtyard, where students go to read and where office workers go for a few moments of relative peace. The experience of sitting in a local shrine is like sitting in a small inner-city park in Central New York – a small piece of community space surrounded by offices, apartment buildings and busy city streets. It is public space in all four senses, because it is openly accessible to all who want to enter; it is supported by donations from local people and local businesses; it has common impacts in that it is a centre for community symbols and the reverence of ancestors and spirits, as well as providing general meeting space; and it is space where public roles are performed, particularly narration of daily collective experience and expression of identity.

At community shrines, one might well encounter a reasonably broad cross-section of that community; but only that community. In fairly homogenous Japan, that might not matter all that much, but in cities with big divides between rich and poor, black and white, male and female, and so on, it would matter a great deal if the only spaces available for meeting the public were these local ones for local public spheres. And thus it is for a great many of the relatively open public spaces in many localities. Even where there are no private security officers keeping away 'undesirables', still a village market in rural North Yorkshire is a very, very different place from the Queen's Crescent Market in Gospel Oak, London, say, while the market in Gospel Oak is very different from one in Islington. This is because these sites are embedded in larger social structures, which means that the denizens of Gospel Oak – a working class and immigrant enclave sandwiched between wealthy Belsize Park and Hampstead – are very different from those in the rapidly gentrifying Islington, let alone those in monocultural, rural North Yorkshire. And thus the denizens of rural North Yorkshire – conservative with a small and capital 'C' – have a very different picture of the *demos* than the denizens of Gospel Oak. Which of these pictures has normative value – which is represented in television dramas, in the pages of the newspapers, and so on – adds another level of complexity, but the contention here is that the range of people that we meet and interact with every day has an important impact on our conception of who counts as a fellow citizen, and thus whose claims we take seriously in the public sphere.

The same applies to what we might think of as mobile public space: the public transport network. When it comes to democracy, public transport is important for three reasons. First, and rather obviously, it transports people into and out of city centres so that they can meet and engage with each other. Second, it is one of the sites where one gets a visual impression of the variety of the *demos*. And third, in many places it constitutes a part of the public sphere itself. As Swiss friends have pointed out to me, elected officials in the federal government often travel by train, and on those trains are often drawn into political discussions with their fellow passengers. However, again one's impression of the *demos* will be very different depending on whether one travels first or second class; on an intercity or local train; what time of the day one travels (with the commuters, with retired folk, after school, on a Saturday before the big football games, on a Sunday morning). At least Swiss trains are reasonably accessible; others are not, so even if one travels at a variety of times by train, one would not encounter disabled people in many cities.

Relative cost is a major factor in the stratification of the *demos* on a train. Table 8.1 gives a rough comparison of the costs of doing a simple journey by metro in each of the cities under study, and they reveal some wide variation,

177

Table 8.1. Affordability of public transport: minutes to earn a ride[a]

Rank	City	Mode	Fare	Fare type	USD fare	USD wage	Ratio	Minutes to earn
1	Mexico	Metro	$3.00	Standard fare	0.25	1.80	0.1389	8.3
2	Cape Town	Metrorail	R5.50	Cape Town to Bellville	0.75	5.10	0.1471	8.8
3	Tokyo	Metro	¥230	12–19 kilometres regular fare	2.46	15.70	0.1567	9.4
4	Washington, DC	Metro	$3.17	Median fare	3.17	19.00	0.1668	10.0
5	Hong Kong	MTR	$11.50	Central to Tsuen Wan	1.48	8.00	0.1850	11.1
6	Berlin	U-Bahn	€2.10	Zones A and B fare	2.86	13.70	0.2088	12.5
7	Canberra	Action bus	$3.80	Standard fare	3.55	14.00	0.2536	15.2
8	Ottawa	OC Transpo bus	$3.25	Standard fare	3.25	12.80	0.2539	15.2
9	Santiago	Metro	$470	Rush hour fare	0.91	3.10	0.2935	17.6
10	Wellington	Metlink	$4.50	Zone 4 basic fare	3.20	8.40	0.3810	22.9
11	London	Underground	£4.00	Standard fare	6.17	13.90	0.4439	26.6

[a] The table ranks cities based on a ratio of the cost of a ride on public transport relative to the average hourly wage. 'Minutes to earn' is the time it would take someone on the mean hourly wage to earn the fare. The mode is underground railway, except for Canberra and Ottawa, which are pretty much bus-only systems; Cape Town, where I have used overground rail; and Wellington, where there is an integrated rail and bus system. The fares are all basic, walk-up adult fares; in some cases (e.g. Mexico), they are the only fares available; in other cases (e.g. London), there are several alternatives, most of which are cheaper, some considerably so. Where there is a difference between the off-peak and rush-hour fare, I have used the latter. Where there is a zone system, I have used the middle zone; for example, Zone A+B fares for Berlin, the 12–19 kilometres fare for Tokyo and the Zone 4 fare for Wellington. Where prices are calculated between individual stations, as in Hong Kong and Cape Town, I have selected a station approximately half way between the centre and the end of the network. Zones and networks, of course, vary considerably in extent and price differential. Fares are converted to US dollars using the xe.com rate at 2:00 p.m., 14 April 2010. Wages are hourly means, in US dollars, net of taxes, calculated by the bank UBS (2009). Every one of these decisions creates problems – for a discussion of many of the problems involved in calculating equity in transport, see Litman (2007).

with it taking a Londoner on the average hourly wage more than three times as long as a Mexican to earn the price of a trip on the underground. While in some countries there is a prejudice that public transport is for the poor – the well-off drive – in other places the poor cannot afford public transport either, and must either walk or be excluded from the central spaces of the public sphere. In my sample, the difference between Mexico and Santiago is especially striking. The Mexico City system is cheap, and all lines seemingly used by a very wide variety of people, from civil servants to street cleaners and many further down the socio-economic ladder. In Santiago, by contrast, the lines seemed clearly stratified, with the white upper-middle classes dominating Line 1 that links the city centre with the eastern suburbs, Lines 2 and 3 seemingly having an entirely different clientele made up of the working classes, but neither having many indigenous passengers. Now, this is partly to do with the striking degree of economic clustering one finds in Santiago (Dockemdorff et al., 2000; Tomic and Trumper, 2005), with Line 1 serving wealthy areas along the city's east–west axis and Lines 2 and 3 linking less-well-off ones on the north–south axis. But it is also to do with the relative expense of the system: in Table 8.1, Santiago has the third cheapest ticket price but is the third least affordable. These facts combine to mean that those whose daily commute is on Line 1 from, say, leafy Los Leones to an office near La Moneda, would have an impression of the Chilean people as being a fairly prosperous, fashionably dressed lot. It does not take much to imagine the subsequent indignant shock felt by the comfortable middle classes when the 'Indios' start agitating for land rights down the main street. They never even rub shoulders with each other, let alone engage seriously with each other, and I will discuss more how that might matter at the end of the next section.

One could find many different examples of this stratification. As noted in Chapter four, Cape Town still struggles under the weight of apartheid planning laws, dividing black from white from coloured areas not by razor wire any more but by infrastructure: barriers of motorways, railway lines, power lines, drainage systems, and golf courses. Still, there are spaces in some strongly divided cities where particular kinds of sacred space perform a more unifying role rather than reinforcing limited, fragmented visions of the demos. In this regard, Santiago's main public cemetery, the Cementerio General, is a fascinating example. Here is a city in miniature, with its wealthy districts featuring huge, ornate family monuments; its middle-class suburbs with smaller but still imposing and often neo-classical family mausoleums; its working class districts with what can only be described as mini apartment blocks of memorials; and its shanty towns of memorials to the poorest of the poor (Figure 8.2). In among all that are military districts and its counterculture, including the large and relatively recent walls listing the names of those murdered and disappeared by the Pinochet regime. It even has graffiti – justice

179

Figure 8.2. A working class district of the *Cementerio General*, Santiago
Photo by Lion Hirth, public domain via Wikimedia Commons.

for so-and-so, rights for the poor, attempts to recall past evils, and so on. And in among all this, hundreds of families from right across the social spectrum make weekend trips to pay their respects, maintain the family plot or palace, take a picnic, chat with the neighbours, or let the kids run about. It is a site for public holidays and public festivals; a site not just for state memorials but contestation over memories (Wilde, 1991). It is a lively place for a deathly place, and while it did not make me want to rush out and build a family mausoleum – 'the final and funniest folly of the rich', according to Ambrose Bierce (1993) – it did make me rue the cheerless, barren uniformity of the modern cemetery in my homeland. In Chile, cemeteries are public spaces in that they are facilities for the living as well as memorials to a sometimes-contested past. In New Zealand, many of them seem public in the same sense that the city dump is public: necessary, managed, regretted, and avoided.

Parks, Encounter, and Escape

Other spaces perform – or were created to perform – similar unifying functions, among them city parks. Parks are enormously important yet surprisingly ambiguous places in cities, and it is worth dwelling on them because they help draw out the major point in this chapter. From eighteenth-century London when the public parks movement began, parks were places where people from a surprisingly broad spectrum of society could walk and if not exactly encounter each other in conversation, at least be seen and acknowledged as fellow citizens. This was part of their purpose (Sennett, 2002: 85). These days parks in Western cities are less likely to be used for such encounter purposes, although that depends on the nature of the park and the aims of the person using it. While they can be, and often are, places for celebrations, performances and public claim-making, more often they are treated as places to *escape*, places to watch people but not to be obtruded upon, places where the norm of public disattendability takes primacy over engagement and visibility (see Chapter 3, page 55; Goffman, 1963: 1063). They can be places for memorials and memorialization – the National Mall in DC is *the* space for public memorials, as is Hyde Park in London – but they can also be places for quiet enjoyment of displays of the gardener's art, with 'keep off the grass' signs prominent in Tokyo's Hibiya Park and in London's St James's Park, for example. They are often places for play (Stevens, 2007): places to take the kids, to meet up with friends, to throw a Frisbee, kick a ball, and fire up the barbecue (publicly funded and maintained around the shores of Lake Burley Griffin in Canberra). They can be seen as 'wild' nature reserves, places that are essential for the environmental sustainability of cities, managed sport and recreational facilities, places to let the dog off the lead and run around happily, places for people to reconnect with nature, places for them to watch others, and places to sit and contemplate (Burgess et al., 1988; Chiesura, 2004). They can also be places where 'others' go to escape supervision and control, either for private encounters (Iveson, 2007), or just to rest, or to represent and express themselves when no other avenues exist (Mitchell, 1995). To the degree that such spaces are used by 'others' – gay men cruising, homeless people sheltering, domestic workers picnicking, the politically radical mobilizing and expressing – to that degree do they become shunned by mainstream society. For these and other reasons, they can be places of fear, places where dangers lurk in hidden corners and down darkened paths. They need not be grandiose affairs: another of the (many) striking things about Santiago was not just the ornamental parks like Cerro Santa Lucia, or the extensive green belt of the Parque Metropolitano, but the dozens of small patches of grass in poor areas, complete with goalposts, where kids could kick a football about. In that respect, although clearly not in others, children from poor families in Santiago seemed better off to me than terrace-dwelling children in many British cities.

The point of this long list of uses is that expectations of parks collide and cause conflict. Conflicts arise when a publicly funded, publicly accessible park is fenced off for a particular event like a demonstration; or, worse, for an event that charges admission, like a concert or an exhibition; or worse still, for corporate entertainment and other events that are by invitation only and inaccessible for any money. The third example is easily dealt with on the principles laid out in Part I: the use of public spaces for private purposes should not be allowed to crowd out other uses of that space. There are plenty of private spaces available for private functions, and in general corporate entertainers should be made to use those spaces and not be permitted to fence off otherwise public facilities, no matter how much money they offer cash-strapped officials for the privilege. Having said that, there should still be room for local variation in what counts as a public event, and local experimentation to allow for mixed use. For example, a common use of the Parliament grounds and function rooms in Ottawa is for wedding receptions, and while the private aspect of weddings has certainly become more dominant in Western societies over the last half-century – my parents would not have even thought 'It's *my* wedding and I'll invite who I want to', let alone said it – it is still in large part a public ritual, state regulated, recorded, and sanctioned. Other parliament managers, such as in New Zealand, treat such things as private matters and refuse applications to use the grounds and rooms, and I see no particular problem either way here – it is a matter of local practice rather than deep principle. By contrast, the first example of fencing off cannot be resolved by appeals to the concept of 'public', but arise from the facts that the label encompasses several different ideas; that two bodies cannot occupy the same space at once; and that the performance of some public activities means that others necessarily cannot be enjoyed. As with any such conflicts, answers only emerge through negotiation based on other values – values of turn-taking, say, or whether a particular society values collective goods over individual ones, or peaceful enjoyment over noisy enjoyment.

The conflict between a park as a place for denizens to enjoy themselves and a park as a more abstract aesthetic entity is seen most clearly in Tokyo. Tokyo has relatively little open green space, certainly when compared with New York, London, or Paris, yet those they do have seem relatively underused. This is partly because they are usually open for limited hours, hours that relatively few hard-working Japanese can manage, while the 'keep off the grass' message is so strong that even picnicking is forbidden. They seem more for display than use. In response, a direct action group has been set up to challenge it – the Tokyo Picnic Club.[3] Run by a collection of architects, urban planners, artists, and others, the Club started with a succession of illegal picnics in parks to highlight the lack of space for ordinary enjoyment of the open air. They have progressed to creative appropriation of urban spaces to continue their 'Fight for the Picnic' by such means as flash-picnics on

---

[3] http://www.picnicclub.org/

'portable lawns', squares of grass on trolleys wheeled out into the Ginza or the upper levels of a hip new tower block.[4]

Other conflicts arise when spaces are colonized by the marginal over long periods of time. These frequently attract violent responses from city and state governments, justified by efforts to reclaim the space for 'all users', followed by efforts to normalize the spaces through open design, fencing, and lighting. This can lead to seemingly wild, 'natural' space losing its wildness, with trees and nooks and crannies replaced by volleyball courts and bright lighting – the example is from Mitchell's discussion (1995) of the taming of People's Park in San Francisco. This kind of conflict has been played out in many big-city parks that feature extensive wooded areas, like New York's Central Park, London's Lincoln's Inn Fields, and, to a lesser degree because of the astonishingly house-proud behaviour of its residents, Tokyo's Yoyogi Park.

One point to emphasize here is how the presence of certain design elements matters in the closure of such conflicts. I showed in the previous chapter how it matters that the plazas outside sites of national symbolic importance, and the sites of actual decision-making, be relatively open expanses, relatively unimpeded by breaks made up of furniture, statues, planters, trees, arcades, fountains, and such like. When it comes to many of the other purposes in the list on page 181, however, what matters are the trees, the grass, the seats, the nooks and crannies, and the view. For another set of purposes, perhaps it is the ball courts, the goal posts, the fitness stations, the skateboard ramps, and the running tracks that matter. In other words, what makes for good design in public space depends on the purposes of that space, but *no single space can perform all those functions*. What makes good space for mass public visibility is terrible space for a quiet sandwich, not much better for letting the dog off the leash, and certainly no good for building a bed for the night. A single space might be able to perform several functions: for example, demonstrations in Hong Kong's Victoria Park tend to use the expanse of tennis and basketball courts because it is the largest open expanse in the Park, and the firm surfaces are more resilient than the central grassed area, especially if it is wet, as it very often is in June. There might also be room for the creative appropriation of space in order to surprise and attract attention: the Aboriginal Tent Embassy in Canberra is one example. But while certain spatial arrangements can perform one or two public functions, it cannot fulfil them all at once. Therefore, in any given public space conflicts are going to arise, conflicts that cannot be closed by appealing to the concept of 'public'. To repeat, the conflicts are opened by that appeal;

---

[4] The Tokyo Picnic Club's fame has spread – they have organized similar events in Newcastle, UK, for instance – although there it is with council sanction and with imported, not local, iconography, and so has more connotations of 'trendy Japanese architects' than 'risky urban activism'.

183

they are closed by the exercise of power, or by appeal to other values, including those that are bundled up in the 'public' label.

That observation has an impact on two complaints frequently encountered in the urban theory literature. From a democratic point of view, two things exercise observers of these urban experiences: one, that the restrictions reinforce a limited concept of who counts as a member of the *demos*, and thus who gets taken seriously when people attempt to press public claims; and two, that democratic claim-making in these spaces is one of the activities that have become delegitimized. With regard to the second complaint, I have argued already (in Chapters six and seven) that the downgrading of purposive publics in favour of accidental publics is a major problem for democratic performance. What is going on is not, perhaps, a fall from a gracious state in which all public claim-making was once seen as legitimate, but rather a very long-running series of battles, over centuries, between those who want to express outrage at the actions of the powerful, and the powerful who want to stop them.

With regard to the first complaint, there is something intuitively right about the idea that a lack of visibility of certain members of the public matters. Take, for example, disabled people. It is a central claim among disabled activists and academics that disabled people are marginalized socially, politically and economically to the degree that they are kept institutionalized, kept out of mainstream society, even if allegedly for their own good (Barnes and Mercer, 2003). If the rest of us never encounter a disabled person in our day-to-day lives – if we do not go to school with them, work with them, engage with them socially, or even just see them on television – then we simply do not take their needs into account in our public decision- and claim-making. We do not include them in our mental map of 'the public' at all.[5] When we do encounter disabled individuals, we tend then to treat them merely as bearers of medical conditions, sometimes even assuming they have mental disabilities as well (Hughes and Paterson, 1997), not as fellow citizens, bearers of legitimate claims in the public sphere. Therefore, it matters to the marginalized that they have places in which to be seen by the wider public; and it matters therefore that many cities prevent such visibility, not just through the policing of public space but its design too.

But while it is important that the marginalized are seen, that cannot be the end of the matter. The claim from the disabled is not about visibility pure and simple, but about active engagement, and the rest of the *demos* treating them as deserving of that engagement. We can link this to the political theory of efficacy: efficacy calculations are made not on the basis of mere visibility, but of perceived effectiveness in the public realm, a sense that 'people like me' are

---

[5] Apologies for the 'us and them' language here, but it helps make the point: the disabled are usually treated as the 'other' in public debate.

184

taken seriously and have their voices heard (Goodin and Dryzek, 1980; Lawless, 2004). While visibility is an important precondition for public claim-making, it is not the sum total of it. As argued back in Chapter three, the deliberative democratic process requires space in which claims can be tested, weighed against each other, and turned into binding collective agreements. While occupying space like People's Park in San Francisco might be a great way of announcing one's presence and claims to an otherwise-oblivious audience (Mitchell, 1995), it is not a good way of performing some of the subsequent roles. Democratic deliberation and decision-making requires that those claims be subjected to representative decision-making processes in an assembly before they have binding force for others. In a deliberative democracy, claims are not self-evidently right; they are right when they survive the processes of public reasoning by legitimate, broadly inclusive representatives.

Therefore, it might very well be important to largely Filipina domestic workers in Hong Kong that they have claimed many central spaces in Hong Kong as their own every Saturday, and that large-scale occupation of these spaces might mean that their presence has become instantly much more visible to the rest of Hong Kong society as a result (Law, 2002). It might even be that this has provoked a development of group political consciousness among domestic workers. But in the long run, what matters from a democratic viewpoint is that such severely marginalized people are taken by other Hong Kongers as fellow claim makers, as people who have a right to a voice in collective decision-making. If that is so, then mass picnicking has hardly been an effective means to that end. For one, it has not generated much in the way of domestic workers' claims on the public, let alone claims to *be* a public. For another, it has provoked years of complaints that Hong Kong's meagre open spaces are now so overrun by domestic workers that no one else can use them, and occasional demands for the police to turf them out. In other words, they are not accepted as legitimate claim makers, not accepted as members of 'us', by other Hong Kongers, and the mass occupation of public spaces reinforces the us/them division. Whether more physical conflict arises, and the attempts to resolve it result in recognition (following Young, 2000, for example), remains to be seen.

To conclude this section, the points I want to re-emphasize here are (*a*) no single public space can possibly be used for all public roles; and (*b*) that appealing to concepts like 'public', 'the public', and 'democracy' is what opens up conflict rather than resolving it. It follows from the first point that we should not be hypnotized by particular cases, but look at the broad sweep of public space available in a city. It matters that there is *some* space for the performance of a given democratic role, but it cannot be the case that *every* public space must perform *every* democratic role. Ought implies can: it is therefore nonsense to criticize a particular space for failing to do that which it cannot possibly do. Instead, and referring back to the summary of democratic roles and spatial criteria that closed Chapter four, what we should be looking at is the degree to which a particular city provides space for narrating a variety of experiences by majorities and minorities alike; that it provides visible space for those same people to make public claim; and that it has single, dignified spaces for making decisions about those claims and scrutinizing the decision-making and implementation processes. What we should *not* be doing is focusing on isolated cases and implying that any given space should fulfil all those roles, or applying truncated accounts of publicity and democracy, which boil down to mere accessibility and visibility.

Representing the Public

So far, I have focused on spaces where people meet each other physically, face to face, and gain an impression of the *demos* that way. But there is another important way in which people get a sense of 'who counts' (Goodin, 2008) in a democracy, and that is through representation of people in the built environment, the symbolic representation of the *demos*.

In September 2005, the Mayor of London unveiled the first in a new series of statues to occupy what is known as 'the Fourth Plinth' in Trafalgar Square. The plinth was originally built in 1841 to carry an equestrian statue of King William IV, but funds ran out and the fourth plinth remained empty until 1999, when a series of three sculptures was displayed. To the delight of some and the utter disbelief of others, what the mayor unveiled to begin the second series was no dead king or long-forgotten general: it was 'Allison Lapper Pregnant', by Marc Quinn.

The statue depicted disabled British artist Allison Lapper. The sculptor said that he was inspired by the fact that there was 'no positive representation of disability in the history of public art' (Cooke, 2005), while the subject said that she regarded it 'as a modern tribute to femininity, disability and motherhood. It is so rare to see disability in everyday life – let alone naked, pregnant and proud' (Fourth Plinth Project, 2005). Not everyone was so positive – the conservative *Daily Telegraph* newspaper felt it looked 'a little out of place' among 'the assortment of military statues that *grace* the square' (Reynolds, 2005, my emphasis); the Conservative Party arts spokesperson condemned the idea when it was first announced, saying that 'the politically correct lobby has prevailed' (Hall, 2004). Others called it 'horrible' and 'repellent', while insisting that it was the execution, not the subject matter, that repelled them.

In their public art, their public iconography, their public spaces, and the built environment more generally, capital cities represent nations and people. To the degree that we think that such representations matter – and I think they *do* matter, a point argued below – then democratic norms might lead us to expect that those representations be relatively 'representative', inclusive of the variety of the *demos*. However, the reality is that representation in public space is often highly selective in subject matter and approach. Not only is it rare to see disabled, pregnant, and many other kinds of people represented in public art, it is also often the case that the symbolic resources of cities speak to some people and not others. At the same time, there are places where competing narratives of a people – their history, values, and identities – are being fought out in the very fabric of the city itself. There are many people in modern democracies who do not recognize themselves or their pasts in their nations' capitals, sometimes despite the strenuous efforts of city planners and political leaders to represent the nation in this way.

In Chapter four, I set out an account of how it is that public space conveys meaning, drawing on a distinction between depictions and symbols. A depiction shares physical characteristics with that which it represents. By contrast, there is no natural, essential link between a symbol and its referent but only what convention, deliberate design, and consistent use build up over a period of time. Thus, we can view 'Allison Lapper Pregnant' not only as a depiction of the person called Allison Lapper, or a depiction of a pregnant disabled woman, but also as a deliberately created symbol of disabled people as strong, 'abled', creative, worthy of respect and dignified status, and thus worthy of their place in Trafalgar Square, a site for 'dignified' national symbols like Nelson's Column, the National Art Gallery and the Admiralty building. These meanings attached to the statue are not 'natural' but applied to it by the artist in his pronouncements on the subject, by reinforcing statements made by the subject and by the commissioners of the work; in reviews in newspapers and magazines; and by local cultural convention that attributes the values of strength and independence to a direct, level gaze and jutting jaw, as well as the value of pride to the open depiction of disability and pregnancy in so public a setting.

Similarly, capital cities have often been deliberately designed as tools of representation. Washington, DC, Canberra, and Ottawa were consciously created to symbolize their respective federations (Sonne, 2003), and they achieve this in various ways. One of these is not exactly subtle: street names. In Canberra, the major routes between the parliamentary, civic, and military zones are Commonwealth Avenue, Constitution Avenue and King's Avenue; those radiating from Parliament are named after the state capitals, Adelaide Avenue, Brisbane Avenue, Hobart Avenue, and so on – all linked by National Circuit, Dominion Circuit, and Empire Circuit. The same applies in Washington, DC: Pennsylvania Ave, Massachusetts Ave, Rhode Island Ave, etc. In Ottawa, regionality is made present in the fabric of the Parliament Building itself, with stained glass windows and frescoes depicting the people, plants, animals, and environments of the Canadian provinces, and by flags and

187

banners for each province and its capital displayed along Wellington Street and in Confederation Square. Thus, in all three of these cities, there is a sense in which visitors from other parts of the country are made to feel present, recognized, and dignified – that the national capital is *theirs* in some way.

There is inevitable friction between the role of a city as national site and symbol, and its role as a home for its residents. This is especially the case in Washington, DC. Many people who work in the city do not live there, commuting in from suburban Maryland, Delaware, and Virginia, yet exercising a great deal of control over the built environment. Washingtonians do not have full national representation – a sore point, and one kept in the public gaze by 'Taxation without representation' slogans on car registration plates since 2000 – and only gained limited local autonomy in 1973 with the delegation of some decision-making responsibility from Congress to an elected mayor. City measures are frequently vetoed by federal congressmen and senators from distant states. Likewise, residents of the Australian Capital Territory were only granted self-government in 1988 and still the federally run National Capital Authority exerts a great deal of control over what can and cannot be done by Canberrans in the 'national triangle'. In all the capital cities I visited, the presence of national institutions and sites limits the freedom of local authorities to organize public space as they see fit. But while the Washington, DC, case is an extreme example – the usual justifications for denying Washingtonians representation do not stand up to a moment's scrutiny – in the other cases the tension is inevitable, and once again not resolvable by appeal to the concepts of democracy and public space.

The concept of democracy *does* give us traction with other issues, however, and one is the symbolic inclusion of groups within the nation. It is not the case that every member of a given state is included in quite the same way in public space. One of the most striking absences in these cities is the absence of native iconography. This is particularly noticeable in Ottawa, where not only is much sign of the aboriginal Algonquin people missing, even the province of Nunavut, created in 1999, is almost entirely absent from official buildings, statues, and memorials. One finds First Nation art in specialist and souvenir stores, but not inscribed in the fabric of Ottawa itself, except in the occasional flag and banner. Even French style and symbolism is hard to discern – the contrast with Montréal is unmistakable – leaving central Ottawa firmly Ontarian. This is despite a significant *Outaouais* population west of the Rideau River and greater efforts to integrate the Quebec city of Gatineau, just across the Ottawa River, into the 'core area' of the national capital. Some of that will change with the transformation of Victoria Island as a 'First Peoples' Centre' as means of expressing native identity, and the redevelopment of parks on the Gatineau side (NCC, 2005), but despite those changes, Ottawa will still feel like an Anglo city on the borders of francophone Canada, with few native traces at all.

Figure 8.3. Memorializing the past – plaque marking 1840 shoreline, Wellington
Photo by 'Br3nda', Licensed by Creative Commons.

In Canberra, attempts to include aboriginal people have been made in recent years. The front of the new federal parliament building includes an extensive mosaic in what white (but not necessarily black) Australians regard as Aboriginal art; sites in the Australian Capital Territory of significance to the local Ngunnawal people are being highlighted by interpretive signs; while in 2002, the Prime Minister opened a space right in the heart of Canberra's main symbolic axis called Reconciliation Place, referring to efforts to integrate black and white Australians into a shared 'public'. Originally, this was criticized by many aboriginals as just another tokenistic depiction in an otherwise white-fella symbolic context, but gradually communities from all over the country are starting to take ownership of the space, filling it with artworks depicting such things as Aboriginal armed service, and memorializing the 'stolen generations' (van Krieken, 1999). In Wellington, too, one can see small shifts in ethnic relations etched on the fabric of the city: not only classic, colonial buildings with no acknowledgement of any culture but their own imported one but also numerous examples of Māori iconography incorporated into space like Civic Square, often designed and developed by Māori artists, and a gradual acceleration of efforts to memorialize Māori settlement and interpret Māori understanding of the city. Examples include the recent preservation of the remains of long-buried houses and storehouses, uncovered during the redevelopment of a site on Taranaki Street and now recovered by see-through flooring. Another is the new gateway outside Parliament showing where an important portage way ran from the shoreline.

In what might be called more 'organic' cities, things are different. With the obvious exception of Paris under Napoleon III, there is not the same scope for large-scale urban redesign as there is when building a city from scratch, and so national symbols must fit in where landowners or appropriation permits; or, in the case of Tokyo and Berlin, the destruction created by war and natural disaster create space for. What large scale redevelopment does exist in liberal democracies is often done by private consortiums rather than public bodies like the national capital authorities. This is one reason why organic cities have paid less attention to the deliberate creation of unifying symbols in quite the same obvious fashion as the designed cities. Unifying symbols there are, but they are symbols that have become such by a more organic process of accretion, the attachment of meaning by centuries of practice and discourse. One example is Big Ben in London, which has come to symbolize British politics.[6] This is because of who works in, and what goes on in, the building under the tower, so that eventually the tower becomes short-hand for the processes, institutions, and individuals associated with it.

One effect of this more organic accretion of ideas may be that the symbols are less readily subject to challenge and change. They take on a naturalness that for many is beyond alteration because that is the way things are done. This is one way of interpreting some conservative reaction to 'Allison Lapper Pregnant': the distaste need not be simply interpreted as loathing of disability, but also a loathing of the disruption of the singularity of national symbolic language. Related to this is the fact that in London there is little trace of anyone feeling the need to 'include' the Scots, Welsh, and Irish in what was for centuries the seat of the English government, although symbols of the four nations are present in the lobby of the Palace of Westminster. Indeed, there is little deliberate 'programming' (the term much used by Ottawa city authorities) of events to emphasize common bonds at all in London. The institutions and their associated rituals are left to speak for themselves – they do not require an event management company to explain them. Clearly, the need to include is a relatively modern impulse, but it is one that is more readily expressed in the newer capitals of the Commonwealth than in the very much older capitals of the Imperial powers because those newer capitals were deliberately designed with expressive, often-unifying symbolism in mind. In the latter, one colonizes and absorbs; one does not 'include'.

The boundary-crossing exception is Berlin: an old city, an Imperial city, and yet also the re-created capital of a united Germany following the Cold War. In

---

[6] And its study: of the twelve British politics undergraduate textbooks on my bookshelf at present, six have Big Ben on the cover; the others have the Union Flag, pictures of political leaders, or the shiny black door of 10 Downing Street. The name, by the way, highlights the distinction between form and symbol: the building is officially called 'St Stephen's Tower', but the symbol is called 'Big Ben', and no amount of pedantry will shift that.

Berlin is being played out not so much a clash of ethnic identities, but a clash of the competing urges to remember and to forget, to freeze and to move on. Berlin is trying to overcome the shadow of a history in which architectural and other symbolism was a core means used by successive regimes to legitimate themselves and their world views; so, Berliners are understandably nervous about 'unifying symbols' in ways that Americans and Australians are not. Still, the case of Berlin shows that while 'organic' symbols might be difficult to change and challenge, it is by no means impossible. The example of the Tempelhof airport terminal is particularly interesting. Designed in 1936 by an architect who 'made the compromises necessary to get Third Reich commissions' (Ladd, 1998: 145), the building was completely redeemed in symbolic terms by its central role in the Berlin airlift of 1948–9. This is a perfect example of the way that events and their associated narratives can shift the meaning of a symbol dramatically in a relatively short space of time. At present, Tempelhof is in disuse and disrepair, but there are serious plans to maintain it and restore it because it serves as a symbol of hope and friendship from afar at a time when nearest neighbours had turned hostile. Compare this with other Nazi era buildings like the Air Ministry next door that has never benefitted from a redeeming event, and thus remains for some a symbol of a past that is best erased.

Erasure is controversial because of the links between memory, identity, and values. In the case of the Nazi past, part of the conflict concerns the wish not only to memorialize the victims of that regime, but also to validate the identity of the survivors and to give them physical touchstones that activate those memories; and also to help ensure that history is not allowed to repeat itself by providing reminders of the horrors that can be unleashed. Berlin is being relatively successful at embodying some memories, with such focal points as the Holocaust memorial and the Topography of Terror exhibition, which focuses on the former buildings of the Gestapo and other 'security' services, although with the passing of time it is getting more and more difficult to get young Germans to take an active interest (Till, 2005: 151). Just as such symbols may be very much more meaningful to some identity groups than others, it is also the case that, for the young, the past is truly 'a foreign country' (Hartley, 1953), another context whose inhabitants share narratives that they do not, or would rather not, partake in.

As already noted in Chapter four (p. 75), the rush to reunify East and West has led some people to feel that their city is being taken away from them; that they no longer have anchor points for their memories because many scenes that greeted them every day on their journeys around the city are just not there any more. Therefore, at Easter 2007, the city government caused uproar in some circles by demolishing an 18-metre section of the Wall near Potsdamer Platz to make way, perhaps ironically, for the new Environment

Ministry building. Others see the Wall as 'a despised symbol of a totalitarian regime [that] should be completely destroyed' (Anonymous, 2007), and are applauding its erasure.

I have mentioned other examples of erasure already, like District Six and the Wellington foreshore. Of a somewhat different kind is Canberra, which has at least two sets of public space, one overlying the other. The one that is visible to Western eyes is the city of Walter Burley Griffin and the National Capital Authority: broad commemorative avenues linking garden suburbs around a triangular core, the axes of which line up with the peaks of key hills. The one that is visible to Ngunnawal eyes is entirely different, consisting of cues for the Dreamings of ancestors and totems, of paths into the Brindabella mountains to catch the bogong moth on its annual migration, of paths to sacred sites (Jackson-Nakano, 2001). Few white Australians would recognize this alternative geography, despite the interpretive signs that are springing up around the territory. The two cities overlap, but they barely intersect.

Demolition and redevelopment is not the only way of dealing with uncomfortable memories. Santiago shows another way: renaming. One of the things I wanted to do was find out to what extent the dictatorship is remembered in physical forms in the city. However, where both Berlin and Cape Town have their memorials, exhibitions, and physical reminders of the past, and attempt to maintain awareness of the mistakes of the past, Chileans, it seems, prefer not to deal with their past openly. Perhaps this is because the cleavages are still so keenly felt (Wilde, 1991). But it was remarkable that, with the exception of La Moneda, its statue of Salvador Allende (round the back) and the bullet holes still pockmarking surrounding buildings, many other markers of the dictatorship have been quietly removed or ignored. Take, for instance, the dozens of sites used around the city to imprison and torture opponents of the regime. One can find websites listing the sites, but try to find them on the ground and frustration awaits. Often there are no memorials, not even a plaque; or there are plaques with messages so oblique that one needs to know the history in order to tell what it is they are referring to; or buildings with changed numbers; or changed street names; sometimes signs of redevelopment, but rarely holes in the ground. Some have all these features: the torture site at what was Av. Republica 517 is a building of the *Universidad de los Lagos*, on a street now called Av. Cummings, with a plaque that commemorates the site 'taking up its role again as a centre for learning, toleration and humanity' (author translation). A search for the former National Intelligence Directorate headquarters at Belgrado 11 was a frustrating one until persistence with maps and a photograph revealed that the street is now called la Periodista Jose Carrasco Tapia, and the building is now the headquarters of the *Federación de Estudiantes Universidad de Chile* – the irony must be bitter-sweet on both sides. At least

192

that street is covered in memorializing graffiti, albeit oblique once again. The National Stadium, scene of numerous atrocities, bears not a single memorial, no graffiti, not a bunch of flowers, nothing. The only exception is the Villa Grimaldi site in Santiago's east, which has been turned into a 'Park for Peace'. Meanwhile, what seemed to some of the Chileans I spoke to as a slap in the face remains: one of the city's main roads is Av. 11 September, commemorating not the date of the terrorist attacks on New York and Washington, DC, but the date of the 1973 coup. The military remains celebrated in street names and in a massive mausoleum in the *Cementerio General*; their dirty war is being erased. From conversations with Chileans, it seems that these physical symbols help deepen the country's polarization; despite some victories over ultra-conservative elements, a sense remains that the old, authoritarian elites maintain their hold on power, and that those with more liberal (as opposed to neoliberal) values do not have a voice in the Chilean formal public sphere (cf. Siavelis, 2009).

What do the concepts of public space and democracy tell us about how to deal with these conflicts of symbolic representation, or memory and forgetting? This time, the answer might seem to be a bit more substantive than the answer to questions about the availability of openly accessible parks, because it is not the case that any space will do. For most public narration, any site is as good as another so long as people can get to it. For claim-making, the requirements are more firm: sites need to be visible to attentive publics and, ideally, endowed with symbols of dignity. By contrast, identities and memories are anchored by very specific sites: the exact square in 1968 where the Mexican military opened fire on demonstrators; the exact balcony where Mandela addressed the crowds on his release from prison; and the exact configuration of streets that one had to navigate in order to get from one isolated corner of a divided Berlin to another. This, however, is not in itself an argument for changeless preservation, because there is nothing in the concepts of democracy or public space that says we must privilege preservation claims over erasure claims. What democratic principles *do* give us is a reason for complaining that certain claims do not get a hearing at all, and that certain identities do not get represented at all. We might then need another theory that tells us which of the multiplicity of identities and experiences should be represented in public space, especially in 'dignified' public space. One available theory is that of Phillips (1995) who argues that gender and ethnicity are the primary sources of disadvantage in democratic societies, although what counts as an ethnicity can itself be fraught, and in other settings one might well think that religion, control of valued resources, and caste might well be the salient cleavages. It is also the case that representing cleavages in formal institutions tends to solidify them, not break them down, which might provide another argument for fluidity rather than preservation (cf. Kriesi, 1998). The balance

193

struck in any particular location between preservation and development should be a dynamic one, dependent on the values involved in specific cases, the overall availability of alternatives, and the changing dynamics of politics.

Thus, it turns out that, once again, the concepts of democracy and public space might alert us to problems with certain voices not being included, certain experiences not being narrated, and certain identities not being symbolized; but it does not tell us precisely which identities to include, how, or where. It is also the case that renaming streets or placing statues might be an important step but it is not normally sufficient to give people a feeling that they are being recognized rather than merely depicted. This is important from a normative democratic theory point of view, because if we want people to gain a sense of efficacy from seeing their symbols made present in capital cities, then large proportions of the symbolism need to line up in some way. Recalling the discussion of the way symbols gain meaning, this requires that the actions of the powerful change with respect to subaltern groups. A new artwork, a new piece of public space, might make an extremely good physical anchor point to mark and call to mind a real change in government policy or ideology – the signing of a treaty, the enfranchisement of a group, the changing of some institutional rules – and might thus act as a cue to formerly excluded groups that it is now worth their while getting involved and participating in public decision-making. But these things cannot *create* inclusion on their own. Symbols are powerful communicators when they line up with actions; when action and symbol are at cross-purposes, tokenism takes over.

Conclusions

There is a great deal more that could be said about the way that democracy plays out in cities. A great deal more *has* been said, especially by scholars who have taken particular cities as their case studies and have gone into a great deal of detail examining their nooks and nuances.[7] The aim in this chapter has been both narrower and higher level, examining the wider fields of democratic narration and claim-making by focusing on capital cities' representative functions.

Capital cities are, by design, by usage or both, symbols of national institutions, values, myths, and norms – they *contain* such symbols and they *are*, in their own right, such symbols. They are also symbols of who constitutes the nation, who is recognized as being a part of the *demos* and who is not. This is

---

[7] I particularly recommend Iveson (2007) for his street-level analysis of the interaction between citizens, city spaces, and the calling of publics into being through expressive acts.

partly on the basis of who gets depicted in dignified, formal settings like Trafalgar Square, Anzac Parade and the halls of the Capitol building; but is also on the basis of whose story lines and memories are given physical anchor points in the very fabric of capital cities.

Some capitals have been deliberately designed to act as symbols of the nation, but all send signals of inclusion and exclusion, deliberately or otherwise. National symbols are constructed by patterns of use and habit as much as deliberate association. A possible implication is that such associations may be hard to change in any deliberate fashion, because would-be symbol changers are up against the 'naturalness' of symbolic associations. It is easier to create new symbols, or appropriate symbols from others. The exception has been Berlin, which shows that changes to the symbolic function of buildings are facilitated by dramatic external events associated with those buildings, such that the narratives associated with them are changed overnight. Such shocks to the narratives that accrete around symbols do not happen every day, but at least they demonstrate that we are not prisoners of our built environment, but can have it mean what we want it to mean by acting in new ways.

At the same time, cities provide facilities for the performance not just of narrations of the *demos*, but of other public claims, other narrations, and even space for getting away from each other and persistent public claim-making. The degree to which different members of the *demos* can enjoy that space depends very much on the background structures of social stratification in a given city, although I found interesting exceptions in the case of some kinds of sacred space, like local shrines in Tokyo and the *Cementerio General* in Santiago. City parks proved an especially fruitful location in which to explore the tensions between all the different things that acting in public can mean, and I argued that different park configurations can have an important impact on people's ability to perform different roles. Indeed, I argued that space that is good for escape is not good for encounter or some kinds of play, but rather than use single case studies to imply that every public space ought to have a certain set of characteristics that encourage democratically valuable pursuits, I argued instead that variety is what is required – urban wild spaces as well as manicured lawns; dusty grounds to kick a football around as well as basketball courts; wide, open spaces as well as nooks and crannies.

When it comes to issues of membership and narration, the concept of democracy helps resolve conflicts to a certain extent, because it provides a presumption that all the members of the *demos* should feel that their group narratives are represented in dignified public space, and that capital cities are theirs in a symbolic sense. That has benefits for their sense of democratic efficacy. The concept of democracy does not tell us precisely which groups to include, where, or how; for that we need other theory, even democratic procedures themselves. When it comes to the conflicts over the multiple uses of park space, however, the concepts of publicity and democracy help us in only very minor ways. They help us rule out the closing of parks for private functions; although what counts as a private function is itself something that depends on other values, going back to the discussion in Chapter three. But while that might be an important gain, there are an awful lot more kinds of conflicts over access to and use of public parks than that. I argued that it is simply a mistake to think that the concepts of democracy and public space resolve such conflicts.

* * * * *

That concludes Part II, in which the theoretical issues have been explored through observations, interviews, and some secondary work on a selection of cases. Throughout this section, I have made a number of evaluative claims about how well or badly certain cities provide certain kinds of space, including the point made above about having a variety of park space for performing a variety of roles. In the final chapter, I will draw all those threads together by coming up with a framework for evaluating the spatial elements of democracy, and offering a preliminary assessment of the democratic strengths and weaknesses of my sample of capital cities.

Part III
Evaluating Democratic Space

9

Conclusions and Implications

When it comes to the provision of public space for the performance of democracy, what makes for a good capital city? That is the question I will try to answer in this concluding chapter. Along the way, I sum up answers to the two major questions of the book: what space does liberal, deliberative democracy require for its performance, and how well is that space provided in a selection of cities? I start by restating the major descriptive and normative claims made in the preceding chapters. I then look at some general issues of the measurement and evaluation of democracy, before refining an evaluative approach and, tentatively, applying that approach to my cases.

The approach I take is generally a qualitative one, not quantitative, for fairly obvious epistemological reasons. I will set these out in detail shortly but, in brief, I have argued throughout that the use of public space depends on the meanings attached to it, and the exploration of meaning requires qualitative work. Nonetheless – and with a due sense of caution, given the criticisms I made of this kind of work back in Chapter five – I think also that certain kinds of space are necessary in a democratic capital city, and the capacity of that space is itself an important factor, so there is no getting away from a certain amount of tape-measure-based evaluation. But even then, a crowd looks big in context: 50,000 people crammed into Hong Kong's Victoria Park looks big; the same number would look a little feeble in DC's National Mall. The Goldilocks question of how much public space is 'just right' is itself something that varies from place to place.

These considerations, and the exploratory nature of this whole inquiry, make generalization dangerous, and in the end I offer some conclusions about the strengths and weaknesses of different capital cities that are more in the way of hypotheses for further detailed testing. Still, I am particularly critical, ironically enough, of those cities and buildings that have been planned and built allegedly with democratic values in mind. Democracy is not something that can be 'built'; but it is something that can be performed more or less effectively on different kinds of stages. Thus, I will argue that

199

urban planners, architects, governments, and security services need to do both more and less: more by way of ensuring that a variety of spaces exist for different public purposes, more by way of providing specific stages for some of those purposes, more by way of dealing with the 'deputization' of the built environment, but less grand gesture. There also needs to be less of providing buildings that are supposed to symbolize and shape democratic values, and more of providing buildings for how people actually behave and engage with each other.

Perhaps what is at issue is the gap between planners', architects', and urban theorists' understanding of what democracy means, and the understanding that underlies the normative claims throughout this book. Therefore, I am going to start by summarizing those claims. But I end with some reflections on the study of politics and policy, and a plea that even if the reader does not buy my claims about the necessity of physical stages for the performance of democracy, he or she will recognize that democracy is a rich and fascinating performance, one that the current focus on varieties of rationality fails to capture.

Stages for Democracy: A Summary

1. *Democracy is a decision mechanism with a supporting culture, not a culture alone*

Throughout this book, I have worked with an account of democracy that in most respects is quite standard as far as political scientists and theorists are concerned, but quite different from the more sociological account implicit in the literature on public space. It is a specifically political account, in that it takes democracy to be a set of principles and procedures that allow groups of people to make binding, collective decisions about how they should live together. Within those terms, it is a reasonably broad, deliberative account in that it considers not just formal institutions but also the wider, social, communicative foundations of democratic engagement. It considers the ways in which narratives and claims are shared around a democratic society, setting the political agenda, structuring the terms on which arguments are held, and translating those arguments into acts of governance, as well as the sites of elected, representative government.

I have taken that standard account and given it a performative twist, not just for analytic purposes but also because democracy really is a performance. It is one of the virtues of urban theory that several branches of it understand the degree to which public life in advanced democracies is narrated, scripted, ritualized, and performed, and yet for the most part political science and political theory persist with models that emphasize formal institutions that structure decisions rather than the informal aspects; or, when considering the informal, focus on psychological factors rather than sociological or anthropological ones – choice, decisions, habits, norms, and values rather than the social and cultural mechanisms by which norms are created and transmitted. I have factored performance into my account of democracy in two main ways: by adding accounts of democratic roles and actors, and of democratic stages. One of the major benefits of the roles and actors distinction was that it helped set up the idea that particular physical stages are required for their performance, following the idea of the scene–act ratio. It also helps make sense of peculiar local democratic practices, institutional arrangements, even spatial resources, much more so than idealized templates can. I have been keen throughout to stress the analytic value of using theories as torches to light up dark corners, not as frames that constrain the practices we take into account.

I have also resisted a narrowly territorial account of which people should be involved in which decisions, and have worked with an 'all affected' account instead. While that can have many different implications, the point in this context was to highlight the fact that it is rarely an easy matter to decide who the relevant *demos* is on any given issue. One can very often dismiss the sufficiency of attempts to restrict decision-making to 'the local community', simply because people living in (or working in, or originally coming from) a particular area are usually not the only ones affected by particular decisions, and not the only ones who have claims on particular spatial resources. Thus, it is not the case that Washingtonians should be the only ones making the decisions about Washington, DC; they should certainly have a voice, a great deal more than they presently do, but DC is the nation's capital, and defining who counts as a Washingtonian is itself fraught with difficulty. But this illustrates neatly a central contention of the book: democracy is one of the ways we sort out conflicts; it does not provide all the answers.

Starting from that base, I have made a number of overall claims in the book, as follows.

2. Space can be 'public' in up to four ways; it can have some apparently private features, yet still be public in other respects

The literature on public space tends to start with two categories, public and private, and then attempts to fit particular spaces into one category or the other, or in ambiguous, liminal space in between. This is a mistake. The categories 'public' and 'private' are bundles of concepts that do not fit neatly together. Thus, when we talk of public space, we are talking about space that has one or more of the following features:

1. it is openly accessible;
2. it consumes collective resources;
3. it has common impacts; and
4. it is a stage for the performance of public roles.

There are spaces that clearly fit one criterion but none of the others. For example, privately owned buildings make up the built environment, which has a collective impact, even if the buildings are inaccessible, are privately resourced (although we might argue about the water, air, and energy they consume), and have no public role functions. The fact that they are public in sense 3 means that they are a legitimate topic of public discussion, in terms of their impact on the streetscape, on the availability of light, air, and space for performing other roles. But it does *not* automatically follow that all the other normative criteria of publicity should apply. It might follow that they should be inspectable by public authorities for health and safety reasons, say; or, on the resource consumption point, efficiency, and compliance with standards. But it does not follow that they themselves should be openly accessible and be made available for the performance of public roles. This is important because, by starting with overly broad analytic categories that focus on accessibility and ownership, some urban theorists draw overly broad normative conclusions about the governance of particular public spaces, and some overly specific recommendations for the design of public space that can limit democratic performance.

Now, it might be thought that this analysis gives license to the restriction of freedom of speech and assembly in shopping malls – it might seem to be similar reasoning to that employed by the US Supreme Court in its notorious public space decision in 1972. It is not – but I will set out why when discussing the availability of public space at point 7.

3. *Political behaviour responds to 'place' as much as 'space'; we are therefore not prisoners of the particular spaces we make and inherit*

While physical forms clearly have some important effects on human action, in many cases they are much less significant than might be thought. While some forms have mandatory effects – walls are one example – most other behavioural effects result from a mix of physical and normative cues or, in some instance, purely normative, habitual ones. In the latter cases, forms act as symbols. Symbols can have powerful cueing effects, but those cues arise through use, habit, and narrative association, and not because of any necessary link between the form itself and that which it symbolizes. Even in examples like desire lines, where behaviour seems to follow physical configurations exactly, behaviour still occurs relative to an observed human propensity for shortcuts. It is also the case that some forms can operate in both mandatory and symbolic ways, the Israel–Palestine Wall and the Berlin Wall being prime examples.

This means that while the configuration of some public spaces matters a great deal, for other spaces it matters more what democratic performances are conducted within them, and thus what symbolic associations are built up over time. Therefore, it does matter that space for large-scale public protest is relatively large, flat, and unimpeded by lots of urban furniture, for example. It does matter that assembly buildings are relatively accessible by the public. But buildings like the Reichstag can have their behavioural impacts radically overturned by new political action, by new normative associations. While some Australian Members of Parliament might think that their new assembly building changed many things about parliamentary life, most of those changes had begun *before* they moved into the new building; for the most part, the new building symbolized, emplaced, their new modes of operating. Thus, we are not always prisoners of the public spaces we find ourselves using: there is no necessary link between a symbol and its referent, or between many political forms and their effects, depending on where they sit on the mandatory–symbolic continuum.

4. For the most part, behaviour setting effects are related to broad setting types, not the details

As well as the mandatory–symbolic distinction, there is also a distinction between the effects of what might be called the 'major' and 'minor' features of space. In this regard, the insights from behaviour setting theory were important. That branch of psychology tells us that behaviour responds to the shared associations of a broad setting type, not to the more minor details of the setting itself. Thus, what little discussion there has been on debating chambers in political science focuses on relatively unimportant details, and overlooks something elementary: that debating chambers are much more alike than they are different. They are all fairly large, and thus do not encourage intimacy; they all feature galleries – media, public, or both – and thus encourage playing to the gallery rather than the 'mild voice of reason' (Bessette, 1994); they are all arenas of party politics, something that cannot be designed out of the room. Within that major setting, the seating arrangement turns out to be a fairly minor detail, although it may come to mean something bigger by virtue of its symbolic associations in a particular context, and *not* because of any direct behavioural virtues. The only other major element that I argued for, along with size, was speaker location, rostrum-focused chambers sending more egalitarian messages than those where members speak from their seats.

The same holds true with committee rooms, which feature more variation in major type, and thus more variation in associated behaviour. Some committee rooms are modelled on courtrooms, and thus provoke similar responses – more tension, more conflict, more fear – because they have the same cues as places where retributive justice is dealt out by powerful agents of the state. Others are more like boardrooms or ordinary meeting rooms and send more business-like behavioural cues; yet others are designed to send messages of inclusion of diversity, to be culturally appropriate, and thus help people from minorities feel dignified in dignified settings. Many committee rooms are a mix of several of these features.

The main point is that if one wants to change politics, changing the seating arrangement in the main chamber is not going to help. Taking the assembly on the road – the ultimate in 'Big Tent politics' – as the South Africans have done might achieve something; having a people's assembly as in the *Landsgemeinden* would probably achieve more.

5. *Democracy requires physical performance*

Politics is a physical pursuit. Starting from the claim that political communication and argumentation requires a narrative form – otherwise there is no way to begin thinking about policy responses – I have argued that narration, even for the modern, virtual, dispersed public sphere, requires some physical embodiment, people occupying space and performing roles. This is partly a matter of direct engagement between political actors; sometimes a matter of attracting the cameras. Sometimes this is a way of communicating a story of ideas; sometimes the actions themselves are the story. That can be deliberate, as in protest action; or inadvertent, as when action is captured on mobile phone cameras and posted on You Tube. Either way, politics involves people, who take up space, doing things to other people. Political conflict is often about accessing and preventing access to space because of exclusive claims to resources that go with space. Combatants thus invoke limited definitions of 'us', limited definitions of the public in sense 3, and attempt to stop 'them' from accessing ('stealing') those resources. The resources might be physical – water, food, minerals, trade routes, etc. – or they might be symbolic – national buildings, plazas, flags, symbolic centres of public action, and spaces for the performance of public roles.

If politics is physical, democracy is too. Even on a fairly standard, liberal understanding, physical engagement matters to democracy in four major ways. First, the narrative and deliberative phases of democracy work best when conducted face to face, because it increases civility, brings in publicity's disciplining force, and allows all the non-verbal cues to be transmitted and received. Second, when it comes to making public claims, it is important that claim-makers be seen in dignified, symbolically rich public space so that their claim-making is made obvious to other citizens; to demonstrate to decision-makers the scale of public displeasure; and so that claim-makers themselves get the efficacy benefits that come with being seen to share views with others. Third, a sense of inclusion and membership of the *demos* is enhanced when one sees one's narratives anchored in symbolic, physical form. Even the presence of the marginal in public places is a necessary (but not sufficient) condition for them to feel and be recognized as fellow claim-makers by other members of the *demos* (Figures 9.1a and 9.1b). Fourth, the physical performance of decision-making helps attentive publics perform their scrutiny role – virtual decision-making can too easily become hidden, back-room decision-making. Forcing decision-*makers* into public view helps force decision-*making* into public view, with all the deliberative benefits of publicity that follow.

Physical performance also matters to politics more generally because it helps claim-makers establish the visual cues that support or undermine their arguments, particularly *ethos* claims. But that takes us onto the next claim.

Figure 9.1a. Recognizing the *demos* 1: Electric Avenue market, Brixton, London
Photo by Matus Benza, GNU Free Documentation License.

205

Figure 9.1b. Recognizing the *demos* 2: Helmsley market, North Yorkshire
Author photo.

6. Different roles have different stage requirements

For the first democratic role, narration, the possibilities are seemingly endless. Experiences are related in all sorts of settings, from pubs to parliaments, and plazas to parlours. As was the case in Eastern Europe before the fall of the Berlin Wall, it is important that a good proportion of those spaces is public only in the sense that public roles are performed in them; they might be private in that they are by invitation only, or not subjected to state surveillance; and so once again a blanket insistence that public space be openly accessible space misses the point of some sites of public discussion. But the city of Berlin also shows that for some kinds of symbolic narration – where the built environment is itself the physical anchor point – only a very specific space will do, and thus conflicts ensue over the competing meanings attached to the built environment and its ongoing production.

For the second democratic role, public claim-making, the requirements are narrower. I have argued that while employing mixed methods is essential to overcome the danger of ritualization and the danger that conflict can itself become the story, it is a requirement of democracy that there be space available that is both open and publicly accessible, and highly visible to attentive publics, especially the regular news media, bloggers, other opinion leaders, and decision-makers. Because it is important that such claim-making be taken seriously in the public sphere – it affects everyone in a given polity, after all – dignified sites are required, although here 'dignified' means 'set apart', not 'grandiose'. This tends to mean that the physical spaces for public claim-making are concentrated in and around sites of national symbolic importance. These tend to be the same sites where the key institutions of the formal public sphere are found. Sometimes those buildings are part of what dignifies the site; in other cases, they were built at those locations because those locations were already of national importance; in other cases it is a bit of both.

For the third and fourth democratic roles, the requirements are narrower again. Here, democracy requires single stages for binding collective decision-making. There are benefits that flow from forcing the physical performance of decision-making onto a single stage; or, at least, a small number of stages that are readily identifiable and accessible by attentive publics. It helps focus scrutiny on the powerful, it helps make the public present in deliberations, and it brings with it the benefits of face-to-face engagement. This feature plays back into the second role above. Having a single stage like this means that mass public engagement with decision-makers should take place nearby so that the public *can* annoy the powerful.

7. Not every stage can support all the roles at once; variety is required, and claim-making should be protected in some sites

As a corollary of point 6, variety is king when it comes to democratic public space – the fact that different roles are performed best on different kinds of stages implies that democratic cities require various kinds of public space. This might seem to be an extraordinarily simple point, but it is worth making because there is a tendency among officials and critics to treat all public space as qualitatively the same, and thus criticize particular spaces for not having qualities that they need not and cannot have. Stopping people from holding political rallies in a certain park, say, is not necessarily a problem so long as that park is not the only large rallying space near symbolically and politically important sites, and so long as the publics activated in that space have other spaces where they can make themselves visible and audible. Indeed, it might open up that park for other public purposes, and for other publics, and there is nothing in the concepts of democracy and public space that allows us to decide in advance which publics and which purposes we ought to privilege in any one space.

Interestingly, this gives us reason to resist the mantra commonly heard in Britain that justifies kicking certain people out of parks and squares on the grounds that the space should be available for 'all users'. If a given square is the primary public space next to the sites of the formal public sphere, then purposive political action, especially public claim-making, should have special status in that space, and should not be trumped by tourists, dog-walkers, picnickers, and Frisbee-throwers. On the same grounds, the US rules on public space are straightforwardly wrong because they fail to ensure the provision of space for public claim-making. Likewise, space for encountering the *demos* is important, although I have argued that unplanned encounters are often a great deal more structured than would appear; that some places meet this need in surprising ways; and that we should worry more about opportunities to act collectively as citizens, something that arises again at point 8.

The case of the Aboriginal Tent Embassy provides an interesting test of this idea. It suggests that democrats have a duty to protect the Embassy's presence on the lawn in front of Old Parliament House, and that claims about it interfering with a site of national symbolic importance are spectacularly beside the point: that is the reason the embassy is *there*, and not somewhere else. There might still be an argument to be had about maintaining the 'dignity' of the site – if too much dignity is lost, then the embassy suffers too – but again I use dignity in a relatively limited sense, and would caution against too readily accepting an argument that elites have used over the centuries to dismiss the claims of the *hoi polloi*.

Democratic performance does not just require gathering points; in some places, it is the marching, not the standing and shouting, that matters. Wide avenues are conducive not just to control, as is frequently said of Haussmann's Paris, but to the gathering of the masses as well. Narrow streets might be harder to control, but they less visibly demonstrate the scale of displeasure, and are thus less effective for the making of public claims. However, this too can be taken too far. Canberra is all broad avenues with relatively little space at the human scale. This makes the Australian Parliament remote and inaccessible, while other features of the security regime delegitimizes, trivializes, and mocks direct action. This is not, let me repeat, a feature solely of the space itself, but of the space combined with a control regime and set in a discursive context, of which more at point 8.

8. *There are multiple barriers to the provision of democratic public space*

In the second half of Chapter four, and in Part II, I considered how likely it was that democracy's spatial conditions would be met; and how well they were in fact met in my cases. There are numerous ways in which space is made unavailable for democratic performance.

Like any public good, public space is subject to the tragedy of the commons. This is especially noticeable in hilly, coastal Wellington and Hong Kong where reasonably flat land for building and open spaces is scarce and therefore pricy. It is no wonder that these places have few open spaces in their urban centres. But in a neo-liberal political economy where even the state values land in private sector terms, it can be very tempting indeed for city governments to hand over control of parts of the city to private sector finance and control. The upshot is space that is managed for certain kinds of publics – shoppers – and not for others – citizens. The state itself can monopolize space by reserving to its office-holders the right to perform their power in state and national celebrations, but deny performative rights to other citizens.

Another set of issues arise with the control of access to the buildings of the formal public sphere. Most buildings are inaccessible to the *demos* in all but the most trivial of senses: one can access them as a tourist but not as a citizen; one can buy knick-knacks from the gift shop but cannot have a conversation with one's representative – and certainly not participate in the debates in any other role than onlooker – although, given the publicity requirements of deliberative democracy, onlooking itself has value. There are good reasons for this exclusivity. There is a desire to maintain these buildings as working spaces, which implies a certain amount of access limitation – the President or Prime Minister would never get anything done if Joe Public could wander and in out of his or her office, or if he or she were forced to work only in the Assembly Chamber, say, as was the case in the early American republic. And that has a democratically good effect, because maintaining these buildings as working spaces helps keep the real work of democracy in the foreground. In those places where the work of democracy has been allowed to slip out the side door and into less accessible office buildings – the US Capitol is the most obvious example, but the same is true of others – it becomes less visible and thus less well-understood. There is thus a tension between allowing a certain amount of public access and involvement in the building, yet not allowing open slather, a tension that the Canadians managed better than others.

The key set of tensions concerned 'deputizing' public space: using features of the built environment to control people and provide security rather than relying on uniformed citizens to do the same job. This has had the perverse effect of creating *more* open space around some public buildings, but space to which access is strictly controlled, large setbacks that are useless for public purposes, and which, when taken to extremes, destroys the intimacy of cities. This is in addition to the more obvious policing of public space, and the tendency to put into police hands decisions over what counts as a legitimate public claim, and who counts as a legitimate public claim-maker. But the negotiated management approach to controlling protest has discouraged occasional activism and encouraged organization and professionalization – perhaps not what the model's managers intended.

9. *Accidental publics are privileged over purposive publics*

Underlying many of these problems, and a thread that has run throughout the book, is the idea that active public citizenship has become delegitimized, while other kinds of public – shoppers, football crowds, and the audiences at big public ceremonies – are encouraged. It is this background preference for public as shopper over public as citizen that underlies the extreme, even fatal, force that meets the modern protestor; that means that the public as tourist can penetrate the Australian Parliament but the public as citizen is viewed with great suspicion and restricted to swipe-card-controlled zones. Even some elected representatives are so restricted.

The same suspicion underlies many other features noted in this book: the US Supreme Court privileging private property over public citizenship; the encouragement of gated communities, skyways, and malls; and the turning of the buildings of the public sphere into historicized tourist experiences instead of sites for active democracy. Securing public space, as Vale (2005) puts it, means securing it from the public more often that securing it for the public. And this is something that certain urban design trends play into, privileging as they do filling open spaces with features that encourage individuals to stop and have a sandwich, and thus making them less useful for large-scale public claim-making.

10. *All this restricts the repertoires of purposive publics and purposive citizens*

One of the conclusions was that activists do not pack up and go away simply because the 'right kind' of stage is not available. They work in creative ways with the space available, although even then what counts as a transgressive, challenging act varies across time and space (Tilly, 2008). But it remains the case that some space is easier to work with, and to control, than other spaces. The city of Canberra is not conducive to large-scale claim-making, and while that does not stop Australians using iconic settings in *other* cities – the Sydney Harbour Bridge and Opera House especially – the analysis here suggests that something is lost in the move, and that is the ability to directly confront the powerful with popular displeasure; to inconvenience them, to rattle their cages. The more distant an elite becomes, the less accountable he or she is, and I have argued that matters in a literal as well as figurative sense.

Furthermore, if protest becomes seen as something that only hooded and masked thugs engage in, and not something that the concerned grandmothers of the world do too, then democracy itself is threatened.

All these points have implications for the comparative evaluation of democratic space. Before setting those out, it is important to reiterate a point of general evaluative approach, which arises from the discussion so far, and that is that the same form can mean different things in different contexts, and thus can have different impacts, different democratic implications in different contexts. This means we cannot evaluate democratic space in just a tape-measure-and-theodolite fashion. We need more qualitative strategies, and that runs counter to a great deal of democratic evaluation in political science, and against the tools used in political discussions of democratic public space. I start by discussing the measurement of democracy before laying out my own approach in more detail. After that, we turn to the comparisons.

Measuring Democratic Space

Measures of the extent of democracy go back at least sixty years, with Downs (1957) and his index, through Dahl and his two major attempts (1956, 1971), to more recent efforts of Arat (1991) and Vanhanen (1997), and the ongoing work of organizations like Freedom House, the Polity IV Project, and the Democratic Audit.[1] Measuring democracy is also big business. Some governments and NGOs make international aid allocation decisions, worth billions of dollars, on the basis of recipients' positions on democracy indices. The best known example of this is the United States' Millennium Challenge Account which targets funds according to a country's position on seventeen indicators, including the explicitly democratic indicators from Freedom House and the Worldwide Governance Indicators from the World Bank Institute (McMahon and Kornhelser, 2010).[2] Efforts to measure the extent of democracy and promote its spread have taken on more importance given the widespread belief in the idea that democracies do not go to war with each other (Russett and Oneal, 2001), in an age where democracies feel themselves threatened the world over.

However, while governments place a great deal of importance on democracy measures in such circumstances, the measures used tend to focus on a very limited range of electoral indicators. Some are mere institutional tick-lists: the presence of elections, multiple parties, and a competitive media, for example. Others are more behavioural: franchise and turnout measures, measures of electoral rights, frequency of peaceful power handovers at elections, and so forth. Some bundle economic and electoral freedoms, but very few go any further in attempting to measure democratic culture. The vast majority take the very thin view that democracy is about the election of leaders.

---

[1] http://www.freedomhouse.org http://www.systemicpeace.org/polity/polity4.htm http://www.democraticaudit.com and Beetham (1994).

[2] See the Millenium Challenge Corportation at http://www.mcc.gov and http://info.worldbank.org/governance/wgi/index.asp

Clearly, my account of democracy is a great deal thicker than that minimal, electoral one. Using the language of narrative and performance, it draws on quite a different tradition of democratic thought that focuses on the public sphere, and the myriad ways in which experiences are shared in public and claims are made on the public. It takes the sites of formal, binding, collective decision-making seriously: one of my central claims is that democracy requires there to be a single, public stage on which decisions are made, tested, and justified. But it goes well beyond those formal sites to include the broader fields in which citizens meet each other as citizens (i.e. performers of democratic roles) and not just as shoppers or picnickers, dog-walkers, or people-watchers.

Therefore, one way of answering the 'how democratic?' question would be simply to add some spatial criteria to the quantitative measures already available. Democracy requires visible, dignified stages for the pressing of public claims, meaning relatively featureless plazas in front of the assembly buildings. OK, so let's get out the maps and rulers, or Google Earth, and compare the physical size of available space for protest. I hope the counterarguments to that are fairly obvious. Mexico City's Zócalo would score very highly on such a measure, yet protest in Mexico is the most ritualized I came across. London would score very poorly, yet the ongoing battles for access to Parliament Square have kept the issue of freedoms of assembly and speech on the public agenda for some years now, the attempted repression being, oddly enough, good for maintaining the issue fresh in the media.[3] Thus, we have reasons to think that it might not be so easy to come up with indicators that mean the same thing in different contexts – which, of course, is a criticism frequently levelled at large-N comparative studies full stop, not just comparative democracy studies (Coppedge, 1999).

Thus, spatial ideas in democracy push us, ironically, away from measuring physical features in a physical, quantitative way and towards more qualitative approaches like Beetham's Democratic Audit. The measures that follow are in that spirit: broad, qualitative questions to ask of democratic cities rather than precise measures. Let us then return to the question that opened the chapter: what do the claims made in this book say about the requirements for an ideal democratic city? First, I set out the requirements for the buildings of the formal public sphere, then space for public claim-making, and then the more general features of the city.

The following points hold for the formal public sphere:

---

[3] For a similar point about the benefits to social movements of a somewhat hostile state, see Dryzek et al. (2003).

212

- Binding collective decisions should be taken on a single stage, preferably the main debating chamber, in full public view. In systems with separation of powers, executive decisions need to be tested on that stage before becoming law.

- The 'stage' will usually be a debating chamber, with speakers operating from one or more equally dignified positions.

- The chamber should be open to all registered voters and the formal news media. At the very least those observers should be clearly visible to Members and possibly have an active role in weekly debates. Educational visits should take place while the assembly is in session. Tourism and the revenue generated by gift shops should be secondary to those functions.

- Members should have offices in the main building and be accessible by constituents at set times in those offices, as well as in their constituencies.

- The buildings should contain a mix of large and small committee rooms that encourage deliberation, using furniture that can be laid out in flexible ways as the occasion demands. The buildings should have one, clear entrance that members and the public both use.

- The symbolic resources of the site need to strike a balance between whatever counts as 'timeless and dignified' in that particular time and place,[4] and inclusivity of the relevant variety of symbolic resources. Because dignity and patterns of cleavage change over time, the buildings should evolve too, rather than being preserved in historicizing aspic.

- The site should have plenty of unimpeded external space to the front for mass public gatherings and public ceremonials, but not be completely surrounded by open space so as to isolate it from the surrounding city streets. Roads should not be closed completely; perimeter security should be addressed in more risky but more humane ways.[5]

- Building managers should not restrict the use of the space to state- or elite-focused events only, but should allow it to be used by voters for the performance of 'dignified' public roles, however that is defined locally.

To the extent that these measures are normative requirements, part of what they aim at is an extension of the senses in which the buildings of the formal public sphere are seen to be public. When assembly buildings are closed to the *demos*, it is easy for them to be seen as public space merely in sense 2, as consumers of public resources. This closes down the range of symbolic

---

[4] See Chapter five for a discussion of how what counts as 'timeless' is very much dependent on particular conditions.

[5] Here, I am thinking of the perimeter security that was used around the 'square mile' of the City of London towards the end of the last big Irish Republican Army bombing campaign in the early 1990s. There, roads remained open, but check points ringed the City and vehicles larger than a standard family car were subjected to searches to guard against truck bombs.

associations of the building – remembering that buildings acquire meaning through use – and makes it easier for the building to be historicized or marginalized in other ways. The work done in them disappears from view. Open up the uses, and the building comes to symbolize the more expansive account of democracy that I defended in Chapter two; less about elite performances and legitimation, more about the wider public generation of debate, deliberation, and policy.

When it comes to the plazas in front of assembly buildings, how much space is 'enough'? That depends: a small space is good for making a small crowd look big; a very large space can make even a large crowd look small. From the point of view of protestors, what they want is impact through the limiting lens of a TV camera, so would probably prefer tight compression, and for that reason as well as others, the choice of location should be a tactical one to be made by the protestors, not something set in legislation. Still, it looks a great deal more impressive when the National Mall is filled to overflowing than when London's Parliament Square is filled to overflowing; there should be space for hundreds of thousands to gather, not just hundreds. And so on any account of 'enough', Hong Kong's Chater Gardens and Statue Square are woefully inadequate, while London's Parliament Square is not much better: too small, increasingly too furnished, and too policed.

The following are the initiatives for the wider democratic city:

- An extensive and low-cost (and thus heavily subsidized) public transport system that operates not just in hub and spoke sense, but with the spokes connected too.[6]

- The public provision of meeting rooms for citizens, fitted out with IT networks and projection equipment, perhaps at libraries, council buildings, colleges, and universities.

- A variety of parks and plazas such that the city as a whole can meet all the different uses of parks without expecting each and every space to meet all of them. Where the city's built heritage does not allow this, otherwise private space should be designated for public claim-making purposes.

- A balance struck in the built environment between preserving memories and rebuilding, representing different peoples and experiences in built form, which in turn implies an open and publicly accountable planning regime.

---

[6] This is a common problem in cities, with the centre connected to most suburbs, but the suburbs not connected to each other. London is attempting to address its failures in this regard with new east–west linkages; Canberra's bus network attempts to address this too, but in almost comical ways, with winding bus routes that greatly multiply point-to-point journey times.

214

- Footpaths and streets designated as public space in sense 1, not to be controlled by private security guards, business associations, or residents' associations, regardless of ownership.

- Serious attempts to promote urban development that integrates rather than stratifies.

There may be other more precise initiatives that one could add to this list, but some of the practices I found were pleasantly surprising, and so I am suspicious of being overly prescriptive here, especially applying injunctions from northern European and American contexts to entirely different ones. Still, the aims of these provisions are to redignify the performance of citizenship; and to challenge moves that emplace hierarchy over membership of a common *demos*. Therefore, I strongly dislike the gated community movement, strongly dislike the restrictions on free speech in favour of private property, and hark back to times and places when social housing was built in prime locations. I am thinking here of 1930s New Zealand, where wealthy suburbs in the latter became host to pockets of well-designed and built state housing in a way that seems almost unthinkable now. A clearer sense of 'we' is, I have argued, important to democracy yet undermined on a daily basis in many places, and democrats should celebrate those cities where such moves are being resisted.

Now, the overall acid test for democracy defined as it is here is this: are the narratives that are told at street level and the claims that they underpin accurately represented and determinative in formal decision-making moments, and are they *seen* to be so? That means that my key measure of the level of democracy in a given state or democratic system is a discursive one, one that traces claims as they live and die in deliberative processes.[7] What I am arguing here is that those claims are emplaced: some because they are claims about physical, symbolic, and imaginative resources; others because they are performed in public space; or a combination of the two.

The Cases Compared

How do my cases stack up against those criteria? To do this job properly, each one of my cities would require a long, qualitative, cross-disciplinary project, so what follows can only be impressionistic. The judgements are offered as hypotheses to be tested, not firm conclusions.

---

[7] This is something that I am taking up in forthcoming work. See Parkinson and Mansbridge (forthcoming) and other contributions to the Deliberative Society conference at the University of York, June 2009 (available at http://www.york.ac.uk/politics/research/conferences/deliberative/).

Table 9.1. The cases compared

	Single stage	Single speaking position	Accessibility	Offices in main building	Committee room style	Symbolic cues	Open plaza	Public purpose availability	Public transport system	Public meeting space	Variety of parks	Memory and rebuilding	Public footpaths	Integration	Total ticks (and queries)
Cape Town			?		✓	✓			✓		–	?			3(2)
Santiago/Valparaíso		✓		✓	–						✓			✓	4(1)
Tokyo	✓		?		–				✓		–	?	✓		✓	4(2)
London	✓		?		✓		?				–	?	✓		✓	4(4)
Mexico City		✓		✓	–				✓			?	✓	✓	5(1)
Hong Kong			✓					✓	✓	✓	?		✓	✓	5(1)
Washington, DC	✓		?			?	✓		✓		✓				5(2)
Canberra	✓		?	?	✓	✓	?	?		✓	?	?	✓	✓	5(6)
Ottawa	✓		✓	✓	✓	?	✓	✓		–	✓	?			7(2)
Wellington	✓		✓	?	✓	✓	?	✓		✓		✓		✓	8(2)
Berlin	✓	✓	?		✓	?			✓		–	✓	✓	✓	–	8(2)

Table 9.1 sets out each of the criteria and gives a simple tick to cases that I have singled out for praise over the course of the analysis so far; a question mark where there are ambivalent features; and a dash where I do not have evidence to hand. A blank square means a negative assessment. I will not plod through every detail here. Instead, let me tease out what I think are the most interesting conclusions.

While not wanting to insist on the quantitative rigour of this, I have put the cities in a rough order from those with the least number of desirable features clearly present to those with the most. Two of the worst are Cape Town and London, but for different reasons. Cape Town has very cheap public transport, along with an effort to include symbolically and some reasonably good committee room space, but otherwise the buildings of the formal public sphere are isolated from the rest of the city by walls, gates, and fences, while what goes on inside the building is the preserve of an elite – public access is achieved much more when Parliament goes on one of its road trips, not in its main site in Cape Town. Parliament is just one of several stages in multi-centred South Africa, even more so when its politics are so dominated by one party. Furthermore, the city itself remains heavily divided, with townships isolated by infrastructure and the barren Cape Flats; gated communities springing up (but being fought by the City Council); and District Six being rebuilt slowly but not for its former residents. What London does well is focusing activity on the one stage, even in a so-called differentiated polity; the relative accessibility of the site, despite the ghastly and inexcusable glass partitions in the public

216

gallery; and the style of its committee rooms. Perhaps controversially, I have given London a tick on the integration score too. While it might not feel this way to close observers of the city, and while there is clearly a north/south divide in the city, come into the centre and one really does encounter all sorts – the British *demos* feels infinitely more varied in central London than does the American *demos* in central Washington, DC, let alone the even-more exclusive Canberra where everyone seems white and middle class. But London is a ferociously expensive city to get around; its public spaces are policed to an extent unmatched except by Washington; and it is indulging in the privatization of footpaths and roadways.

Ottawa does not get an integration tick either, because of the degree to which it is so firmly an Anglo city. There are a few Outaouais neighbourhoods to the East, but the city's dignified spaces all speak with English symbolic language, not French, and certainly not any native languages. Symbolically, it is really only Canberra, Cape Town, and Wellington that make much effort to include a variety of symbolic resources in their designs. While both Ottawa and London make symbolic references to constituent parts, it is all done in a single symbolic language, which is certainly not the language of a subordinate group.

However, Ottawa comes near the top of my list overall. In terms of the formal public sphere's accessibility and availability for other public purposes, I have given ticks to Ottawa because of the efforts made to maintain public access, to redesign committee rooms for more deliberative purposes and to meet constituents in the building, the arrangements made for the media, its willingness to hold both large and small-scale public celebrations on the Hill and in the buildings, and also the efforts made to permit protest in the grounds. Wellington gets a tick too because of its presumptions of access by the media into the heart of the executive wing, its use of ceremonial spaces for a large range of public functions, its attempts to include people in the design of committee rooms, and the toleration of some performances by some New Zealanders in the open public galleries. Both the Ottawa and Wellington assemblies are working buildings rather than merely symbolic entities. However, these comments should not be taken as unqualified, ringing endorsements. Access is getting tighter, behavioural restrictions are severe, the galleries are out of sight, and there is little public performance of citizenship. These are the best of a bad lot, and far from the ideal.

One feature worth praising in Wellington is the provision of public meeting space in libraries and city council buildings. Community groups have long been supported with information infrastructure and meeting spaces. Where Wellington falls down is in its extensive but relatively expensive public transport system, and the increasing private control of footpaths, elements of the waterfront, parks, and other formerly public spaces. Given its physical geography, it is a city in which open space is at a premium and city and central governments have rarely been minded to preserve or create it except in the form of the Town Belt, a ribbon of wooded space that covers many of the steep hillsides, and Midland Park, a tiny central city park that would hardly rate a mention were it not for the fact that it resulted from a public campaign for some open city space following the demolition of an old hotel in the 1970s. Other cities in the sample present similar challenges, but it is in Hong Kong where these reach an extreme degree, and public parks are to be found squeezed under road flyovers, or wedged into the corners between buildings and steep, stepped streets. And yet these are fairly free spaces. Certainly, there are lots of 'no dogs, no ball games' signs in them, and yet these rules are often more honoured in the breach. Contrast Tokyo where space is more formalized, and certainly more patrolled. Yoyogi Park, while not exactly central, is an astonishingly extensive but also empty space in such a densely populated city, more to be looked at than used, and certainly not used for a picnic. The result is that in Hong Kong one gets the sense that public space is the domain of the people, a public resource; whereas in Tokyo the sense is more that it is a state resource, and 'people' are rather beside the point.

When it comes to the provision of single stages, strongly presidential systems are clearly at a disadvantage, because their main deliberative assembly simply does not matter all that much. I have ticked Washington, DC, on this score because in the United States, presidential measures must be tested on the floor of Congress, and are frequently thrown out or heavily amended; unlike in Chile, Hong Kong, Mexico, or South Africa where the legislature has less power, or is sometimes a mere rubber stamp. But Washington, DC, has a major problem in that the Congress building is becoming historicized, with democratic work moving out of the frame and heritage and tourism moving in. The buildings make what seem to me to be rather ham-fisted attempts at inclusion in the shape of the National Statuary Collection, for example. Overall, Washington, DC, stands as a warning about what happens when 'dignity' is allowed to take precedence over democratic work: it feeds elitism, becomes a reason to exclude the people who ultimately pay for it all, and make the work of democratic re-engagement even harder. It has the wonderful resource of the National Mall, but squanders that resource by making the Congress building a mere backdrop; a magnificent one, certainly, but a backdrop nonetheless.

In the end, Berlin has ticked many of the boxes not, I suspect, because it is the perfect democratic city, but because it has been the site for so long of battles over the use of public space for political purposes. Issues of public space have been salient for decades because it is in public space that various German regimes have attempted to inscribe their dominance. In Canberra and Wellington, one side won the battle, decisively, with the result that the precolonial spaces were almost completely erased, concreted over by the new colonial

218

capitals. In Berlin, the victories have never been so utterly complete. The legacy of several previous phases of contestation remains, too dominant to tear down and erase completely. And thus public space is a matter of discussion in Berlin in a way that it is simply not in Wellington, say. The big problems in Berlin include the fact that the Reichstag too makes the tourism mistake, with access more symbolic than actual, and with the building oddly isolated from the rest of the city, *surrounded* by open space, avenues, and the river, rather than having, ideally, just one face to a large open space. It is not a building one just happens upon.

And despite being designed with democratic imperatives in mind, and despite having a parliament that was supposed to embody democratic values, Canberra has a very mixed scorecard. In its favour are the excellent parks for public relaxation, exploration, and celebration. However, it is not a city built at the human scale, but for grand vistas. Like Berlin, its public sites are thus too isolated from the city that surrounds them (to say nothing of the isolation of the city itself), while the current policing regime makes direct public engagement with politics a humiliating, futile experience. The parliament building itself appears to allow a great deal of access, but to spaces that are not used by parliamentarians, while even parliamentarians are sorted into insiders and outsiders by the separation of ministerial offices from the rest of the building. It is like Tokyo in that public space feels like a state resource, not a popular resource, despite the opposite population densities of the two cities. While Washington is an object lesson in elitism, Canberra is an object lesson in the folly of thinking that one can design democracy in a grand sense, abstracted from actual people, their concerns, and behaviour.

Implications

As I have already stressed, these are preliminary impressions based on greatly varying degrees of familiarity with the cities in question, and are thus offered more as hypotheses for further investigation than firm conclusions. Nonetheless, they have some interesting implications for the evaluation of democracy more generally. Does this analysis mean that Berlin is a more democratic city than Cape Town? Yes, in my view it does. Does that mean that Germany is a more democratic state than South Africa? Now I am really going to stick my neck out and say yes; on these measures, it is. If public space matters at all to democracy – and I have argued at length that it does – then German democracy is enhanced to the extent that battles over the public representation of the German *demos* are played out in its built environment and other public spaces, and not hidden away under a uniformity of design. It is enhanced to the extent that its primary building of the formal public sphere is an

219

egalitarian and open forum, despite the problems of its siting. It is enhanced to the degree that Germans can access that space via cheap public transport and footpaths that are not privately controlled. It could be better, but it could be worse, and in Cape Town, and in Santiago/Valparaíso, it *is* worse, with the public heavily stratified, the formal public sphere shunted off into a corner, policed and otherwise inaccessible, competing histories overwritten and denied.

These are relatively easy contrasts to draw. Things get tougher when the focus shifts to the 'mid-table' cities because my approach is not conducive to fine-grained, quantitative distinctions. Does this analysis mean that Berlin is a more democratic city than London? Again, in some ways the answer is yes. I have mentioned some of its features already, but in London the assembly is inaccessible in important ways and heavily, overwhelmingly policed; the space available for public protest is small and highly controlled; the city has pockets where the very streets are privatized; and public transport is privatized, patchy, and expensive by comparison with the other cities in the sample. On the plus side, while there are many areas that have been 'regenerated' out of all recognition – the Docklands especially, but there are lots of other examples – there are also many parts of the city where the physical anchors of memory remain, and where the variety of experiences and narratives are memorialized in art works and the built environment itself. There is an enormously rich variety of parks in London, and while too many of them are inaccessible, many could so easily become more democratically valued if the policing approach were modified. And, like Berlin, the restrictions on access to public space, and the policing of protest, have themselves become topics of public debate, with efforts afoot in recent years to overturn some of the restrictions. This means that while Parliament Square is really inadequate for democratic purposes, the fact that it is a centre of contention means that issues of access to public space are on the agenda, just as in Berlin where battles over the built environment have put a different set of spatial issues in the public realm.

Still, if we are going to pursue measures of democracy in either qualitative or quantitative ways, then an implication of this book is that we need to add spatial elements to our measures. No measure of democracy that I am aware of does so, and yet it would be a relatively simple task. I am not going to attempt to create some quantitative measures for the reasons already specified, but the ease can be illustrated by taking the Democratic Audit, the most qualitative example, which poses a total of thirty questions on the health of democracy in four broad sets: the electoral process, open and accountable government, civil and political rights, and civil society. To Beetham's second set of questions (1994: 37–8), one could add:

- to what extent are decision-makers forced to perform their roles in the assembly? and

- to what extent is the public able to witness and engage in scrutiny and accountability?

To the fourth set of questions (1994: 39), one could add:

- are there suitable places available for public contestation, expression, and claim-making?

These questions capture the main thrust of the two sets of questions on pp. 213–14 above, yet are in the spirit of the Audit because they leave plenty of room for qualitative, context-sensitive judgements.

What can a *demos* do with a city that fails to deliver the requisite spaces? The grand events that present windows of opportunity for the wholesale redesign and rebuilding of cities are few and far between, and I do not recommend embracing some of those means anyway – the destruction caused by war and natural disaster is one such window, but I will not be quite so mad as to argue in their favour on those grounds. Most people, therefore, are going to have to work with the built environment they have been bequeathed, but they can do so in two ways. On the one hand, assembly buildings can be refurbished and committee rooms reorganized so that their 'major' and 'mandatory' design elements – the size of the chamber, the layout of committee rooms – help express desired values. Plazas can be redesigned if not necessarily enlarged, removing the furniture from claim-making plazas and ensuring that other parks have a variety of forms to meet a variety of needs, for kids on skateboards as well as parents pushing prams, as well as book lovers and the homeless sheltering – although surely there is something perverse about ensuring park space caters for the homeless rather than building more social housing.

On the other hand, I have stressed throughout that buildings and the built environment change meaning with changes of use, especially spaces that operate more at the symbolic end than the mandatory end of the scale. Therefore, grand design (as seen in Canberra, for instance), besides having unintended and anti-democratic results, may not be necessary in the first place. One embeds new values in an old place by turning it to a new use. More often than not, it is the use and habit that creates buildings' meaning and the behaviours that follow those cues, not simply the arrangement of the bricks.

Finally, there is a broader implication for the study of politics and policy, which is that it should start to attend to performative aspects a great deal more than it does at present. There are a few branches of political science where this call would not surprise: the study of social movements and contentious politics, especially through the work of

221

Tilly (2004, 2007, 2008); the narrative, argumentative branches of policy studies (Stone, 2002; Hajer, 2009; among others); and political communication studies, following Edelman (1976, 1988). But as a specialist in deliberative theory and practice, it strikes me as increasingly problematic that current democratic theory emphasizes the give and take of reasons and rational selection of alternatives as its normative and descriptive standards. This emphasis is fascinating and fruitful, but all around us we see a rich pageantry of democratic performance, a surprisingly narrow range of scripts that allegedly free, rational actors follow, yet a wonderfully creative variety of ways in which democratic performers act out their roles. Even if the sceptical reader does not buy my main claim that democracy really does require physical stages for its performance, I hope at the very least that this work will prompt some to think about the performance of democratic politics. It *is* a rich and fascinating performance, and one worthy of serious attention.

References

Adams, Douglas. 1979. *The hitch hiker's guide to the galaxy*. London: Pan.

Agnew, John. 1987. *Place and politics: the geographical mediation of state and society*. Boston: Allen & Unwin.

Allen, Edward. 2005. *How buildings work: the natural order of architecture*. New York: Oxford University Press.

Almond, Gabriel, and Sidney Verba. 1963. *The civic culture*. Princeton: Princeton University Press.

Anderson, Benedict. 1991. *Imagined communities*. Revised ed. London: Verso.

Anonymous. 2002. Sinn Féin challenges Stormont symbols. *An Phoblacht*, 16 May.

——2003. Unsightly security on the Hill. *Canberra Times*, 28 May.

——2007. One of last remaining chunks of Berlin Wall disappears. *Deutsche Welle World*, 11 April.

Arat, Z. F. 1991. *Democracy and human rights in developing countries*. London: Lynne Rienner.

Arendt, Hannah. 1958. *The human condition*. Chicago: University of Chicago Press.

Au, Wagner James. 2007. Fighting the front, 15 January 2007. In *New world notes*. http://nwn.blogs.com/nwn/2007/01/stronger_than_h.html

Backscheider, Paula. 1993. *Spectacular politics: theatrical power and mass culture in early modern England*. Baltimore: Johns Hopkins University Press.

Baechler, Jean. 1980. Liberty, property and equality. In *Property: Nomos 22*, ed. J. R. Pennock and J. Chapman. New York: New York University Press, pp. 269–88.

Bandura, Albert. 1982. Self-efficacy mechanisms in human agency. *American Psychologist* 37 (2):122–47.

Barber, Benjamin. 1988. Participation and Swiss democracy. *Government and Opposition* 23 (1):31–50.

——2001. Malled, mauled and overhauled: arresting suburban sprawl by transforming suburban malls into usable civic space. In *Public space and democracy*, ed. M. Hénaff and T. Strong. Minneapolis: University of Minnesota Press, pp. 201–20.

Barber, Lucy. 2002. *Marching on Washington: the forging of an American political tradition*. Berkeley, CA: University of California Press.

Barker, Rodney S. 2001. *Legitimating identities: the self-presentations of rulers and subjects*. Cambridge: Cambridge University Press.

Barker, Roger G. 1968. *Ecological psychology: the environment of human behavior*. Stanford, CA: Stanford University Press.

Barnes, Colin, and Geof Mercer. 2003. *Disability*. Cambridge: Polity Press.

Barnes, Colin, and Michael Oliver. 1995. Disability rights: rhetoric and reality in the UK. *Disability and Society* 10 (1):111–16.

Barnes, Marian. 1997. *Care, communities and citizens*. London: Longman.

Barnett, Clive. 2003. *Culture and democracy: media, space and representation*. Edinburgh: Edinburgh University Press.

Barthes, Roland. 1981. The theory of the text. In *Untying the text: a post-structuralist reader*, ed. R. Young. Boston: Routledge & Kegan Paul, pp. 31–47.

Bassett, Michael. 1972. *Confrontation '51: the 1951 waterfront dispute*. Wellington: Reed.

BBC. 2005. Historical churches. Radio 4, 8:52 a.m., 24 June.

—— 2009. Obama's inauguration. *BBC News*, http://news.bbc.co.uk/1/hi/world/americas/obama-inauguration/7837927. stm 20 January.

Beck, Haig, ed. 1988. *The architecture of Australia's Parliament House*. Sydney: Watermark.

Beetham, David, ed. 1994. *Defining and measuring democracy*. London: Sage.

Bell, Daniel. 1993. *Communitarianism and its critics*. Oxford: Clarendon Press.

Bellah, Robert N. 1967. Civil religion in America. *Daedalus* 96 (1):1–21.

Bender, Barbara, ed. 1993. *Landscape: politics and perspectives*. Providence, RI: Berg.

Benhabib, Seyla. 1992. Models of public space: Hannah Arendt, the liberal tradition, and Jürgen Habermas. In *Habermas and the public sphere*, ed. C. Calhoun. Cambridge, MA: MIT Press, pp. 73–98.

Benjamin, Walter. 1999. *The arcades project*. Cambridge, MA, and London: Belknap Press/Harvard University Press.

Benton-Short, Lisa. 2007. Bollards, bunkers, and barriers: securing the National Mall in Washington, DC. *Environment and Planning D: Society and Space* 25 (3):424–46.

Berlin, Isaiah. 1958. *Two concepts of liberty*. Oxford: Clarendon Press.

Bessette, Joseph M. 1994. *The mild voice of reason: deliberative democracy and American national government*. Chicago: University of Chicago Press.

Beyme, Klaus von. 1998. *The legislator: German parliament as a centre of political decision-making*. Aldershot: Ashgate.

Bickford, Susan. 2000. Constructing inequality: city spaces and the architecture of citizenship. *Political Theory* 28 (3):355–76.

Bierce, Ambrose. 1993. *The devil's dictionary*. Mineola, NY: Dover.

Black, John W. 1961. The effect of room characteristics upon vocal intensity and rate. *Journal of the Acoustical Society of America* 22:174–6.

Block, Lisa, and Garnett Stokes. 1989. Performance and satisfaction in private versus nonprivate work settings. *Environment and Behavior* 21 (3):277–97.

Borden, Iain. 2001. *Skateboarding, space and the city: architecture and the body*. Oxford: Berg.

Bragdon, Claude. 1918. *Architecture and democracy*. New York: Alfred Knopf.

Burgess, Jacquelin, Carolyn Harrison, and Melanie Limb. 1988. People, parks and the urban green: a study of popular meanings and values for open spaces in the city. *Urban Studies* 25:455–73.

Burke, Kenneth. 1969. *A grammar of motives*. Berkeley, CA: University of California Press.

Byers, Jack. 1998. The privatization of downtown public space: the emerging grade-separated city in North America. *Journal of Planning Education and Research* 17 (3):189–205.

CABE. 2002. *The value of good design: how buildings and spaces create economic and social value*. London: Commission for Architecture and the Built Environment.

Calhoun, Craig, ed. 1992. *Habermas and the public sphere*. Cambridge, MA: MIT Press.

Cannadine, David. 2000. The Palace of Westminster as palace of varieties. In *The Houses of Parliament: history, art, architecture*, ed. C. Riding and J. Riding. London: Merrell, pp. 11–29.

Catt, Helena. 1999. *Democracy in practice*. London: Routledge.

Chambers, Simone. 1996. *Reasonable democracy: Jürgen Habermas and the politics of discourse*. Ithaca: Cornell University Press.

Chapple, Geoff. 1984. *1981: the tour*. Wellington: Reed.

Cheng, Joseph Y. S., ed. 2005. *The July 1 protest rally: interpreting a historic event*. Hong Kong: City University of Hong Kong Press.

Cheung, Chor Yung. 2005. The Principal Officials Accountability System: not taking responsible government seriously? In *The July 1 protest rally: interpreting a historic event*, ed. J. Y. S. Cheng. Hong Kong: City University of Hong Kong Press, pp. 151–84.

Chiesura, Anna. 2004. The role of urban parks for the sustainable city. *Landscape and Urban Planning* 68 (1):129–38.

Childs, Sarah. 2004. A feminised style of politics? Women MPs in the House of Commons. *British Journal of Politics and International Relations* 6 (1):3–19.

——Mona Lena Krook. 2008. Critical mass theory and women's political representation. *Political Studies* 56:725–36.

Christman, John. 1994. *The myth of property: toward an egalitarian theory of ownership*. Oxford: Oxford University Press.

CNN. 2009. CNN live events special: ordinary citizens make extraordinary plans to attend historic inauguration. http://transcripts.cnn.com/TRANSCRIPTS/0901/17/se.10.html

Cohen, Jean. 1996. Democracy, difference, and the right of privacy. In *Democracy and difference: contesting the boundaries of the political*, ed. S. Benhabib. Princeton: Princeton University Press, pp. 187–217.

Cohen, Joshua. 1989. Deliberation and democratic legitimacy. In *The good polity: normative analysis of the state*, ed. A. Hamlin and P. Pettit. Oxford: Blackwell, pp. 17–34.

Coleman, Clive. 2006. Heads, we extradite. Tails, you don't. *The Times*, 29 June.

Collier, Richard. 2005. Fathers 4 justice: law and the new politics of fatherhood. *Child and Family Law Quarterly* 17 (4):511–34.

Connolly, William. 1991. *Identity/difference: democratic negotiations of political paradox*. Ithaca: Cornell University Press.

Cooke, Rachel. 2005. Bold, brave, beautiful. *The Observer*, 18 September 2005.

Coppedge, Michael. 1999. Thickening thin concepts and theories: combining large and small in comparative politics. *Comparative Politics* 31 (4):465–76.

Cybriwsky, Roman. 1999. Changing patterns of urban public space: observations and assessments from the Tokyo and New York metropolitan areas. *Cities* 16 (4):223–31.

Dahl, Robert. 1956. *A preface to democratic theory*. Chicago: University of Chicago Press.

—— 1971. *Polyarchy: participation and opposition*. New Haven: Yale University Press.

—— 1989. *Democracy and its critics*. New Haven: Yale University Press.

Davies, Jonathan. 2003. Partnerships versus regimes: why regime theory cannot explain urban coalitions in the UK. *Journal of Urban Affairs* 25 (3):253–69.

Davis, Mike. 1990. *City of quartz: excavating the future in Los Angeles*. London: Verso.

Dean, Jodi. 2001. Publicity's secret. *Political Theory* 29 (5):624–50.

della Porta, Donatella, and Herbert Reiter, eds. 1998. *Policing protest*. Minneapolis: University of Minnesota Press.

Dewey, John. 1924. *The public and its problems*. New York: Holt.

Dockemdorff, Eduardo, Alfredo Rodríguez, and Lucy Winchester. 2000. Santiago de Chile: metropolitization, globalization and inequity. *Environment and Urbanization* 12 (1):171–83.

Dovey, Kim. 1999. *Framing places: mediating power in built form*. London: Routledge.

—— 2001. Memory, democracy and urban space: Bangkok's 'Path to Democracy'. *Journal of Urban Design* 6 (3):265–82.

Dow, Coral. 2000. Aboriginal tent embassy: icon or eyesore? *Chronology 3: 1999–2000*. Canberra: Social Policy Group, Parliamentary Library.

Downs, Anthony. 1957. *An economic theory of democracy*. New York: Harper & Row.

Dryzek, John. 1987. Complexity and rationality in public life. *Political Studies* 35 (3):424–42.

—— 1990. *Discursive democracy*. New York: Cambridge University Press.

—— 1996. *Democracy in capitalist times: ideals, limits, struggles*. Oxford: Oxford University Press.

—— 1997. *The politics of the earth: environmental discourses*. Oxford: Oxford University Press.

—— 2000. *Deliberative democracy and beyond: liberals, critics, contestations*. Oxford: Oxford University Press.

—— 2006. *Deliberative global politics*. Cambridge: Polity.

—— David Downes, Christian Hunold, David Schlosberg, and Hans-Kristian Hernes. 2003. *Green states and social movements: environmentalism in the United States, United Kingdom, Germany, and Norway*. Oxford: Oxford University Press.

—— Simon Niemeyer. 2008. Discursive representation. *American Political Science Review* 102:481–93.

Duncan, Hugh Dalziel. 1989. *Culture and democracy: the struggle for form in society and architecture in Chicago and the Middle West during the life and times of Louis H. Sullivan*, 2nd ed. New Brunswick: Transaction.

Dunsire, Andrew. 1973. Administrative doctrine and administrative change. *Public Administration Bulletin* 15 (December):39–56.

Earl, Jennifer, and Sarah Soule. 2006. Seeing blue: a police-centered explanation of protest policing. *Mobilization* 11 (2):145–64.

Eco, Umberto. 1986. *Travels in hyperreality*. San Diego: Harcourt Brace.

Edelman, Murray. 1976. *The symbolic uses of politics*. Urbana: University of Illinois Press.

—— 1988. *Constructing the political spectacle*. Chicago: University of Chicago Press.

Elkin, Stephen. 1987. *City and regime in the American republic*. Chicago: University of Chicago Press.

Elliot, Larry. 2010. Mervyn King warned that election victor will be out of power for a generation, claims economist. *The Guardian*, 29 April.

Emrich, Cynthia, Holly Brower, Jack Feldman, and Howard Garland. 2001. Images in words: presidential rhetoric, charisma, and greatness. *Administrative Science Quarterly* 46 (3):527–57.

Estlund, David. 1993. Making truth safe for democracy. In *The idea of democracy*, ed. D. Copp, J. Hampton, and J. E. Roemer. New York: Cambridge University Press, pp. 71–100.

Feldman, Ofer. 1996. The political personality of Japan: an inquiry into the belief systems of Diet members. *Political Psychology* 17 (4):657–82.

Ferris, John, Carol Norman, and Joe Sempik. 2001. People, Land and sustainability: community gardens and the social dimension of sustainable development. *Social Policy and Administration* 35 (5):559–68.

Fewtrell, Terry. 1985. A new Parliament House: a new parliamentary order. *Australian Journal of Public Administration* 44 (4):323–32.

—— 1991. A new parliamentary order? *Australian Journal of Public Administration* 50 (1):84–93.

—— Clement McIntyre, and John Uhr. 2008. Roundtable summaries and transcript. *Architecture and parliament: how do buildings help shape parliamentary business?* Canberra: Parliament of Australia.

Field, Cynthia, Isabelle Gournay, and Thomas Somma, eds. 2007. *Paris on the Potomac: the French influence on the architecture and art of Washington, DC*. Athens, OH: Ohio University Press.

Field, Sean. 2001. *Lost communities, living memories: remembering forced removals in Cape Town*. Cape Town: Centre for Popular Memory, University of Cape Town.

Fischer, Frank. 1990. *Technocracy and the politics of expertise*. London: Sage.

—— 2009. *Democracy and expertise*. Oxford: Oxford University Press.

—— John Forester. 1993. *The argumentative turn in policy analysis and planning*. Durham: Duke University Press.

Fishkin, James S. 1997. *The voice of the people: public opinion and democracy*, 2nd ed. New Haven: Yale University Press.

Flinders, Matthew, and Jim Buller. 2006. Depoliticisation: principles, tactics and tools. *British Politics* 1 (3):293–318.

Flint, Anthony. 2005. Both safe and sorry? Second generation security measures could be degrading what's best about our cities. *Planning* 71 (6):4–9.

Forester, John. 1984. Bounded rationality and the politics of muddling through. *Public Administration Review* 44:23–30.

Fourth Plinth Project. 2005. *Unveiling*. Fourth Plinth Project/Greater London Authority [cited 3 May 2007]. http://www.fourthplinth.co.uk/unveiling.htm

Franklin, Benjamin, and William Temple Franklin. 1818. *Memoirs of the life and writings of Benjamin Franklin*. London: Henry Colburn.

Freeman, Joanne Barrie. 2004. Opening Congress. In *The American Congress: the building of democracy*, ed. J. E. Zelizer. Boston: Houghton Mifflin, pp. 25–37.

Fung, Archon. 2003. Survey article: recipes for public spheres: eight institutional design choices and their consequences. *Journal of Political Philosophy* 11 (3):338–67.

Geertz, Clifford. 1985. Centers, kings, and charisma: reflections on the symbolics of power. In *Rites of power: symbolism, ritual, and politics since the Middle Ages*, ed. S. Wilentz. Philadelphia: University of Pennsylvania Press, pp. 13–38.

Geuss, Raymond. 2001. *Public goods, private goods*. Princeton: Princeton University Press.

Gibson, Rachel, and Sarah Miskin. 2002. Australia deliberates? A critical analysis of the role of the media in deliberative polling. In *Constitutional politics: the republic referendum and the future*, ed. J. Warhurst and M. Mackerras. St Lucia: University of Queensland Press, pp. 163–75.

Gieryn, Thomas F. 2000. A space for place in sociology. *Annual Review of Sociology* 26:463–96.

Goffman, Erving. 1963. *Behavior in public places: notes on the social organization of gatherings*. New York: Free Press.

Goodin, Robert. 1992. *Green political theory*. Cambridge: Polity.

—— 2003. *Reflective democracy*. Oxford: Oxford University Press.

—— 2007. Enfranchising all affected interests, and its alternatives. *Philosophy and Public Affairs* 35 (1):40–68.

—— 2008. *Innovating democracy: democratic theory and practice after the deliberative turn*. Oxford: Oxford University Press.

—— John Dryzek. 1980. Rational participation: the politics of relative power. *British Journal of Political Science* 10 (3):273–92.

—— Christian List. 2006. A conditional defense of plurality rule: generalizing May's theorem in a restricted informational environment. *American Journal of Political Science* 50 (4):940–9.

Goodsell, Charles T. 1988a. The architecture of parliaments: legislative houses and political culture. *British Journal of Political Science* 18 (3):287–302.

—— 1988b. *The social meaning of civic space: studying political authority through architecture*. Lawrence, KA: University Press of Kansas.

Gorringe, Hugo, and Michael Rosie. 2008. It's a long way to Auchterarder! 'Negotiated management' and mismanagement in the policing of G8 protests. *British Journal of Sociology* 59 (2):187–205.

Gournay, Isabelle, and Jane Loeffler. 2002. Washington and Ottawa: a tale of two embassies. *Journal of the Society of Architectural Historians* 61 (4):480–507.

Grapard, Allan. 1982. Flying mountains and walkers of emptiness: toward a definition of sacred space in Japanese religions. *History of Religions* 21 (3):195–221.

Habermas, Jürgen. 1984. *The theory of communicative action*. Trans. T. McCarthy. Boston: Beacon Press.

—— 1989. *The structural transformation of the public sphere: an inquiry into a category of bourgeois society*. Cambridge: Polity Press.

—— 1996. *Between facts and norms: contributions to a discourse theory of law and democracy*. Trans. W. Rehg. Cambridge: Polity Press.

Hajer, Maarten. 1993. Discourse coalitions and the institutionalization of practice: the case of acid rain in Britain. In *The argumentative turn in policy analysis and planning*, ed. F. Fischer and J. Forester. Durham, NC: Duke University Press, pp. 43–76.

——2003. A frame in the field: policymaking and the reinvention of politics. In *Deliberative policy analysis: understanding governance in the network society*, ed. M. Hajer and H. Wagenaar. Cambridge: Cambridge University Press.

——2005. Setting the stage: a dramaturgy of policy deliberation. *Administration and Society* 36 (6):624–47.

——2009. *Authoritative governance: policy-making in the Age of Mediatization*. Oxford: Oxford University Press.

——Hendrik Wagenaar, eds. 2003. *Deliberative policy analysis: understanding governance in the network society*. Cambridge: Cambridge University Press.

Hall, Tim. 2004. Disabled statue for Trafalgar Square. *Daily Mail*, 16 March.

Hardin, Garrett. 1968. The tragedy of the commons. *Science* 162 (3859):1243–8.

Harrington, John, and Elizabeth Mitchell, eds. 1999. *Politics and performance in contemporary Northern Ireland*. Amherst, MA: University of Massachusetts Press.

Harris, Aroha. 2004. *Hīkoi: forty years of Māori protest*. Wellington: Huia.

Harris, Ian. 2003. Attempts to encourage interactive debate in the Australian House of Representatives. Paper read at 34th Presiding Officers and Clerks Conference, July, at Nuku'alofa.

Hartley, L. P. 1953. *The Go-between*. London: Hamish Hamilton.

Hawkes, Terence. 2003. *Structuralism and semiotics*, 2nd revised ed. London: Routledge.

Hay, Colin. 2002. *Political analysis: a critical introduction*. Basingstoke: Palgrave.

Hayek, Friedrich A. von. 1960. *The constitution of liberty*. London: Routledge and Keegan Paul.

Heffernan, Richard. 2002. 'The possible as the art of politics': understanding consensus politics. *Political Studies* 50 (4):742–60.

Held, David. 2006. *Models of democracy*, 3rd ed. Cambridge: Polity Press.

Hénaff, Marcel, and Tracy Strong, eds. 2001. *Public space and democracy*. Minneapolis: University of Minnesota Press.

Hendriks, Carolyn. 2006. Integrated deliberation: reconciling civil society's dual role in deliberative democracy. *Political Studies* 54 (3):486–508.

Hindson, Paul, and Tim Gray. 1988. *Burke's dramatic theory of politics*. Aldershot: Avebury.

Hirst, Paul Q. 2005. *Space and power: politics, war and architecture*. Cambridge: Polity Press.

HMIC. 2009. *Adapting to protest: nurturing the British model of policing*. London: Her Majesty's Inspectorate of Constabulary.

Hood, Christopher. 1998. *The art of the state: culture, rhetoric and public management*. Oxford: Oxford University Press.

——Michael Jackson. 1991. *Administrative argument*. Aldershot: Dartmouth.

House of Commons, Canada. 1999. *Building the future: House of Commons requirements for the Parliamentary precinct*. Ottawa: House of Commons.

Hughes, Bill, and Kevin Paterson. 1997. The social model of disability and the disappearing body: towards a sociology of impairment. *Disability and Society* 12 (3):325–40.

229

Inglehart, Ronald, and Christian Welzel. 2003. Political culture and democracy: analyzing cross-level linkages. *Comparative Politics* 36 (1):61.

Ireland, Tim. 2008. *My submission to the Home Office for the public consultation on SOCPA* [Video submission]. Bloggerheads [cited 20 October 2009]. http://www.bloggerheads.com/archives/2008/01/my_socpa_submission.asp

Iveson, Kurt. 2007. *Publics and the city*. Malden, MA: Blackwell.

Iyengar, Shanto, and Donald R Kinder. 1987. *News that matters: television and American opinion*. Chicago: University of Chicago Press.

Jackson-Nakano, Ann. 2001. *The Kamberri: a history from the records of aboriginal families in the Canberra-Queanbeyan district and surrounds 1820–1927 and historical overview 1928–2001*. Canberra: Aboriginal History.

Jaeger, Suzanne. 2006. Embodiment and presence: the ontology of presence reconsidered. In *Staging philosophy: intersections of theater, performance, and philosophy*, ed. D. Krasner and D. Saltz. Ann Arbor: University of Michigan Press, pp. 122–41.

Kateb, George. 1981. The moral distinctiveness of representative democracy. *Ethics* 91 (3):357–74.

King, Gary, Robert Keohane, and Sidney Verba. 1994. *Designing social inquiry*. Princeton: Princeton University Press.

King, Michael. 2003. *The Penguin history of New Zealand*. Auckland: Penguin.

King, Mike, and David Waddington. 2005. Flashpoints revisited: a critical application to the policing of anti-globalization protest. *Policing and Society* 15 (3):255–82.

Kingdon, John W. 1984. *Agendas, alternatives and public policies*. Boston: Little, Brown.

Klein, Norman. 1997. *The history of forgetting: Los Angeles and the erasure of memory*. London: Verso.

Kock, Ned. 2007. Media naturalness and compensatory encoding: the burden of electronic media obstacles is on senders. *Decision Support Systems* 44 (1):175–87.

Kohn, Margaret. 2004. *Brave new neighbourhoods: the privatization of public space*. New York: Routledge.

——2008. Homo spectator: public space in the age of the spectacle. *Philosophy & Social Criticism* 34 (5):467–86.

Kraus, Wolfgang. 2006. The narrative negotiation of identity and belonging. *Narrative Inquiry* 14 (1):103–11.

Krieger, Alex. 2003. 'Deputizing' the streetscape. *Places* 15 (3):66.

Kriesi, Hanspeter. 1998. The transformation of cleavage politics: the 1997 Stein Rokkan lecture. *European Journal of Political Research* 33 (2):165–85.

Kyle, Chris R., and Jason Peacey. 2002. 'Under cover of so much coming and going': public access to parliament and the political process in early modern England. In *Parliament at work: parliamentary committees, political power, and public access in early modern England*, ed. C. R. Kyle and J. Peacey. Woodbridge: Boydell Press, pp. 1–24.

Ladd, Brian. 1998. *The ghosts of Berlin: confronting German history in the urban landscape*. Chicago: University of Chicago Press.

Lam, Wai-man. 2004. *Understanding the political culture of Hong Kong: the paradox of activism and depoliticization*. Armonk, NY: M. E. Sharpe.

Laswell, Harold. 1958. *Politics: who gets what, when, how*. New York: Meridian.

Lau, Siu-kai. 1982. *Society and politics in Hong Kong*. Hong Kong: Chinese University Press.

Law, Lisa. 2002. Defying disappearance: cosmopolitan public spaces in Hong Kong. *Urban Studies* 39 (9):1625–45.

Lawless, Jennifer. 2004. Politics of presence? Congresswomen and symbolic representation. *Political Research Quarterly* 57 (1):81–99.

Lefebvre, Henri. 1991. *The production of space*. Oxford: Basil Blackwell.

Leftwich, Adrian. 2004. *What is politics? The activity and its study*. Cambridge: Polity.

Lehmann-Haupt, Hellmut. 1954. *Art under a dictatorship*. New York: Oxford University Press.

Li, Zhen. 2009. Public participation and social movements in environmental policy-making in China. Department of Politics, University of York, York.

Library of Congress. n.d. *Inaugurals of Presidents of the United States: some precedents and notable events*. Library of Congress [cited 21 August 2009]. http://memory.loc.gov/ammem/pihtml/pinotable.html

Lijphart, Arend. 1999. *Patterns of democracy: government forms and performance in thirty-six countries*. New Haven: Yale University Press.

Linz, Juan J. 1994. Presidential or parliamentary democracy: does it make a difference? In *The failure of presidential democracy*, ed. J. J. Linz and A. Valenzuela. Baltimore: Johns Hopkins University Press.

Litman, Todd. 2007. *Evaluating transportation equity: guidance for incorporating distributional impacts in transportation planning*. Victoria: Victoria Transport Policy Institute.

Lofland, Lyn. 1998. *The public realm: exploring the city's quintessential social territory*. New York: Aldine de Gruyter.

Longstreth, Richard. 2006. Washington and the landscape of fear. *City and Society* 18 (1):7–30.

Low, Setha. 2006. How private interests take over public space: zoning, taxes, and the incorporation of gated communities. In *The politics of public space*, ed. S. Low and N. Smith. New York: Routledge, pp. 81–103.

MacIntyre, Alasdair. 1984. *After virtue: a study in moral theory*, 2nd ed. London: Duckworth.

Madanipour, Ali. 2003. *Public and private spaces of the city*. London: Routledge.

Maddison, Sarah, and Sean Scalmer. 2006. *Activist wisdom*. Sydney: University of New South Wales Press.

Majone, Giandomenico. 1989. *Evidence, argument, and persuasion in the policy process*. New Haven: Yale University Press.

Malone, Paul. 2004. It's wall to wall security with plenty of room to play. *Canberra Times*, 5 August.

Mansbridge, Jane. 1992. A deliberative theory of interest representation. In *The politics of interests: interest groups transformed*, ed. M. Petracca. Boulder, co: Westview Press.

—— 1999. Everyday talk in the deliberative system. In *Deliberative politics: essays on 'Democracy and disagreement'*, ed. S. Macedo. New York: Oxford University Press, pp. 211–39.

—— 2003. Rethinking representation. *American Political Science Review* 97 (4):515–28.

May, J. D. 1978. Defining democracy. *Political Studies* 26:1–14.

McIntyre, Clement. 1997. Designing debate: the implications of parliamentary architecture. *Legislative Studies* 12 (1):43–8.

——2008. Parliamentary architecture and political culture. Canberra: Australian Senate, Occasional Lecture Series, 9 May 2008.

McMahon, Edward, and Emilie Kornhelser. 2010. Assessing the assessors: correlating democracy methodologies. *Social Indicator Research* 97:269–77.

Mill, James. 1992 [1819]. *Political writings*, ed. T. Ball. Cambridge: Cambridge University Press.

Mitchell, Don. 1995. The end of public space? People's Park, definitions of the public, and democracy. *Annals of the Association of American Geographers* 85 (1):108–13.

——Lynn Staeheli. 2005. Permitting protest: parsing the fine geography of dissent in America. *International Journal of Urban and Regional Research* 29 (4):796–813.

Mulcahy, Linda. 2009. Legal architecture and restraint of the uncontrollable impulse of the feminine. At Architecture and political representation, ACRP workshop, Birkbeck, University of London, 15 July.

Nagel, Thomas. 1991. *Equality and partiality*. New York: Oxford University Press.

——1995. Personal rights and public space. *Philosophy and Public Affairs* 24 (2):83–107.

National Assembly for Wales. 2009a. *Senedd>Access*. National Assembly for Wales [cited 27 July 2009]. http://www.assemblywales.org/sen-home/sen-access.htm

——2009b. *Senedd>Project History>Design Concepts*. National Assembly for Wales [cited 27 July 2009]. http://www.assemblywales.org/sen-home/sen-projecthistory/sen-design-concepts-link-3

National Capital Authority. 2003. *Urban design guidelines for perimeter security in the national capital*. Canberra: National Capital Authority.

NCC. 2005. *Reflecting a nation: creating a capital experience for all Canadians*. Ottawa: National Capital Commission.

NCPC. 2005. *National Capital urban design and security plan*, 3rd ed. Washington, DC: National Capital Planning Commission.

New Zealand Parliament. 2009. *Visiting and tours: access*. New Zealand Parliament [cited 2 September 2009]. http://www.parliament.nz/en-NZ/AboutParl/Visiting/Access/9/2/8/00VisitVisitingAccess1-Access.htm

Noakes, John, Brian Klocke, and Patrick Gillham. 2005. Whose streets? Police and protestor struggles over space in Washington, DC, 29–30 September 2001. *Policing and Society* 15 (3):235–54.

Nogueira Alcala, Humberto. 2008. The political-constitutional evolution of Chile 1976–2005. *Estudios Constitucionales* 6 (2):325–70.

Norton, Philip. 1997. Roles and behaviour of British MPs. *Journal of Legislative Studies* 3 (1):17–31.

Nozick, Robert. 1974. *Anarchy, state, and utopia*. New York: Basic Books.

NZ House of Representatives. n.d. *Māui Tikitiki-a-Taranga: information about the Māori Affairs Select Committee Room*. Wellington: Visitor Services, Parliament Buildings.

O'Neill, John. 1998. Rhetoric, science and philosophy. *Philosophy of the Social Sciences* 28 (2):205–25.

Office of the Clerk. 2009. *Cannon House Office Building: a congressional first*. Office of the Clerk of the House of Representatives [cited 22 July 2009]. http://clerk.house.gov/art_history/art_artifacts/Cannon_Centennial/index.html

Olson, Mancur. 1965. *The logic of collective action: public goods and the theory of groups*. Cambridge, MA: Harvard University Press.

Orgel, Stephen. 1975. *The illusion of power*. Berkeley: University of California Press.

Parker, Simon. 2004. *Urban theory and the urban experience: encountering the city*. London: Routledge.

Parkinson, John. 2006a. *Deliberating in the real world: problems of legitimacy in deliberative democracy*. Oxford: Oxford University Press.

——2006b. Rickety bridges: using the media in deliberative democracy. *British Journal of Political Science* 36 (1):175–83.

——2007a. The House of Lords: a deliberative democratic defence. *Political Quarterly* 78 (3):374–81.

——2007b. Localism and deliberative democracy. *The Good Society* 16 (1):23–9.

——Jane Mansbridge, eds. forthcoming. *Deliberative systems: deliberative democracy at the large scale*. Cambridge: Cambridge University Press.

Parliament of Australia. 1980. *Parliament House, Canberra: two stage design competition. Assessors' final report, June 1980*. Canberra: Commonwealth Government Printer.

——2007. *Operating policies and procedures no. 16 – protests and other assemblies in the Parliamentary precincts*. Canberra: Department of Parliamentary Services.

Pasley, Jeffrey. 2004. Democracy, gentility, and lobbying in the early US Congress. In *The American Congress: the building of democracy*, ed. J. E. Zelizer. Boston: Houghton Mifflin, pp. 38–62.

Pennock, J. Roland. 1980. Thoughts on the right to private property. In *Property: Nomos 22*, ed. J. R. Pennock and J. Chapman. New York: New York University Press, pp. 171–86.

Peschel, Kurt. 1960. Council chambers of the great parliaments. *Parliamentary Affairs* 14:518–33.

Peters, B. Guy. 1999. *Institutional theory in political science*. London: Pinter.

Philip, George. 2003. *Democracy in Latin America*. Cambridge: Polity.

Phillips, Anne. 1995. *The politics of presence*. Oxford: Clarendon Press.

Pierre, Jon, ed. 2000. *Debating governance: authority, steering, and democracy*. Oxford: Oxford University Press.

Pitkin, Hanna. 1967. *The concept of representation*. Berkeley, CA: University of California Press.

——1972. *The concept of representation*. Berkeley, CA: University of California Press.

Pollitt, Christopher. 1993. *Managerialism and the public services*, 2nd ed. Oxford: Blackwell.

Porter, Henry. 2009. The crushing of eco-protest brings shame on our police. *The Observer*, 19 April.

Przeworski, Adam. 1999. Minimalist conception of democracy: a defense. In *Democracy's value*, ed. I. Shapiro and C. Hacker-Cordón. Cambridge: Cambridge University Press, pp. 23–55.

Rae, Douglas. 2003. *City: urbanism and its end*. New Haven: Yale University Press.

Rapaport, Amos. 1982. *The meaning of the built environment*. Beverly Hills, CA: Sage.

Rawls, John. 1971. *A theory of justice*. Oxford: Oxford University Press.

—— 1996. *Political liberalism*, 2nd ed. New York: Columbia University Press.

Raz, Joseph. 1986. *The morality of freedom*. Oxford: Oxford University Press.

Rehfeld, Andrew. 2006. Towards a general theory of political representation. *Journal of Politics* 68 (1):1–21.

—— 2009. Representation rethought: on trustees, delegates, and gyroscopes in the study of political representation and democracy. *American Political Science Review* 103 (2):214–30.

Reinisch, Charlotte, and John Parkinson. 2007. Swiss Landsgemeinden: a deliberative democratic evaluation of two outdoor parliaments. In *European Consortium for Political Research Joint Sessions*. Helsinki.

Reynolds, Jonathan. 1996. Japan's Imperial Diet building: debate over construction of a national identity. *Art Journal* Fall:38–47.

Reynolds, Nigel. 2005. Whatever would Nelson think? *Daily Telegraph*, 17 September.

Rhodes, Rod. 1997. *Understanding governance: policy networks, governance, reflexivity, and accountability, public policy and management*. Buckingham: Open University Press.

Riker, William H. 1982. *Liberalism against populism: a confrontation between the theory of democracy and the theory of social choice*. San Francisco: Freeman.

Ritchie, Donald. 2004. The press coverage of Congress: reporting Johnson's impeachment. In *The American Congress: the building of democracy*, ed. J. E. Zelizer. Boston: Houghton Mifflin, pp. 239–49.

Rogers, Robert, and Rhodri Walters. 2006. *How parliament works*, 6th ed. Harlow: Pearson Longman.

Rogers Stirk Harbour and Partners. 2007. *National Assembly for Wales* [cited 27 July 2009]. http://www.richardrogers.co.uk/work/buildings/national_as sembly_for_-wales/completed#test2

Rosie, Michael, and Hugo Gorringe. 2009. What a difference a death makes: protest, policing and the press at the G20. *Sociological Research Online* 14 (5). http://www.socresonline.org.uk/14/5/4.html

Ruane, Michael, and Aaron Davis. 2009. D.C.'s inauguration headcount: 1.8 million. *Washington Post*, 22 January, B01.

Russell, Jonathan. 2008. The Duke of Westminster hit by vacancies at Liverpool One. *Daily Telegraph*, 6 April.

Russett, Bruce, and John Oneal. 2001. *Triangulating peace: democracy, interdependence, and international organizations*. New York: W.W. Norton.

Sanders, Lynn. 1997. Against deliberation. *Political Theory* 25 (3):347–76.

Sartori, Giovanni. 1962. *Democratic theory*. Detroit: Wayne State University Press.

Saussure, Ferdinand de. 2006. *Writings in general linguistics*. Trans. C. Sanders and M. Pires. Oxford: Oxford University Press.

Sauter, Willmar. 2000. *The theatrical event: dynamics of performance and perception*. Iowa City: University of Iowa Press.

Saward, Michael. 1998. *The terms of democracy*. Cambridge: Polity Press.

—— 2003. Enacting democracy. *Political Studies* 51 (1):161–79.

—— 2006. The representative claim. *Contemporary Political Theory* 5:297–318.

—— 2010. *The representative claim*. Oxford: Oxford University Press.

Schon, Donald, and Martin Rein. 1994. *Frame reflection: toward the resolution of intractable policy controversies*. New York: Basic Books.

Schudson, Michael. 1999. *The good citizen: a history of American civic life*. Cambridge, MA: Harvard University Press.

—— 2004. Congress and the media. In *The American Congress: the building of democracy*, edited by J. E. Zelizer. Boston: Houghton Mifflin, pp. 650–63.

Schumpeter, Joseph. 1962. *Capitalism, socialism and democracy*, 3rd ed. New York: Harper & Row.

Scott-Heron, Gil. 1971. The revolution will not be televised. In *Home is where the hatred is*, B side. New York: Flying Dutchman.

Scott, M. M. 2005. A powerful theory and a paradox: ecological psychologists after Barker. *Environment and Behavior* 37 (3):295–329.

Scott, Pamela. 1995. *Temple of liberty: building the Capitol for a new nation*. New York: Oxford University Press.

Sen, Amartya. 1985. *Commodities and capabilities*. Oxford: Oxford University Press.

Sennett, Richard. 2002. *The fall of public man*. London: Penguin.

Shils, Edward. 1965. Charisma, order, and status. *American Sociological Review* 30 (2):199–213.

Shiratori, Rei. 1995. The politics of electoral reform in Japan. *International Political Science Review* 16 (1):79–94.

Shirlow, Peter. 2001. *Mapping the spaces of fear in Ardoyne and Upper Ardoyne*. Belfast: North Belfast Partnership Board.

Siavelis, Peter M. 2000. *The President and Congress in post-authoritarian Chile: institutional constraints to democratic consolidation*. University Park, PA: Pennsylvania State University Press.

—— 2009. Enclaves of the transition and Chilean democracy. *Revista De Ciencia Politica* 29 (1):3–21.

Simmel, Georg. 1950. The metropolis and mental life. In *The sociology of Georg Simmel*, ed. K. H. Wolff. Glencoe, IL: Free Press, pp. 409–26.

Sinclair, R. K. 1991. *Democracy and participation in Athens*. Cambridge: Cambridge University Press.

Singer, Brian. 1996. Cultural versus contractual nations: rethinking their opposition. *History and Theory* 35 (3):309–37.

Smith, Graham. 2005. *Beyond the ballot: 57 democratic innovations from around the world*. London: The Power Inquiry/Short Run Press.

—— 2009. *Democratic innovations*. Cambridge: Cambridge University Press.

Soja, Edward. 1989. *Postmodern geographies: the reassertion of space in critical social theory*. London: Verso.

Sokal, Alan, and Jean Bricmont. 1997. *Intellectual impostures*. London: Profile Books.

Sonne, Wolfgang. 2003. *Representing the state: capital city planning in the early twentieth century*. Munich: Prestel.

Soule, Sarah, and Christian Davenport. 2009. Velvet glove, iron fist, or even hand? Protest policing in the United States, 1960–1990. *Mobilization* 14 (1):1–22.

Southworth, Michael. 2005. Reinventing Main Street: from mall to townscape mall. *Journal of Urban Design* 10 (2):151–70.

Spragens, Thomas A. 1990. *Reason and democracy*. Durham: Duke University Press.

Starr, Amory, Luis Fernandez, Randall Amster, Lesley Wood, and Michael Caro. 2008. The impacts of state surveillance on political assembly and association: a socio-legal analysis. *Qualitative Sociology* 31:251–70.

Stevens, Quentin. 2007. *The ludic city: exploring the potential of public spaces*. Abingdon: Routledge.

——Kim Dovey. 2004. Appropriating the spectacle: play and politics in a leisure landscape. *Journal of Urban Design* 9 (2):351–65.

Stoker, Gerry. 2006. *Why politics matters: making democracy work*. Basingstoke: Palgrave.

Stone, Clarence N. 1993. Urban regimes and the capacity to govern – a political economy approach. *Journal of Urban Affairs* 15 (1):1–28.

Stone, Deborah. 1988. *Policy paradox and political reason*. Glenview: Scott, Foresman.

——2002. *Policy paradox: the art of political decision making*, revised ed. New York: Norton.

Sudjic, Deyan. 2005. *Edifice complex: how the rich and powerful shape the world*. London: Allen Lane.

——Helen Jones. 2001. *Architecture and democracy*. London: Lawrence King/Glasgow City Council.

Sunstein, Cass. 2001. *Republic.com*. Princeton: Princeton University Press.

——2002. The law of group polarization. *Journal of Political Philosophy* 10 (2):175–95.

Thomas, Mark. 2007. Demonstrations of victory. *The Guardian*, 26 June.

Thompsett, Adela Ruth. 2005. 'London is the place for me': performance and identity in Notting Hill Carnival. *Theatre History Studies* 25:43–60.

Thurley, Simon. 2007. Houses of power. Channel 4, 7:35 p.m., 5 May.

Till, Karen. 2005. *The new Berlin: memory, politics, place*. Minneapolis: University of Minnesota Press.

Tilly, Charles. 2004. *Contention and democracy in Europe, 1650–2000*. Cambridge: Cambridge University Press.

——2008. *Contentious performances*. Cambridge: Cambridge University Press.

——Sidney Tarrow. 2007. *Contentious politics*. Boulder, CO: Paradigm.

Tomic, Patricia, and Ricardo Trumper. 2005. Powerful drivers and meek passengers: on the buses in Santiago. *Race and Class* 47 (1):49–63.

Toolin, Cynthia. 1983. American civil religion from 1789 to 1981: a content analysis of presidential inaugural addresses. *Review of Religious Research* 25 (1):39–48.

Torre, Susana. 1996. Claiming the public space: the Mothers of Plaza de Mayo. In *Sex of architecture*, ed. D. Agrest, P. Conway and L. K. Weisman. New York: Henry N. Abrams, pp. 241–50.

Towers, Graham. 1995. *Building democracy: community architecture in the inner cities*. London: UCL Press.

Tulis, Jeffrey K. 1988. *The rhetorical presidency*. Princeton: Princeton University Press.

UBS. 2009. *Prices and earnings: a comparison of purchasing power around the globe*. Zürich: UBS AG.

Uhr, John. 1998. *Deliberative democracy in Australia: the changing place of parliament.* Cambridge: Cambridge University Press.

US Capitol Visitor Center. 2009. *Plan a visit.* Office of the Architect of the Capitol [cited 26 August 2009]. http://www.visitthecapitol.gov/Visit/

Vale, Lawrence J. 2005. Securing public space. *Places* 17 (3):38–42.

van Krieken, Robert. 1999. The barbarism of civilization: cultural genocide and the 'stolen generations'. *British Journal of Sociology* 50 (2):297–315.

Vanhanen, Tatu. 1997. *Prospects of democracy: a study of 172 countries.* London: Routledge.

Versteeg, Wytske, and Maarten Hajer. 2009. Democratic authority in the Age of Mediatization: an analysis of the London G20-summit as an instance of our deliberative society. In *Democracy and the Deliberative Society.* York, 24–26 June.

Waddington, Peter. 1994. *Liberty and order: public order policing in a capital city.* London: UCL Press.

Waldron, Jeremy. 1988. *The right to private property.* Oxford: Clarendon Press.

Walgrave, Stefaan, and Joris Verhulst. 2009. Government stance and internal diversity of protest: a comparative study of protest against the war in Iraq in eight countries. *Social Forces* 87 (3):1355–87.

Walker, Greg. 1998. *The politics of performance in early renaissance drama.* Cambridge: Cambridge University Press.

Walzer, Michael. 1981. Philosophy and democracy. *Political Theory* 9 (3):379–99.

Warden, James. 1995. Parliament, democracy and political identity in Australia. *Constitutions, rights and democracy: past, present and future.* Canberra: Parliament of Australia, pp. 47–62.

Watson, Sophie. 2006. *City publics: the (dis)enchantments of urban encounters.* Abingdon: Routledge.

Weber, Max, Guenther Roth, and Claus Wittich. 1978. *Economy and society: an outline of interpretive sociology.* Berkeley, CA: University of California Press.

Whitehead, Laurence. 1999. The drama of democratization. *Journal of Democracy* 10 (4):84–98.

—— 2002. *Democratization: theory and experience.* Oxford: Oxford University Press.

Wikileaks. 2010. *Collateral murder* [cited 3 May 2010]. http://www.collateralmurder.com/

Wilde, Alexander. 1991. Irruptions of memory: expressive politics in Chile's transition to democracy. *Journal of Latin American Studies* 31 (2):473–500.

Wilentz, Sean, ed. 1985. *Rites of power: symbolism, ritual and politics since the Middle Ages.* Philadelphia: University of Pennsylvania Press.

Wilson, Richard Guy. 2000. The historicization of the US Capitol and the Office of the Architect, 1954–1996. In *The United States Capitol: designing and decorating a national icon*, ed. D. R. Kennon. Athens, OH: Ohio University Press/United States Capitol Historical Society, pp. 134–68.

Wise, Michael. 1998. *Capital dilemma: Germany's search for a new architecture of democracy.* New York: Princeton Architectural Press.

Wright, Frank Lloyd. 1939. *An organic architecture: the architecture of democracy.* London: Lund Humphries.

Young, Carolyn A. 1995. *The glory of Ottawa: Canada's first parliament buildings.* Montreal: McGill-Queen's University Press.

Young, Iris Marion. 1999. Justice, inclusion, and deliberative democracy. In *Deliberative politics: essays on 'Democracy and disagreement'*, ed. S. Macedo. New York: Oxford University Press, pp. 151–8.

—— 2000. *Inclusion and democracy.* Oxford: Oxford University Press.

—— 2001. Activist challenges to deliberative democracy. *Political Theory* 29 (5):670–90.

Zaller, John. 2003. A new standard for judging news quality: burglar alarms for the monitorial citizen. *Political Communication* 20 (2):109–30.

Zelizer, Julian E, ed. 2004. *The American Congress: the building of democracy.* Boston: Houghton Mifflin.

Zhao, Dingxin. 1998. Ecologies of social movements: student mobilization during the 1989 prodemocracy movement in Beijing. *American Journal of Sociology* 103 (6):1493–529.

Zick, Timothy. 2009. *Speech out of doors: preserving first amendment liberties in public places.* New York: Cambridge University Press.

Index

access:
  authenticity of 123–4, 135
  educative function 124, 127
  media access 130–1
  requirement for democracy 10, 26, 41–2,
    51–2, 54–5, 58
  symbolic function 142
  see also assembly, access; scrutiny
accountability 86
activism 42–3, 69
  see also Greenpeace; protest
actors, *see* Roles, distinct from actors
adversarial, *see* conflict; *see also* debating chamber
agendas 37
Agnew, John 77, 80
Allende, Salvador 137
American Civil Liberties Union 166
Ampelmännchen 75
Any Answers?, Any Questions? 144
Appenzell 14, 45, 67, 132–3, 174
  Landsgemeinde, ~platz 41, 45, 94, 105, 132–3,
    143–4, 170, 174, 204
  symbolic function 133, 170
approach and methods 9–15, 87–9, 119,
  200–1, 212–15, 221–2
arcades 54
architecture 6
  classical 95–6
  community architecture movement 86
  gothic 96
  see also democracy, architecture of
Arendt, Hannah 51, 53
Asimov, Isaac 64
assembly, freedom of 146, 163–4
Assembly
  access 117–18, 123–45, 209
  aural environment 111–12, 125
  banqueting and other spaces 117–19
  committee rooms 113–19
  deliberative site 94, 127
  dignity 18, 94, 144–5, 160–1, 205

  encounters within 115–16
  entrance cues 137–8
  functions 94–5, 111–12, 117, 119–21, 124, 127
  as heritage and tourism site 114–15, 117, 144
  libraries 118
  as politicians' building 118, 160–1
  in presidential systems 137
  public celebration 144–5, 209
  as public space 52, 117–19, 137, 142, 161,
    213–41
  and scrutiny 95, 122–3, 209
  seating arrangement 5, 81, 105–12, 115, 203
  separation of work and public spaces
    123–4, 135
  as stage 99–104, 144–5
  as symbol 93, 95–9, 116–17, 119, 136,
    144–5, 213–14
  women in 106
  as working space 94, 114–15, 118, 123–5,
    137–8, 144, 209
  see also debating chambers; Athens, Berlin,
    Canberra, Hong Kong, Isle of Man,
    Mexico City, London, Ottawa, Santiago
    de Chile, Tokyo, Washington DC,
    Wellington
assembly rooms 125
Athens (ancient) 34, 174–5
  agora 125
  ecclesia 34, 41, 174
  Pnyx 34, 125, 174–5
  Theatre of Dionysus 34
Athens (modern):
  access to parliament 117
  Exarchia 157
  Hellenic Parliament 108, 136
  privatized space 164
  protest in 150
  Syntagma Square 164
audience 34, 41, 43–4, 205
  attention requirement 41–3, 44, 69, 109,
    122, 142, 147, 184

Index

Index